Right Across the World

"John Feffer is our 21st-century Jack London."
—Mike Davis, author of *Planet of Slums*

"John Feffer brings [...] a rich store of experiences and a wise perspective."
—Adam Hochschild, author of *King Leopold's Ghost*

"An important book [...] the Trump world is part of a transnational story that won't go away. Feffer knows this international ground well and covers it skillfully."
—Lawrence Rosenthal, Chair and Lead Researcher of the Berkeley Center for Right-Wing Studies

"Clearly lays out the challenges societies are facing from an increasingly mobilized transnational far right movement. Unique, because he also provides solutions."
—Heidi Beirich, co-founder of the Global Project Against Hate and Extremism

"An urgent warning to progressives that while they may consider themselves to be the true internationalists, the nationalist right has stolen a march on them and now threatens to overrun their values of global justice and solidarity."
—Walden Bello, International Adjunct Professor of Sociology at the State University of New York at Binghamton

Right Across the World

The Global Networking of the Far Right and the Left Response

John Feffer

First published 2021 by Pluto Press
New Wing, Somerset House, Strand, London WC2R 1LA

www.plutobooks.com

Copyright © John Feffer 2021

The right of John Feffer to be identified as the author of this work has been asserted in accordance with the Copyright, Designs and Patents Act 1988.

British Library Cataloguing in Publication Data
A catalogue record for this book is available from the British Library

ISBN	978 0 7453 4188 0	Hardback
ISBN	978 0 7453 4189 7	Paperback
ISBN	978 1 78680 855 4	PDF
ISBN	978 1 78680 856 1	EPUB

This book is printed on paper suitable for recycling and made from fully managed and sustained forest sources. Logging, pulping and manufacturing processes are expected to conform to the environmental standards of the country of origin.

Typeset by Stanford DTP Services, Northampton, England

Simultaneously printed in the United Kingdom and United States of America

Contents

Acknowledgments vi

Introduction 1
1. Origins of the new right 15
2. Transnational organizing of the new right 44
3. The new right's pandemic pivot 66
4. Responding to the new right 87
5. Transnational progressive organizing 104
6. Conclusion 127

Notes 141
Index 171

Acknowledgments

This book draws on interviews with more than 80 thinkers and activists around the world. Quotations without citations are from those interviews, conducted between June and October 2019.

An earlier version of some of the material in this book appeared in the Institute for Policy Studies report, *The Battle for a New World*, produced with the Transnational Institute and Focus on the Global South and supported by the Rosa Luxemburg Foundation. Other portions appeared originally in articles for *The Nation*, TomDispatch, and Foreign Policy In Focus.

The author would like to thank Kristin Henderson for research assistance, Maresi Starzmann for feedback, and Peter Certo for copy-editing the original IPS report. Andreas Gunther and John Cavanagh can't be thanked enough for their commitment to this project. And Ken Barlow provided invaluable help in turning this manuscript into a publishable book.

Introduction

THE RISE AND FALL OF STEVE BANNON

A Nationalist International should be a contradiction in terms, but that didn't stop Steve Bannon from trying to create one.

Steven Bannon was the head of Breitbart News and a darling of the alt-right when he took over as Donald Trump's campaign CEO in August 2016. He was captaining what virtually all U.S. political observers believed to be a sinking ship. And yet, in the space of a few months, he managed to right the foundering vessel on the way to achieving one of the most remarkable electoral surprises in American history. The victory contributed to his confidence that he could accomplish virtually anything he envisioned.

Bannon subsequently joined the Trump administration as a spin doctor, strategic advisor, and conduit to what he liked to call the "deplorables," an ironic reference to Hilary Clinton's infamous disparagement of a certain subset of Trump supporters.[1] One year later, as a result of political infighting, the sole member of Trump's brain trust left the administration, with the president himself declaring that Bannon had "lost his mind."[2] Even this ignominious departure didn't dim Bannon's enthusiasm for his commander-in-chief. He would later return to Trump's aid in the autumn of 2019, launching a daily radio show and podcast to rally support for the president in the face of congressional impeachment and, later, the coronavirus crisis.[3]

In between these efforts on behalf of his chosen Prince, the Machiavellian Bannon set off in early 2018 on an extended world tour. His mission was even more ambitious than getting Trump elected. Bannon hoped to build a loose network of right-wing populists with a strong transatlantic link and branches in ideologically sympathetic outposts elsewhere in the world. In grand fashion, he wanted to replicate on the global stage his success in building bridges within the U.S. right.

Bannon believed very strongly in his own timing. With the Breitbart media empire, which injected far-right ideas on immigration, politics, and culture into the American mainstream, Bannon had created a platform for Donald Trump's candidacy. In his role as vice president of Cambridge Analytica, Bannon also worked behind the scenes in 2015 to lay the groundwork for what seemed at the time to be a longshot attempt to pull the United Kingdom out of the European Union.[4] As with Trump's election, the successful Brexit referendum in 2016 turned out to be an upset victory for the far right and a vindication of Bannon's foresight.

In 2018, which Bannon thought was the perfect moment to create a Nationalist International, the far right hadn't just been winning in the United States and the United Kingdom. In the 2010s, far-right politicians made unprecedented leaps into power throughout Europe. In Eastern Europe, right-wing populists took over in Hungary in 2010, Poland in 2015, and the Czech Republic in 2017. Ideologically similar leaders entered coalition governments in Austria in 2017 and Italy in 2018. Even in notoriously tolerant Scandinavia, the far right made significant headway. The True Finns acquired enough votes after the 2015 election to enter a coalition government with center-right parties, while the Sweden Democrats, a party with neo-Nazi roots, came close on several occasions to becoming that country's most popular party. In Germany, the extremist Alternative für Deutschland (AfD) became the third-largest party in 2017 even as the government was banning neo-Nazi organizations.

In celebration of its success that year, the AfD sponsored a convention in Koblenz that brought together a group of these like-minded European leaders. Movement headliners Marine Le Pen from France, Geert Wilders from the Netherlands, and Matteo Salvini from Italy all participated. It took place shortly after Donald Trump's inauguration, which prompted Wilders to comment, "Yesterday a free America, today Koblenz, tomorrow a new Europe."[5] Two years later, in the European Parliament elections in May 2019, far-right parties were the top vote-getters in the UK, France, Italy, and Hungary. It seemed as though Wilders's prediction was coming true.

Although they'd existed in Europe for several generations, far-right parties had always hovered on the fringes of politics: boycotted by mainstream politicians, mocked in the mainstream media, and ignored in the broader culture. In the late twentieth century, huge demonstrations thronged the streets of France, the Netherlands, Austria, and other European countries to block the far right's entrance into mainstream politics. By the 2010s, it was the far right bringing people out onto the streets as they evolved into serious political players and, in some cases, governing parties. Bannon intended to build on this dramatic reversal of fortune by providing the European far right—a motley crew of parties, movements, and marginal figures—with an organizing upgrade.

Furthermore, the success of the far right was not restricted to the United States and Europe. In the Philippines, "Asia's Donald Trump" Rodrigo Duterte won the presidential election in May 2016, prefiguring Trump in many ways with his profane and sexist rhetoric, assaults on the rule of law, crackdowns on dissent, and direct criticisms of Barack Obama. In December 2016, Duterte signaled a shift in policy toward the United States by congratulating Trump on his electoral victory. "We both like to swear," Duterte said. "One little thing, we curse right away; we're the same."[6] The president-elect returned the favor by praising the Philippine leader's drug policy, which had attracted widespread criticism for involving thousands of extrajudicial killings.

After 2016, other parts of the world experienced a Trumpification of politics, and again Bannon could justifiably claim some credit, if only indirectly. Jair Bolsonaro, who took the reins in Brazil in 2017, "copied a lot from Trump: his online politics, his speeches against political correctness, his anti-feminist and hate speech," explains Esther Solano of the Federal University of São Paulo.

Elsewhere right-wing leaders began to bend toward Trump like flowers to the sun. In Israel, Benjamin Netanyahu had been pushing politics inexorably to the right since becoming prime minister in 2009, but he managed to achieve some of his key dreams—such as moving the U.S. embassy from Tel Aviv to Jerusalem—only after his friend Donald Trump took power in Washington. Two long-serving leaders, Vladimir Putin in Russia and Recep Tayyip Erdoğan in Turkey, turned more fully to the right the longer they stayed in office, and both gravitated toward Trump as well. So did Narendra Modi, whose Hindu fundamentalist party came to power in India in 2014. Even Japanese Prime Minister Shinzo Abe, although he didn't pattern his politics after the U.S. president, tried to leverage his relationship with Trump to bolster his more hardline nationalist stance.

These leaders looked to Trump as a model. They copied his attacks on the elite status quo, his use of social media to connect directly with his base, his strategic incorporation of racist and sexist rhetoric, and his frankly authoritarian style. They echoed his skepticism of economic lockdowns in response to the COVID-19 pandemic and supported his claims of fraud following his loss in the 2020 presidential election. Some, like Vladimir Putin, even withheld congratulations to the winner of the 2020 presidential election, Joe Biden, out of deference to Trump's wounded ego. In this way, Trump's influence could be felt beyond America's borders, thanks in part to Bannon's illiberal philosophy and toolbox of tactics.

Although he would only serve one term in office, Trump left his mark on U.S. and global politics. For instance, he expanded the boundaries of what is acceptable for a U.S. president on the international stage. By inviting autocrats to the White House and routinely flouting global norms, "Trump has created space for the international far right," Paris-based political consultant Ethan Earle argues. "He's given *carte blanche* to people further down the pecking order in geopolitics to continue to push their politics further and further to the right knowing that there's political coverage coming from the very top." In fact, these illiberal rulers played a game of follow-the-leader. As Barbarina Heyerdahl, the Vermont-based manager of the Acorn Fund notes,

> There is a cabal of authoritarian, racist leaders—Trump, Modi in Kashmir, Xi in Hong Kong, Putin acting against protesters in Russia, Bolsonaro against indigenous communities in Brazil, and Erdoğan against the Kurds in Syria—who are just watching each other to see what the others are getting away with to calculate what they can get away with in their own countries.

Although other right-wing leaders looked to him for inspiration, Trump showed neither the interest nor the capacity to head up a new Nationalist International. Others, however, have been eager to rush in where Trump fears to tread. Certain leaders, like Putin in Moscow and Hungary's Viktor Orbán, have put themselves forward as potential leaders of an axis of illiberalism.

But in 2018, believing that he had the time and the skills necessary to organize such an axis, Steve Bannon threw his hat into the ring.

Despite his attacks on globalism and globalists, Bannon has an ideology well-suited to building a global movement. His worldview has been shaped by three major founts of internationalism: Catholicism, Hollywood, and Wall Street. Raised Irish Catholic, he attended Catholic schools and, after a flirtation with Buddhism, eventually settled on a more fundamentalist, medieval version of the Vatican's teaching.[7] With a degree from Harvard Business School, Bannon began to work with Goldman Sachs, eventually moving to Los Angeles to handle investments in the entertainment industry. Over time, he has come to believe in a holy trinity of capitalism, nationalism, and Christianity. But all three, he argues, have been infected by liberalism of one sort or another, represented by the "party of Davos," the transnationalism of the European Union, and religious reformers like Pope Francis.[8]

Although Bannon consorted with the extreme right during his days at Breitbart, his own philosophy has its roots in more traditional Burkean conservatism. However, as an organizer who dreams not only of a new Europe but a new world, Bannon has a different role model in mind than a statesman and philosopher like Edmund Burke. He sees himself as something of a right-wing Lenin, an international activist committed to destroying rather than conserving the status quo.[9] Like Lenin, he aspires not simply to control a single state but to spur a worldwide revolution. His philosophy of state, however, is the opposite of Lenin's. An advocate of small government, Bannon is eager to seize control of the levers of state and transfer power to non-state actors like the corporate sector and religious institutions.[10] At the global level, he is doubly suspicious of anything that smacks of world government, like the United Nations.

Bannon is a populist, not a statist. Despite his elitist background, he always speaks of the power of the People. "It's not a question of whether populism is on the rise and going to be the political future," Bannon has said, nodding in the direction of Donald Trump and presidential aspirant Bernie Sanders. "The only question before us is: is it going to be populist nationalism or populist socialism."[11]

To ensure that his version of populism triumphs, Bannon has been pushing coordination not only across international borders but across ideological borders within the world of his political co-religionists. Political scientists distinguish between the "radical right" and the "extreme right." The latter, which includes terrorists, neo-Nazis, and white nationalists on the fringes, is contemptuous of democracy overall and refuses to engage in electoral politics. The radical right, which is critical of *liberal* democracy with its emphasis on legislative safeguards and the protection of minority rights, is content to win power through the ballot box. "In essence, the radical right trusts the power of the people, the extreme right does not," writes political scientist Cas Mudde.[12]

By helping to create a new alternative right—or alt-right—Bannon was instrumental in blurring the distinction between these two categories. At Breitbart News, he smuggled some of the content of the extreme right, particularly on immigration and identity issues, into the radical right. Meanwhile, he consistently pushed a populist line against the anti-democratic extreme. And he latched onto Donald Trump, whose political views were hitherto all over the map, as a figure he could mold into a politician acceptable to both the radical right and the extreme right—and ultimately the conservative mainstream as well.

In this way, Bannon has been instrumental in creating a "new right" that merges elements of extremism, radicalism, populism, and conventional conservative thinking even as it attempts to distance itself from Nazism—just as a "new left" emerged in the 1960s from an amalgam of communist, socialist, progressive, and liberal thinking that deliberately rejected Stalinism. And unlike its parochial predecessors, the new right is well-suited to become a global ideology.

THE MOVEMENT

To consolidate this "new right" globally, Bannon teamed up with right-wing Belgian politician Mischaël Modrikamen in 2018 to establish a bulkhead in Europe with something they called the Movement. Hoping to take advantage of surging dissatisfaction with European integration, Bannon rolled his Trojan horse into the very heart of the enemy's camp. They located their new organization in—of all places—Brussels, the home of the European Union. With the Movement, Bannon wanted to wrest the EU from the control of social democrats and pallid conservatives, the Vatican from the reforms of the too-permissive Pope Francis, and the West from the clutches of immigrants and multiculturalists.

To create a new generation of leaders for his Movement, Bannon pinned his hopes on what he called a "school for gladiators." With the help of conservative British Catholic Benjamin Harnwell, he leased a thirteenth-century monastery south of Rome from the Italian government. Here the two men planned to establish a training academy that, according to Harnwell, would "institutionalise the thoughts and political insights of Steve Bannon."[13] Italy held a special fascination for Bannon because of its lineage of right-wing populist leaders, from Silvio Berlusconi to Matteo Salvini of Lega Nord. When the latter did surprisingly well in the 2018 parliamentary elections, which enabled Lega to form a government with the more politically ambiguous Five Star Movement, Bannon was effusive: "Nobody has been more engaged in the European project than the political leaders in Italy. Yesterday, what you had was a total rejection by the Italian voters, and I think that was the earthquake; the tremor is going to continue."[14]

Bannon journeyed to the epicenter of the earthquake to meet with like-minded colleagues and build institutional infrastructure. Finding enough money for this new venture, however, posed something of a challenge (much later, money would ultimately prove the undoing of Bannon). Key funders abandoned him when he was driven out of the Trump administration and published a book containing critical remarks about his former boss. But the silver-tongued Bannon found other sources of money, including a million-dollar-a-year contract from the Chinese billionaire, Guo Wengui.[15]

Now all Bannon needed were the troops. For that, he had to persuade the various radical right parties and movements to line up behind him. He started things off with a dinner in London in July 2018, which included his Belgian pal Modrikamen and Brexiteer Nigel Farage, representatives of Belgian and French far-right parties, and a former member of the far-right Sweden Democrats.[16] Filmmaker Alison Klayman was at the dinner to gather footage for her documentary about Bannon, *The Brink*. She called her husband afterwards and told him, "Either I just filmed the Wannsee Conference [a meeting of senior Nazis in 1942], or I filmed a bunch of jerks having dinner."[17]

Bannon's ambitions reached far beyond Europe. In Latin America, he appointed Bolsonaro's youngest son as his regional representative to help build on the right's electoral successes in Brazil, Colombia, Guatemala, Honduras, and Paraguay.[18] With Guo Wengui, he created a Rule of Law Fund as the point of a spear aimed at the regime in Beijing and began filming what he called a "devastating takedown of the 'myth of Chairman Xi' including the Wall Street and corporatist faction that props up the regime."[19] He visited Japan at the invitation of the Happiness Realization Party, a political cult that embraces Japanese militarism.[20] Israel, too, was part of the alt-right archipelago because Bannon, a self-professed "Christian Zionist," sees Prime Minister Benjamin Netanyahu as a key link in a future anti-Islamic front. Also figuring prominently in his thinking is Russia, a vast country led by a critic of Western liberalism and "radical Islam" that alt-right leader Richard Spencer has called "the sole white power in the world."[21]

Bannon talks big and grabs headlines. As a politico and filmmaker, he's a master illusionist. Despite all these efforts, however, Bannon never managed to turn his illusions into reality.

The Movement Bannon hoped to create in Brussels never became operational, having repeatedly postponed its promised launch throughout 2019 and then disappearing from the news altogether. Most of the political parties that Bannon and Modrikamen expected to line up behind them simply refused. After an embarrassing failure in the Belgian elections in May 2019, Modrikamen dissolved his right-wing Francophone party and grumbled that he might give up his own political career as well.[22] Bannon's much-hyped training center for right-wing politicians in Italy didn't get off the ground either as the 19-year lease the government provided to Bannon's organization—and then subsequently annulled—is now entangled in litigation.[23]

Bannon's European grand tour in 2018 was a basically a bust, and that London dinner in 2018, in retrospect, was just a Wannsee wannabe.

One of Bannon's chief selling points—that he was an American who could mediate among different European actors—turned out to be a major drawback. "For some people it was a complicated game to play: Anti-Americanism is an integral part of many nationalisms in Europe," Jordi Vaquer of the Open Society Foundations points out. "Bannon wanted to oversell what he was doing. It was more about the announcement than a carefully crafted strategy."

Bannon's prominent failures have attracted nearly as much attention as his promised successes.[24] Those failures followed Bannon back to the United States. On the morning of August 20, 2020, federal postal inspectors and representatives of the U.S. attorney's office in Manhattan raided Guo Wengui's yacht near Westbrook, Connecticut, and arrested Bannon for fraud. He'd been involved in an elaborate scheme to bilk investors who contributed to We Build the Wall, a private initiative supposedly set up to help Trump erect his long-promised wall along the southern border with Mexico.[25]

Then, in November, Bannon's Prince lost the 2020 presidential election, despite Bannon's confident predictions, up to and including the night of the election, that Trump would win.[26] In the aftermath of the vote, Bannon continued to trumpet his loyalty to the soon-to-be-ex-president by spinning outlandish conspiracy theories about election fraud. Two days after the election, he went further in his defense of Trump by calling for the beheading of two administration officials—FBI head Christopher Wray and top health official Anthony Fauci—for their perceived disloyalty to the president. "I'd put the heads on pikes," Bannon said on his live podcast. "Right. I'd put them at the two corners of the White House as a warning to federal bureaucrats. You either get with the program or you are gone." The comment prompted both Facebook and YouTube to remove the video and Twitter to permanently suspend his account.[27]

Bannon's rise and fall eerily paralleled that of Trump. The November election might not have seemed close by either the popular vote (a difference of more than 7 million votes and 4 percent of the ballots cast) or the Electoral College results (306 to 232), but the margin in the key swing states was razor close: only 43,000 votes. From this near-win on election day, Trump quickly spiraled downward and out of control. He launched an ill-advised effort, with Bannon's support, to overturn the election through a mixture of legal challenges, pressure tactics against state officials, and the incitement of his base.

This latter strategy culminated on January 6 with the president urging his followers—many of them fired up by global right-wing ideologies and conspiracy theories—to march to Capitol Hill where Congress was scheduled to certify the results of the 2020 election. Thousands of those followers overwhelmed local police, broke into the Capitol building, and came close to confronting the vice president and the assembled legislators. One police officer was killed, and four protesters died.

In the aftermath of this failed insurrection, the social media giants did to Trump what they'd done to Bannon: canceled his accounts. Congress voted to impeach him a second time. Like Bannon, he also faced a number of serious criminal charges. The parallel lines intersected once more when, during this time, Trump reached out to Bannon by phone as part of a reconciliation with his former advisor.[28] In one of his last acts as president, Trump issued a pre-emptive pardon of Bannon. Unlike their collaboration in 2016, the two men were now united in defeat, not victory.

Yet, it would be a mistake to project these failures backward and assume that Bannon's attempts to organize a Nationalist International, inspired in part by Trump, have had no impact. "Bannon might fail to build a coherent alliance across the Atlantic," French human rights activist Yasser Louati explains. "Nevertheless, the discourse he and his natural allies are pushing has become the ruling ideology in their countries—the United States, the UK, Italy, Hungary. White nationalism is in power in those countries."

Bannon's failure to establish a political bulkhead in Europe for a transatlantic far-right movement and Trump's failure to win a second term obscures a disturbing reality: both men were on to something. Even without Bannon at the fore or Trump as a symbolic figurehead, the new right has patiently been building its global connections—at the level of political parties, through civil society organizations, in the digital realm, and at the level of discourse. Bannon, like Lenin, tried to usurp an emergent project and make it seem like a mainstream concern rather than a minority sentiment.[29] For once, Bannon's timing was off, much like Lenin and his calls for revolution in Russia in 1905.

History, of course, gave Lenin a second chance. Will the same hold true for Bannon and his political revolutionaries?

THE BIG PICTURE

Whatever his talents as a political organizer, Steve Bannon has always been an acute seismologist. He understood that a succession of social upheavals over the last decade has radically realigned political power throughout the world. As a result of these tectonic shifts, what had once been on the furthest fringes of the right has now moved toward the center while the left has been pushed to the margins.

"Things fall apart; the centre cannot hold," poet William Yeats wrote at a time of similar political churn in 1919. "The best lack all conviction, while the worst are full of passionate intensity."

Today, a century after the publication of Yeats's poem, those who are full of passionate intensity now rule over considerably more than half the world's population. "The right is full of belief," Transnational Institute organizer Brid Brennan observes. "The left is full of doubts." Many of these right-wing leaders have come to power democratically but are determined to undermine democratic institutions. Their political rise has often been supported by more conventional conservative parties. They have aligned themselves on an *ad hoc* basis with other authoritarian leaders who owe their positions to military coups, one-party deliberations, or dynastic succession. Further to the extreme, a set of avowedly racist organizations and networks provide ideas, messaging, and sometimes muscle for these leaders of the new right. These ideas have also inspired a series of mass shooters to embark on racist killing sprees in the United States, throughout Europe, and even in New Zealand.

This is not a normal oscillation in electoral power. The new right wants to permanently reorder the political landscape. Mainstream parties have lost credibility. Politics have become even more polarized. Not just liberalism but democracy itself is under attack. Even where leaders have lost power, as Trump has in the United States, their supporters continue to push their agenda, on the streets as well as in the corridors of power, to prepare the ground for a successor of similar mindset.

Nor will the guardrails of democratic governance necessarily contain the ambitions of these new right leaders, for they have challenged constitutional, legislative, and judicial restraints. They have attacked the cornerstones of civil society, including the press and other watchdog institutions. They aspire to become leaders for life (like Vladimir Putin, in charge since 1999) or to establish parties that govern with little opposition for decades on end (like Japan's Liberal Democratic Party, in power almost continuously since 1955).

Rhetorically, the new right is focused on securing borders, protecting sovereignty, and challenging global elites. These leaders use the language of nationalism and particularism. They speak in the name of imagined majorities that are racially or religiously homogenous.

Yet, despite this obsession with strengthening the nation-state, this new right has increasingly been active across borders. States and parties have created international alliances. Extremist civil society organizations have worked transnationally to promote a climate of intolerance that nurtures the political ambitions of right-wing populist leaders. White nationalists in particular have created alternative digital platforms to spread their messages and recruit new members across the globe.

Progressives have organized locally and nationally to respond to the new right. But ironically, given their historic internationalism, progressives have been slow to work across borders—in a sustained, coordinated manner—in response to the new transnational assault on democracy. This dilute internationalism coincides with both the new right's attacks on global institutions and an intensification of various global threats such as climate change, pandemics, widening economic inequality, and weapons proliferation.

"Internationalism is now a problem for the left," observes Gadi Algazi of Tel Aviv University, "and a reality for the right."

FOUR ARGUMENTS

This book, which benefits from interviews with more than 80 activists, analysts, and academics around the world, will analyze the rise of the global new right and its political pivot during the coronavirus pandemic. It will highlight some of the effective responses to the new right. It will survey the current state of transnational progressive organizing. It will outline the challenges to that organizing and identify some of the lessons learned. And it will conclude with a discussion of what's missing from a robust, multi-issue, progressive transnationalism and how to fill those gaps. In the process, I will be making four key arguments.

First, the new right has made significant gains politically because it has effectively channeled discontent with economic globalization. This liberal development project, supported by mainstream political parties of the center left and center right, certainly provided benefits to some. But many more people have been "left behind" by globalization—or they feel increasingly insecure as a result of this global project—and the new right has reached these constituencies in ways that the internationalist left simply hasn't.

A second key to the new right's success has been a story that can be applied effectively across borders: the "great replacement." The argument that minorities and immigrants, with help from "globalists," are "stealing" the privileges of the dominant group has proven appealing to both an extremist fringe and more mainstream conservatives. Indeed, this narrative has provided the glue binding together the new right alliance of extreme right, radical right, populists, and mainstream conservatives.

A third element is the new right's authoritarian opportunism. These leaders have promised quick, simple solutions to complex problems. Because they are not interested in building consensus, they can effectively navigate in polarized political environments. Despite their populist pretensions and anti-corruption rhetoric, they have also used their offices to leverage state power on behalf of themselves and their political cronies. The coronavirus pandemic in 2020 provided leaders like Donald Trump, Viktor Orbán, and Benjamin Netanyahu an even greater opportunity: to operate in states of emergency that allowed them to seize more powers and implement policies that hitherto encountered legislative or judicial resistance.

Finally, the new right has a major Achilles heel. It has nothing to say about global crises like pandemics and the ever-worsening climate crisis—or what it does have to say is demonstrably wrong. For the latter, progressives and liberals can put together their own new coalition, centered around a Global Green New Deal. Such a plan, if constructed according to principles of equity, wouldn't just address the environmental crisis. By creating enormous numbers of well-paying jobs, it would also speak to those left behind by economic globalization. Such a narrative would undermine the new right's anti-globalist appeals while offering up a positive vision to rally around within and across borders.

As the twenty-first century began, progressives famously proclaimed that "another world is possible." They imagined a world beyond rote democracy and the rapacious market.

With the longstanding liberal-conservative status quo now crumbling, the new right has not only taken up this call, it is also putting it into practice. The new right's construction of "another world"—an intolerant, anti-democratic, unsustainable world—can and must be stopped before it is too late. But it requires that the best of us regain the conviction that Yeats described, not just to counter the new right but to save the planet from ruin.

This book is about that battle for another world.

1
Origins of the new right

He was a wealthy businessman who suddenly decided to run for president. Nobody in the political elite took him seriously. After all, as an outsider, he'd never been successful in politics. Plus, he trafficked in outlandish conspiracy theories, which led him to say the craziest things. Given these handicaps, there was no way he could beat the established parties and their candidates to become president.

But Stan Tymiński surprised everyone. Long before Donald Trump scored his electoral upset in the United States, Tymiński upended politics in Poland in 1990.

As a successful entrepreneur in Canada, Tymiński had made millions.[1] He proved luckless, however, in Canadian politics. His Libertarian Party never received more than 1 percent of the vote. In 1990, he decided to return to his native Poland, then preparing for its first free presidential election since the 1920s.

In June of the previous year, as the Warsaw Pact was beginning to unravel, Poland had held a relatively open parliamentary election, producing a solid victory for candidates backed by the independent trade union, Solidarność. These dissidents-turned-politicians governed for a year, under the leadership of their prime minister, Solidarność intellectual and pioneering newspaper editor Tadeusz Mazowiecki. During that first year of transition, former Communist general Wojciech Jaruzelski retained considerable authority as president. In 1990, the general finally decided to step aside.

Two political giants hoped to replace Jaruzelski as president. Mazowiecki thought he could trade on his year of experience as prime minister plus his status as a member of Solidarność's intellectual elite. Also in the running was former trade union leader Lech Wałęsa, who had done more than any other Pole to take down the Communist government (receiving a Nobel Prize for his efforts).

Compared to these famous figures, Tymiński was a nobody.

All three candidates made promises. Wałęsa announced that he would provide every Pole with $10,000 to invest in new capitalist enterprises. Mazowiecki swore he'd get the Rolling Stones to perform in Poland. Tymiński had the strangest pitch of all. He carried around a black briefcase inside which, he claimed, was secret information that would blow Polish politics to smithereens.[2]

Tymiński managed to get a toehold in national politics because, by November 1990, many Poles were already fed up with the new status quo Solidarność had created. They'd suffered the early consequences of the "shock therapy" economic reforms that would soon be introduced across much of Eastern Europe and, after 1991, Russia. Although Poland's macroeconomic indicators had finally stabilized by the end of 1990, unemployment had shot up from next to nothing to 6.5 percent, while the country's national income had fallen by more than 11 percent.[3] Though some were doing well in the new business-friendly environment, the general standard of living had plummeted as part of Poland's price for entering the global economy. The burden of transition had fallen disproportionately on workers, pensioners, small farmers, and sunset industries.

Mazowiecki, the face of the new political elite, would, like Hillary Clinton many years later, go down to ignominious defeat. Tymiński, meanwhile, garnered support from areas hardest hit by the dislocations of economic reform. He made it to the second round of voting to square off against the plainspoken, splenetic Wałęsa who pledged to take an ax to what remained of the Communist status quo.[4] Although he would ultimately accuse Wałęsa of collaborating with the secret police during the Communist era, Tymiński would lose in the second round of voting by a margin of three to one.

Stan Tymiński eventually took his wild conspiracy theories and populist pretensions back to Canada, a political has-been. And yet he was prescient in so many ways (including those charges against Wałęsa, who probably did collaborate briefly with the secret police).[5] The liberal reforms that Poland and the rest of Eastern Europe implemented after the transformations of 1989 were supposed to be a one-way journey to a future as prosperous as Scandinavia's. Instead, the immediate post-1989 was a nightmare for a huge number of people in the region, and they responded in politically unpredictable ways.[6]

After Poland's initial experiment in shock therapy, one country after another in Eastern Europe embraced fast-track free-market reforms and rapid privatization, which together represented a condensed version of economic globalization. Like Poland, they plunged into crises characterized by high unemployment and a sharp polarization of wealth. The major political parties—liberal, conservative, post-socialist—by and large supported these disruptive economic reforms. Future loans from international financial institutions and membership in the European Union depended on it. Meanwhile, with the explosion of far-right extremism came an uptick in intolerance and an escalation of attacks on minorities, particularly Roma.[7]

Tymiński was not the only politician in the region to gesture in the direction of this grimmer, unpredictable future. In Slovakia, Vladimir Mečiar steered his country out of its union with the Czech Republic in 1993, away from integration with Europe and down an insular, more nationalist path. Populist leaders in Serbia and Croatia were so determined to expand their national boundaries and homogenize their populations that they tore apart former Yugoslavia in a succession of wars in the 1990s.

With the exception of the former Yugoslavia, the prospect of joining the transnational European Union initially limited the spread of these political tendencies in Eastern Europe. When offered a choice between candidates promising eventual European citizenship plus access to EU resources versus those espousing narrow nationalism, voters unsurprisingly chose the former. But once most of the countries in the region became EU members, the anti-liberal alternative no longer carried with it that particular political or economic cost. On top of that, the financial crisis of 2008–2009 eroded what remained of popular faith in liberal economic reforms and the parties promoting them. As a result, nationalist and populist tendencies reemerged to become dominant in the region—and increasingly around the world.

Tymiński's "children" now govern nearly every country in Eastern Europe: Jarosław Kaczyński and the Law and Justice Party in Poland, President Miloš Zeman and Prime Minister Andrej Babiš in the Czech Republic, Prime Minister Igor Matovič in Slovakia, Prime Minister Viktor Orbán in Hungary, Prime Minister Boyko Borissov in Bulgaria, President Aleksandar Vučić in Serbia, and Prime Minister Janez Janša in Slovenia. The Polish-Canadian demagogue anticipated the rise of new post-Cold War populists in Western Europe as well. Silvio Berlusconi, an even wealthier outsider with no political experience, came to power in Italy in 1994 while far-right leader Jörg Haider brought his Freedom Party into a coalition government in Austria in 2000. Even the United States, where a stable two-party system was supposed to safeguard against extremism, would eventually fall into the grip of a Tymiński-like leader.

What had once seemed to be a paranoid dead end in politics has turned out to be a royal road to power. More disturbing, Tymiński's "children" are now working together across borders to build an illiberal superhighway that circles the globe.

BAND OF BROTHERS

Right-wing populism is nothing new. In the Anglo-American tradition, it can be found in the anti-Communist firebrand Joseph McCarthy in the United States in the 1950s and the fire-breathing nationalist Enoch Powell in the UK in the 1960s. Several longstanding European parties like the French National Front (now National Rally) have relied on right-wing populism to attract voters. Echoes can also be found in movements in the Global South, from the Baathist party in Syria to the Hindu nationalist Bharatiya Janata Party (BJP) in India.

But right-wing populists like Donald Trump in the United States and Jair Bolsonaro in Brazil are something different. For one thing, they have helped to create a new right by uniting a rising "identitarian" movement that focuses on racial and religious identity with more conventional right-wing parties that see political opportunity in the shift rightward.[8] This new right makes appeals to the majority—the "people"—even as it dog-whistles to a specific subset of the population, such as whites or, in the case of Indian leader Narendra Modi, upper-caste Hindus. Unlike run-of-the-mill authoritarianism or direct-action extremism, the new right seeks power through the ballot box by promising to go after the political elite and its economics of austerity. Once in power, however, the new right looks for ways to stay in office by short-circuiting the usual mechanisms of democratic governance.

In this media-saturated era, modern right-wing populism is more of a style—or, more precisely, a performance—than a coherent set of policy proposals.[9] Political figures like Trump and Bolsonaro are performers who create daily theater pieces for their audience of fans. They alter the content of their performances according to the needs of the political moment rather than the requirements of ideology. To elevate the drama of their governance, they identify one crisis after another which only they can resolve, manufacturing cliffhangers just as streaming TV shows draw in audiences primed to binge watch. To engage new audiences, they create fictional plots—about a "deep state," a threatening wave of immigrants, or a liberal conspiracy to seize all firearms—and rely on the mainstream media to amplify these plots even as careful journalists attempt to debunk them.

A key difference between the new right and conventional authoritarian leaders is their respective relationship to institutions. "Authoritarianism is a governance system," observes Jan Nederveen Pieterse, a Dutch sociologist at UC Santa Barbara. "Right-wing populism is a governance crisis." The new right, to use a motto of Steve Bannon, wants to "deconstruct the administrative state."[10] Authoritarian regimes, meanwhile, rely on such administrative apparatuses as part of their governance strategy: "they don't just control institutions, they *are* the institutions," Pieterse adds.

Despite this significant difference, the new right bears a family resemblance to right-wing authoritarian leaders, and they often collaborate on an *ad hoc* basis. These authoritarians also benefit from a general dissatisfaction with liberalism and a yearning for simple solutions to complex solutions. But unlike the new right, authoritarians are not so interested in membership in the community of democracies. Some, like Prayut Chan-o-cha in Thailand, owe their positions to military coups. Other authoritarians have come to power through one-party systems (Xi Jinping of China) or royal succession (Mohammed bin Salman of Saudi Arabia). Many stay in power through rigged elections (Paul Biya of Cameroon).

There are also authoritarian figures on the left, like Daniel Ortega in Nicaragua and Nicolas Maduro in Venezuela, who have as much distaste for liberalism as those on the far right. "There's a tendency on the left to assume that authoritarianism is a feature of the right," observes sociologist Edgardo Lander of the Central University of Venezuela. "But some leftist governments have become very authoritarian."

Rounding out these numbers are the religious fundamentalists that challenge internationalism, multiculturalism, and inclusive democracy, from the Islamic State and the Union of the Right-Wing Parties in Israel to the Christian fundamentalists in the United States who formed a core of support for Donald Trump.

Today's illiberal leaders are a band of brothers—and they are almost all of them male—when it comes to their shared preference for top-down, nationalist governance. Despite these structural similarities, however, the content of their ideologies sometimes diverges. In the Philippines, for instance, Rodrigo Duterte has attacked the Catholic Church for defending the sanctity of human life and challenging his campaign of extrajudicial murder. In Nicaragua, however, one-time revolutionary Daniel Ortega has courted the Catholic Church as a pillar of his undemocratic rule. Vladimir Putin presents himself and his country as the saviors of Christianity, while Turkey's Recep Tayyip Erdoğan promotes his own brand of political Islam, Narendra Modi has ridden to power thanks to Hindu nationalism, and Xi Jinping eschews religion altogether. Some right-wing nationalists like Bolsonaro have ambitious plans to privatize state assets, while others want to nationalize major properties, as Lega proposed for the Bank of Italy.[11] Hungary's Viktor Orbán expresses concern about climate change, but most right-wing populists like Donald Trump insist that the threat doesn't exist and want to extract ever more fossil fuels.

Although these illiberal leaders may not rhyme, they all dance to the same rhythm. They share a distaste for the constitutional constraints of liberalism, the oppositional stubbornness of civil society, and the watchful eye of a free media. In forming a larger anti-democratic and illiberal political ecosystem, these leaders have also become the world's most dominant political life form: these populists, authoritarians, and fundamentalists now rule over half the world's population. Democracy, by contrast, is in retreat—by a number of different measures. "Of the 41 countries that were consistently ranked Free from 1985 to 2005, 22 have registered net score declines in the last five years," notes Freedom House in its 2019 report.[12] In the 2020 Rule of Law index from the World Justice Project, more countries declined than improved for the third year in a row.[13] The Economist Intelligence Unit's Democracy Index in 2019 registered its lowest score—the least democratic outcome—since the ranking began in 2006.[14]

The new right provides a new twist to the old illiberalism of the authoritarians and religious fundamentalists. It represents a modern synthesis of authoritarian style and superficially democratic practices, with an assist from the latest information technologies. The authoritarians of the last century controlled television and film. Today's illiberals gravitate toward websites and social media. If Silvio Berlusconi, a media tycoon, created a new telepopulism in Italy, his successor Beppe Grillo today is better known for his cyberpopulism. Both Donald Trump and Narendra Modi use Twitter effectively to reach out to their followers. "Each new communications technology has its own form of populism," concludes historian Marco Revelli.[15]

Most importantly, the new right is a calculated response to the most salient dynamic of the post-World War II era: globalization. New right politicians have identified three crises in the globalization project—the failure of economic globalization to benefit the majority, the lack of political legitimacy of the parties that supported neoliberal reforms, and the challenges that immigrants and minorities of all kinds represent to an enforced culture of homogeneity.

AGAINST GLOBALIZATION

The new right is, at least rhetorically, skeptical about globalization and critical of the political and economic elite that supports the neoliberal project of reducing barriers to trade, investment, and financial flows. Against this "globalist" agenda, the new right emphasizes nationalism, sovereignty, and conservative values. "There has never been so much open friction between national and globalist forces," Hungarian Prime Minister Viktor Orbán put it starkly in 2018:

> We, the millions with national sentiments, on the one side, the citizen-of-the-world élite on the other side. We who believe in nation-states, in the defense of borders, in the value of the family and work on the one side and in opposition to us those who want an open society, a world without borders and nations, a new kind of family, devalued work and cheap workers over which an opaque and unaccountable army of bureaucrats reigns.[16]

The new right is capitalizing on some authentic grievances. Although the more interconnected global economy has helped both billionaires and nearly a billion Chinese, many people in between have been left behind. In 2018, the richest 1 percent of people owned nearly half of the world's wealth, while the poorer 50 percent of the global population owned less than 1 percent.[17] The rich just keep getting richer: in 2019, the 500 richest individuals increased their wealth by an extraordinary 25 percent over the previous year.[18] It's hard to track how much the world's poorest have lost in this polarizing environment, though the bottom 50 percent saw their collective wealth drop by more than 8 percent in 2018.[19]

A political backlash was inevitable. When Eastern Europeans experienced the pain of their compressed version of economic globalization—which rapidly restructured their economies so that they could enter the global financial system—they switched their political allegiances to illiberal leaders. The negative impact of globalization that Eastern European countries experienced in the 1990s didn't start hitting more advanced economies in a more sustained way until after 2005. According to a 2016 McKinsey report, *Poorer Than Their Parents*, fewer than 10 million people in 25 advanced economies—approximately 2 percent of households—experienced a flatlining or falling income between 1993 and 2005. Over the next nine years, between 2005 and 2014, that figure rose to 540–580 million people, or 65–70 percent of households.[20] Such an extraordinary increase in the number of families experiencing economic distress, from 2 percent to 70 percent, is certain to have a political impact. And indeed, right-wing populism rose sharply in precisely those countries that have experienced the greatest drop in family income between 2005 and 2014: Italy (97 percent of households), the United States (81 percent), the United Kingdom (70 percent), and France (63 percent).[21]

The financial crisis of 2008–2009, which took place in the middle of this critical period, focused popular resentment on the global economic elite. Some of that anger could be found in the mobilizations against Wall Street by the Occupy movement or against European Union financial policies by the Spanish *indignados*. But it was even more widespread. According to an exhaustive study of protests by the Friedrich Ebert Foundation, 164 protests took place around the world between 2006 and 2013 that targeted international financial institutions and their policies.[22] Since that time, another wave of anti-austerity protests swept through Lebanon, Tunisia, Chad, Sri Lanka, Haiti, Argentina, Ecuador, and Chile, among other countries.

Unlike the World Bank protests at the end of the 1990s or the Occupy gatherings after the 2008 financial crisis, it wasn't the left that took advantage of the more recent discontent with global economic institutions and their austerity programs. "At the root has been the right wing's capacity to harness people's sense of alienation—the discontents of globalization," observes Fiona Dove of the Transnational Institute in Amsterdam. This alienation has caused a political shift in working-class loyalties—for instance, from the French Communist Party to Marine Le Pen's far-right National Rally or the surge of support in proletarian Rotterdam for Geert Wilders.[23] The deindustrialization of Germany, particularly in the eastern regions, has pushed previous supporters of the Social Democrats into the ranks of the Alternative für Deutschland.[24]

To attract supporters of left parties, the far right offered what amounted to a leftish economic program. Beginning in 2015, the Polish right-wing Law and Justice Party (PiS) pushed through classic Keynesian stimulus measures and popular redistribution policies to woo supporters of the post-Communist Party as well as Solidarność trade union loyalists. "When PiS came to power it implemented a number of pro-worker economic policies, such as generous childcare payments that have cut poverty rates and strengthened the labor-market position of single mothers," writes political scientist David Ost. "It has increased minimum wages, lowered the retirement age, and cut back on the use of 'junk' job contracts. It has imposed new taxes on foreign banks and insurance companies to pay for these programs."[25] PiS has also offered free medicine to those over the age of 75 and dropped the income tax requirement for those under the age of 26.[26]

Another example is the swing among many Labour voters in the United Kingdom in favor of the 2016 referendum to leave the European Union. The Labour Party was fatally conflicted about whether to support withdrawal from the European Union, since many members—and leader Jeremy Corbyn—had long attacked the EU for diluting its commitment to social-democratic values, such as a more equitable distribution of wealth among member countries, in favor of a newer neoliberal emphasis on reduced barriers to the flow of capital. These "Lexiteers" joined with some conservatives newly converted to anti-globalization, like Conservative MP Iain Duncan Smith, who began lambasting the very big business ethos he'd earlier celebrated.[27]

The UK could not have exited the EU without a spavined Labour Party and the swing votes of a disgusted working class.

Neither the alienation of the working class nor the populist right's opportunism is confined to the Global North. Authoritarian populism has widespread appeal throughout the Global South, thanks to a bevy of charismatic leaders. "Their appeal to the electorate and their huge support comes from at least a rhetorical anti-neoliberal agenda," notes Wolfram Schaffar of the International Institute for Asian Studies in Leiden. "You see that with Thaksin Shinagawa in Thailand. He introduced universal health care coverage in Thailand, which made him hugely popular." Philippine President Rodrigo Duterte, a student of Communist-Party founder Jose Maria Sison, initially appointed several prominent leftists to his cabinet and made some economic overtures to the traditional working-class constituency of the left, qualifying him as a "fascist original" in Walden Bello's terms.[28] Duterte "came to power with anti-neoliberal and pro-welfare promises," Schaffar adds. "That's why he has the stable support of more than 80 percent of the population." In Brazil, urban working-class supporters of Bolsonaro abandoned the left because of surging unemployment and the pervasive crime in the cities.[29] Pinochetism—the right-wing free-market ideology embraced by Augusto Pinochet in Chile in the 1970s and 1980s—lives on in certain leaders, like Colombia's Iván Duque, but is not an appealing program for most voters.

Central to this political shift of both working-class and blue-collar middle-class voters has been the decline of labor unions. In the Organization of Economic Cooperation and Development (OECD)—36 of the wealthiest countries in the world—trade union membership has fallen by half since 1985, from 30 percent to 16 percent.[30] Globally, for workers in the formal sector, the density of trade union membership is 17 percent—not counting China, Belarus, and Cuba—with dramatic declines in Eastern Europe over the last 30 years.[31] In Poland, for instance, where the independent Solidarność trade union once boasted a membership of 10 million people in a country of 40 million, union membership has dropped to around 10 percent.[32]

In the United States, the drop has been equally dramatic. Unions were "the central piece supporting the welfare state in the United States," points out political economist and historian Gar Alperovitz, co-founder of the Democracy Collaborative. Union membership has "gone from 34.2 percent to 11 percent—only 6 percent in the private sector. The institutional powerbase that once sustained the so-called liberal program is gone." Without union pressure, wages for the average U.S. worker are the same today as they were back in 1973 (adjusted for inflation), and the situation has been much worse for those who have lower annual earnings.[33]

Union guarantees of job security have been central to forestalling the "fear of falling" of the working and middle class.[34] A growing fear of relinquishing hard-won economic gains has been central to the rise of the new right, representing, for instance, a greater predictor of support for Donald Trump in the 2016 elections than economic status alone.[35] "The crucial group are those not yet at the bottom who fear social and economic declassification," observe Lorenzo Marsili and Niccolo Milanese.[36] This is a familiar conclusion in the literature of political science. As Robert Jensen has written, "status loss is one of the most important drivers for the emergence of the radical positions within the electorate."[37]

In this way, the critique of globalization appeals not just to the have-nots but to the have-somes as well. Traditionally seen as the motor for democratization, the middle class has provided an "active consensus" behind right-wing movements in countries like the Philippines, Thailand, and Brazil, suggests sociologist and former member of the Philippines parliament Walden Bello. "The lower classes tend to get swept up with authoritarian politics, but they don't have the same kind of approach or response," he notes. "The middle class, especially the urban middle class, provides a more active consensus."

There is also a geographic factor behind the new right's popularity, at least in the Global North where neoliberal policies have generally benefited urban and suburban workers at the expense of those who live in the countryside. It's no surprise, then, that the new right has also done well in rural areas and small towns—the Polish countryside, the American farm belt, the Anatolian heartland—that did not traditionally benefit from the economic growth in more liberal urban centers.[38] Economic globalization has made the livelihoods of farmers more precarious, and the countryside tends to be more culturally conservative and less cosmopolitan than the cities. As sociologist Walden Bello argues, rural areas frequently provide a base for a populist and occasionally fascist "counter revolution" to liberal democracy.[39]

The new right has also attracted support from particular economic sectors, such as the fossil-fuel industry, where policies addressing climate change threaten jobs from the executive boardroom all the way down to the coal mine. These constituencies, too, are concentrated outside the cities. In her book *Strangers in Their Own Land*, sociologist Arlie Hochschild has explored why even environmentalists support the new right in heavily polluted Louisiana, where the oil and chemical industries have joined conservative politicians to portray pro-immigration and pro-environment liberals as anti-job.[40] "It feels like we're living through the last gasps of not just a dying industry but a whole economic order around extraction," explains May Boeve of 350. org in Oakland. "This intense right-wing surge is a reaction."

The new right has directed much of the anger of those who have not benefited from globalization toward the presumed architects of the project: transnational institutions and elites. In this way, Bannon's platform of "deconstructing the administrative state" has translated into campaigns against the "globalist structures" in Brussels (the EU) and Washington (the IMF) responsible for pushing neoliberal economic policies. In particular, new right leaders want to reduce the power of international institutions and accords that impinge on the sovereignty of the nation-state and restrict the power of national corporations. They are suspicious of any global institutions, like the World Health Organization, that claim to be acting in the common good.

Nor have the failures of globalization been lost on the managers of the global economy. Even the IMF has acknowledged that worsening economic inequality has called into question the capacity of economic globalization to lift all boats in a rising tide (but without engaging in the necessary institutional overhaul to address the problem).[41] Also eroding faith in globalization has been "slowbalization."[42] Over the last decade, the portion of trade as part of global GDP has fallen. Multinationals have seen a drop in their share of global profits. Foreign direct investment tumbled from 3.5 percent of global GDP in 2007 to 1.3 percent in 2018.[43] Globalization, in other words, was having problems not just distributing the wealth but producing it in the first place.

Finally, a set of technological transformations, particularly automation, has threatened to make the global assembly line obsolete, which puts at risk the jobs and livelihoods of millions of workers, including 65 percent of Nigerian workers and 69 percent of Indian workers, according to World Bank projections.[44] Economists who have examined how automation has spiked at times of recession expect a similar surge as a result of the economic downturn associated with the coronavirus pandemic, with low-income workers, the young, and workers of color at greatest risk.[45] COVID-19 alone will not be responsible for causing an economic transformation analogous to the massive reduction of the agricultural workforce in the industrial era, but it could very well represent a moment of punctuated equilibrium in this technological evolution.

Economic globalization, even before the pandemic hit in 2020, was failing to deliver on many levels. But the economic crisis also offers a wealth of political opportunities.

ATTACKING THE POLITICAL CONSENSUS

The political forces that hitched their wagons to economic globalization faced a crisis of their own after the 2009 financial recession. Voters had had enough of their promises of prosperity, which so obviously did not correspond with their reality. This disgust was directed at parties across the political spectrum, not just the Tories in the UK and Republicans in the United States, but also the liberals that embraced "Third Way" politics, French Socialists that pushed austerity economics, even former Communist parties from Eastern Europe that supported versions of "shock therapy."

After 2009, angry voters were casting around for alternatives. "The main establishment parties—Republicans and Democrats in the United States, Social Democrats and Christian conservatives in Europe—all of them were giving the same response, which was to bail out the finance sector and cut social spending to cover the costs of those bailouts," Sol Trumbo Vila of the Transnational Institute points out. "Most people felt that they had only two choices: follow the neoliberal globalization model, which has now been exposed as dysfunctional, or go back to nationalist projects and frames, which are outmoded but familiar."

Progressives might have represented a third option for voters rejecting mainstream parties in the wake of the financial crisis. The upswell of support for Bernie Sanders in the United States, Jeremy Corbyn's rise to the leadership of the UK Labour Party, and the electoral surge of the Greens in the 2019 European parliament elections all reflected this dissatisfaction.

But many on the left have remained suspicious of electoral politics. A 2012 study on "subterranean politics" in Europe reviewed the activism going on at the time—the Occupy movement, the anti-fascist organizing—and concluded, as the London School of Economics' Mary Kaldor put it, that "it was very anti-political because people didn't want anything to do with the political class."[46] This disillusionment was reinforced by the center left's flirtation with Third Way politics, which had pushed the Labour parties in the UK, Australia, and New Zealand, the Democratic Party in the United States, the Swedish Social Democratic Party, and others toward neoliberalism. After 2008, as Sheri Berman writes in a study of *Why the Left Loses*,

> the centre-left lacked a convincing message for dealing with the crisis, or a more general vision of how to promote growth while protecting citizens from the harsher aspects of free markets. Instead, it kept on trying to defend outdated policies or proposed watered-down versions of neoliberalism that barely differentiated it from the centre-right.[47]

While the left was compromised by its history, other political actors were prepared to take advantage of the vacuum created by the financial crisis. "The right wing that was waiting in the wings basically stepped in and harvested the arguments and the resistance organized by movements and unions around the world against corporate globalization," explains Shalmali Guttal of Focus on the Global South in Thailand. "But they changed the enemy. The enemy was not mainly global capitalism and neoliberalism and corporations. They created this 'other.' The enemy were the globalizers, the ones who put free trade before national interests. and those who talked about national interest in the language of justice, equality, and peoples' rights."

Hungary's Viktor Orbán is a case in point. In the late 1980s, Orbán started his political career by co-founding a new party, Fidesz, that embodied the hopes of a new generation of liberal and radical youth. When support for liberalism collapsed in the wake of the country's economic reforms, Orbán found a new home on the opposite end of the political spectrum. Thanks in part to his sharpened critique of globalism, he became prime minister for the second time in 2010. Once a prominent opponent of Russian imperialism and an ardent supporter of European integration, Orbán took advantage of his second shot at power to guide Hungary further away from European liberalism and toward Russian absolutism. It was an astonishing ideological reversal, particularly in a country with a historically strong anti-Russian and pro-European tilt, which had emerged as the poster child for liberalism after 1989.

It wasn't the only example of political opportunism. "There's an enormous number of people who feel deeply let down by the existing political establishment who are very vulnerable to nationalist, populist, racist calls to power," notes Ethan Zuckerman of MIT's Center for Civic Media. "These opportunistic political leaders are masterfully grabbing that sentiment. And once they grab it, they fully believe it. Politicians are salespeople. They have to persuade themselves of something so that they can sell it."

The backlash against liberalism in the wake of the financial crisis was slow in building in some countries. In the United States, even before quintessential liberal Barack Obama won the presidential election in the midst of the downturn in 2008, he was a target of extremist ire. In 2008, David Adkisson was motivated by his hatred of the Democratic candidate—"He is a joke," he declared of Obama in his manifesto, "He is dangerous to America"—to walk into a Unitarian Universalist Church in Knoxville, Tennessee, where children were rehearsing the musical *Annie*, pull out a shotgun, and kill two people before he was wrestled to the ground. "Liberals are evil," Adkisson concluded in his manifesto, "Kill liberals."[48]

Approximately a quarter of the American population formed a nascent resistance to Obama as soon as he took office. This was the 26 percent of Americans "who still approved of George W. Bush in the waning days of his presidency; the 26 percent who in 2009 said they'd like to see Sarah Palin as Obama's successor in 2012 ... and the 26 percent who believed that Obama's 2008 election was not legitimate," writes journalist Will Bunch.[49] The resistance would find political form in the Tea Party almost immediately after Obama's inauguration, a vehicle for the radical right that helped to take over the Republican Party and win power through electoral means.

Some of the disgruntled also found a home among white nationalists and other extremists, whose groups multiplied.[50] Much of this expansion took place online where widely dispersed and otherwise isolated extremists could find community. Between 2012 and 2016, according to a report by George Washington University's Program on Extremism, "there was a 600 percent increase in followers of American white-nationalist movements on Twitter."[51] By the summer of 2015, the alt-right was all over the internet, thanks to Steve Bannon and Breitbart News.

But, as journalist David Neiwert points out, the alt-right "lacked a real leader—a charismatic political figure around whom it could finally coalesce, whom its members could devote their energies to electing to office."[52] The backlash against Obama needed someone who could bridge the gap between the radical Tea Partiers and the racist extremists.

Donald Trump was just that bridge. He was the first president to be memed into office, as writer Dale Beran puts it, courtesy of the alt-right, 8Chan jokesters, and a sympathetic conservative media, with a big assist from WikiLeaks and Russian hackers.[53] These armchair activists put forward Trump as a representative of "the America of the peripheries, of all the isolated peripheries forgotten by the centres" while simultaneously portraying Hillary Clinton as the candidate of a wealthy, urban elite.[54] This carefully curated backlash downplayed Trump's cultivation of wealthy donors and promises of big kickbacks to Wall Street. In the 2016 election, Trump was improbably presented as a man of the people even though it was his opponent, Hillary Clinton, who won decisively among those who earned less than $30,000 a year.[55] The pattern was repeated in 2020, with Biden doing even better among those earning less than $50,000; despite his populist persona, Trump only won among those earning more than $100,000.[56] At the same time, the rural and white working class continued to support Trump, pointing to a longer-term transformation of the bases of the two major parties, with the Republican Party following the pattern of new right parties in other parts of the world by attacking cosmopolitan elites, including the financiers that have generally supported conservative politics, in favor of the "people."[57]

Trump is but one of the new charismatic, populist leaders. In the Philippines and India, for instance, "we're moving away from politics as usual or democracy as usual and moving into a period of charismatic politics," explains Walden Bello. "The source of authority is charismatic rather than rational-legal or traditional. People might say, for instance, 'We have too much deadlock and we need a strong leader to break those deadlocks.'" These charismatic leaders tend to be outsiders or, at least, present themselves as outsiders like Donald Trump or career politicians like Modi and Bolsonaro who remade themselves into anti-establishment figures. The rejection of conventional politicians has been so categorical that voters have even flocked to support well-known comedians, like Jimmy Morales in Guatemala, Beppe Grillo in Italy, and Volodymyr Zelensky in Ukraine.

What unites the new right is its exploitation of popular anger at the political and economic status quo. But it has been even more successful in taking advantage of cultural grievances and thereby gaining the support of those who face little or no economic challenges.

CULTURAL STRUGGLE

The new right has flourished in countries that have not prospered economically over the last 15 years. But it has also done well in places such as Austria and the Scandinavian states, which made out quite well.

Although the rejection of economic globalization and the embrace of charismatic, anti-establishment politicians explain much of the new right's appeal, many supporters are responding to factors that are not precisely political or economic. "Decades of academic research have shown that cultural backlash is much more important than economic anxiety," writes Cas Mudde. "In short, there are few far-right voters who are informed only by economic anxiety, while there are many who are only expressing a cultural backlash."[58] As Melissa Ryan, the editor of the Ctrl Alt-Right Delete newsletter, points out, voters are responding to something visceral. The new right is "fighting a cultural war first, and a political war second," she says. "A lot of the time, policy doesn't even enter into it. I closely follow Trump's online army, which is both American and international. It's hard to get them excited about policy but easy to get them amped up around cultural cues: racist, misogynistic, anti-immigrant, and Islamophobic views."

These cultural issues all involve a policing of some type of border. White nationalists are focused on preserving white privilege and maintaining white "purity" in the face of challenges from minorities at home and migrants from non-white countries. Religious extremists want their religion—and only their religion—to be fused with the nation-state. Gender activists are concerned about the loss of heterosexual privileges and male supremacy. This larger effort by the new right to police cultural and physical borders can also be understood as a rejection of Enlightenment values of rationality, progress, and equality.[59] The goal is to rewrite an entire historical trajectory devoted to breaking down barriers and distributing political and economic power more equitably throughout society.

That historical trajectory extends to the gains made by social movements in the modern era, beginning with the victories of feminism. "The ways in which women's movements have challenged the fundamental assumptions of patriarchy have created a set of fears about what will replace it," Kavita N. Ramdas of Open Society's Women's Rights Program points out. "The language of nationalism and hypermasculinity are tied to each other—there's a reason it's called patriotism." The Proud Boys in North America and other masculinist groups fret that men are under siege from the feminist movement, while right-wing populist leaders emphasize their virility and machismo, disparaging women and feminists as Donald Trump and Jair Bolsonaro have repeatedly done. Their misogyny extends even toward gender studies. "Viktor Orbán prohibited gender studies in Hungarian universities in 2018," notes Birgit Sauer of the University of Vienna, so the European far right wants "to use Hungary as an example to cut off the financing of gender studies."

Immigration has long been a preoccupation of the far right, which has demonized outsiders for "stealing" jobs, diluting dominant culture, and even threatening the health of society. It wasn't only despair over economic conditions that motivated German voters to support the far-right Alternative für Deutschland. The anti-immigrant sentiment of many supporters of the post-Communist Party of Democratic Socialism—plus a belief that immigrants were taking their jobs as well as government benefits—pushed them to support the far right.[60] The same holds true throughout Europe.[61]

The new right's anti-immigrant discourse is suffused with Islamophobia, particularly in Europe. According to the myths of "Eurabia" and "Europistan," Muslims are waging both a demographic and an ideological campaign to take over the continent.⁶² These myths motivated Norwegian mass shooter Anders Breivik in 2011 and his would-be acolyte Philip Manshaus, who attacked a Norwegian mosque in summer 2019. They helped generate movements like the English Defence League in the UK and Pegida in Germany. The roots of this Islamophobia run deep, an amalgam of Crusader nostalgia, Orientalist misreadings of history and culture, anger over post-World War II guest worker programs, and concerns about terrorism.⁶³

Nor can this Islamophobia be separated from the geopolitics of the last half-century, beginning with the Soviet invasion of Afghanistan and the Iranian revolution of 1979 through the cultivation of the mujahideen opposition and the rise of the Taliban and al-Qaeda to the U.S. wars in Afghanistan and Iraq. The collapse of the Taliban-led government in Afghanistan and Saddam Hussein's regime in Iraq, followed by the Arab Spring uprisings and the civil wars in Syria and Libya, precipitated a huge outflow of migrants and refugees from North Africa, the Middle East, and Central Asia. The transformation of the demographics of Europe and the United States by an influx of Muslims—fleeing wars and conflicts that were more often than not instigated or at least aggravated by U.S. military intervention—produced a cultural backlash that anti-Islamic movements weaponized politically.

Today, ground zero of this Islamophobic campaign is France, where a succession of governments has used strict secularism, the country's famous *laïcité*, to impose bans on anything that might be construed as promoting religion in public spaces. In practice, these laws have targeted Muslim women who wear head coverings. France is also home to novelist Michel Houellebecq, who has turned anti-Islamic sentiment into bestselling novels, and Renaud Camus, who developed the "great replacement" doctrine. The attacks in Christchurch, New Zealand in March 2019 "show that France has been the promised land for many white supremacists," says French human rights activist Yasser Louati, referring to the killer's manifesto entitled The Great Replacement. "The Christchurch terrorist said that he was inspired or motivated by what is happening in France. France has the largest Muslim minority in the West—and it is the country that has passed the greatest number of laws targeting the Muslim community."

Trump tried to import something similar into the United States with his Muslim travel ban, which lower courts successfully blocked before the Supreme Court upheld it in a narrow 5–4 decision. The Indian and Israeli governments are focused on keeping Muslims at arm's length through stricter citizenship laws. Some Buddhist governments, too, have jumped on the bandwagon, forming an anti-Muslim International that connects Sri Lanka, Myanmar, and Thailand. Even Nobel Prize winner Aung San Suu Kyi has joined the fray by visiting Hungary and discussing with Viktor Orbán their shared concern over "continuously growing Muslim populations."[64] The EU made only a lukewarm statement on Myanmar's ethnic cleansing of the Muslim Rohingya minority "because Orbán did not want to have a clear statement on that," says Wolfram Schaffar. "Orbán said that he could understand Myanmar expelling what it considers illegal immigrants." In other words, Orbán could understand genocide as long as it applied to Muslims.

Islamophobia is a subset of a more encompassing xenophobia associated with populism. Much media focus has been on anti-immigrant sentiment in Europe. But attacks on foreigners have become so acute in South Africa that more than a thousand refugees camped out in front of UN offices in Cape Town in October 2019 demanding that they be relocated to a third country because they feared for their lives.[65] Venezuelan refugees have faced xenophobic backlash throughout Latin America.[66] Hatred of ethnic Chinese periodically resurfaces throughout southeast Asia and has spread more widely in the wake of the COVID-19 pandemic.[67] Anti-immigrant parties have also attracted significant support in Australia and New Zealand.

The border crosser, according to this anti-globalization ideology, is suspect, whether a globetrotting financier, a cosmopolitan liberal, a family seeking a better life in another country, or a desperate refugee fleeing a warzone. The coronavirus pandemic has only further stigmatized border crossers as potential vectors of infection.

GOING MAINSTREAM

Immigration has proven to be the gateway issue for many extremists to enter the mainstream. To do so successfully, they needed the assistance of mainstream media figures. In Europe, for instance, fringe parties and movements couldn't have weaponized the immigration issue to boost their vote totals without a corresponding boost from the media.

"Mainstream media and politicians chose to frame the influx of asylum seekers as a 'crisis' thereby providing ammunition to the already mobilized far right," writes Cas Mudde.[68]

The media has facilitated this mainstreaming in other ways. Because it proved useful for ratings, TV networks in the United States devoted considerable airtime to the outrageous statements of Donald Trump during his presidential campaign, thus effectively providing him free political advertising for his proposals to build a wall along the Mexican border and kick out all undocumented workers. The internet, meanwhile, has provided a megaphone for fringe personalities who would otherwise have narrow appeal. In the United States, Peter Brimelow, formerly a senior editor at *Forbes*, set up the VDare blog in 1999 to showcase his anti-immigration views and those of like-minded white nationalists (though Brimelow himself, British born and now living in the United States, is an immigrant).

The far right has moved into the mainstream through a variety of tactics and not just by creating successful political parties. "The real danger today is not that we have an unstoppable wave of far-right populism," notes Princeton professor Jan-Werner Mueller. "The real danger is the opportunism of the mainstream: other parties that outright collaborate with these far-right populist parties or *de facto* copy at least some of their rhetoric and even some of their policies."

Mainstream political parties in Europe have long maintained a practice of quarantining the far right, allowing their political parties to run for parliament but refusing to partner with them to form coalition governments. In 1991, for instance, Belgian parties agreed to a *cordon sanitaire* to keep the far-right Vlaams Blok out of government. Despite street protests, this agreement has held, even as the Vlaams Blok has changed its name to Vlaams Belang and witnessed a resurgence of support that has prompted the mainstream right-wing parties to challenge the restriction.[69]

A similar *cordon sanitaire* is still holding in the European parliament, where mainstream parties are blocking the far right from chairing any important committees. But the rising number of far-right deputies is putting pressure on this strategy.[70] Also, political isolation has its unintended consequences. "Seeking legal recourse to mute a party that gains voice for its anti-system message through institutionalized channels of participation and representation, however, may itself be seen as being of dubious democratic merit and so risks further alienating a portion of the electorate already suspicious of the establishment," writes political scientist William Downs.[71]

Whether because of this unintended consequence of fueling populism or the sheer increase in the new right's vote totals, conservative parties have begun to renege on their informal non-cooperation pacts. In Austria, for instance, the far-right Freedom Party led by Jörg Haider entered a coalition partnership with the conservative People's Party in 2000. Hundreds of thousands of Austrians demonstrated on the streets, and the EU pledged not to cooperate with the new government.[72] Eighteen years later, when the Freedom Party returned to government, fewer demonstrators showed up on the streets and the EU made no so such threats. "It was an indication of the normalization of incorporation," concludes Cas Mudde.[73]

The Freedom Party was eventually embroiled in a corruption scandal, and the government collapsed. But the far right had already had its impact, for the People's Party standard bearer, Sebastian Kurz, adopted much of the far right's rhetoric. Kurz "has a quite authoritarian agenda," Alexandra Strickner of the Austrian chapter of Attac points out. "It's important to look at how the center—the Christian Democrats and even the Social Democrats—is shifting much more to the right" in Austria.

Something similar has happened in Japan, where right-wing nationalist Shinzo Abe has injected what had once been fringe views about Japanese history into the mainstream. "Since Abe took office the second time at the end of 2012, he has really shifted the whole society to the right," Satoko Norimatsu of the Peace Philosophy Centre in Vancouver explains. "For example, something that would have been controversial 10 or 20 years ago is no longer controversial. If a cabinet member had denied that the Nanjing Massacre ever happened 10 or 20 years ago, he'd have been dismissed immediately. Now, almost the whole cabinet accepts this." In Israel, Prime Minister Benjamin Netanyahu likewise "started supporting far-right activists and candidates and mainstreaming their ideas in order to keep himself in power," reports Ran Cohen of Israel's Democratic Bloc. The resignation of Abe in August 2020 and the collapse of the Netanyahu coalition government in December 2020 did not substantially alter the overall hard right-wing political consensus in either country.

In Russia, some activists of the extreme right chose ideology over the nation when they joined explicitly fascist Ukrainian brigades *against* Russian-aligned separatists. But Vladimir Putin has done much to lure the far right back into his fold, for instance, by using a subtle shift in vocabulary to signify his appropriation of a more exclusionary nationalist project. In the Russian language, the term "Russian" can be translated as either *russky* (ethnic Russian) or *rossisky* (Russian by citizenship). "Since 2012, Putin started using *russky*," explains Ilya Matveev, a founding editor of Openleft.ru living in St. Petersburg. "Previously Putin supported the civic nation. But since the annexation of Crimea, nationalism became more ethnicized. This is precisely what the nationalists wanted, and they became semi-allies of the regime."

In the United States, meanwhile, the victory of Trump in the 2016 elections, but more so his transformation of the Republican Party into a haven for the new right, meant that "the line between the fringe and the right is starting to collapse," notes Heidi Beirich of the Global Project Against Hate and Extremism. "Over the last year, there has been a deepening of the alliance between the Republican Party and these groups that were never accepted in the GOP. The Republicans would dog-whistle a lot about Blacks and immigrants. But now they're openly working with extremists who were beyond the pale before." In the past, a rather marginal figure like Ron Paul, a Republican Congressman from Texas who ran unsuccessfully for president in 2008 and 2012, was the conduit for the far right into the Republican Party mainstream.[74] Trump proved to be a much more successful pipeline.

Sometimes a right-wing populist party will even align with more extremist civil society. In Poland in 2018, for instance, government officials for the first time joined the Independence Day march organized by the far-right National Radical Camp.[75] The following year, local politicians from the Law and Justice Party (PiS) also showed up in support of an anti-LGBT demonstration in Białystok. "Everyone was quite shocked that this collaboration happened in Białystok," reports Igor Stokfiszewski of Krytyka Polityczna. "Until now, we had the impression that PiS was trying to keep at least a little distance, but now they are directly collaborating with the far right."

Indeed, the new right is breaking out of quarantine in many different ways. "An anti-immigration right-wing populist party like Alternative für Deutschland or a grassroots movement like Pegida functions as an incubator or hub where people from the conservative right meet highly violent extremists that they would normally not meet," explains Daniel Koehler of the German Institute in Radicalization and De-Radicalization Studies. "These populist right-wing parties systematically bring down the social barriers that would normally prevent extremist groups from interacting with the political mainstream."

Another path to the mainstream is through the military. Neo-Nazi organizations and the KKK have made inroads in the U.S. military, particularly during the 2000s when recruiters were desperate to fill quotas for the post-9/11 wars. White nationalism persists in the ranks at disturbingly high levels.[76] The arrest of a Coast Guard lieutenant in 2019 accused of stockpiling weapons to start a race war, the training of white supremacists by active-duty U.S. military personnel and veterans, and a plot uncovered in 2020 involving a young Army soldier coordinating with a neo-Nazi group to kill members of his own unit all testify to the close links between the extreme right and members of the military.[77] Germany has been busy trying to purge the far right from the ranks of the Bundeswehr and has been investigating 450 cases of identitarians and neo-Nazis.[78] The German government was even forced to disband an elite special forces unit in 2020 because of far-right infiltration.[79] Australia, New Zealand, and South Africa: all have struggled with white supremacists in the ranks of their militaries. The problem extends to police departments as well.

To move into the mainstream requires money. Right-wing civil society organizations and foundations have facilitated this flow of money. The far-right embrace of climate denial, for instance, has gotten a big global lift from the likes of ExxonMobil and the Koch brothers. The U.S. climate-denial thinktank the Heartland Institute works closely with European partners. At the UN climate conference in Katowice, Poland in 2018, according to German journalist Susanne Götze, "the Heartland Institute connected with the Polish trade union, Solidarność. They signed a contract of collaboration. They did it officially. They don't hide." Solidarność represents Poland's dwindling number of coal miners.

In Spain, where the stigma attached to former fascist dictator Francisco Franco hitherto restricted the emergence of far-right political parties, the new Vox party took advantage of considerable international support to get off the ground.[80] Campaign finance laws in the

EU make it difficult for foreigners to contribute money to elections. As in the United States, however, foreigners could support like-minded organizations that spread Vox-like messages.[81] During the parliamentary elections in April 2019, the party went from zero to 10 percent (and 24 MPs) in record time and then, in a second election in November, doubled its seats to become the country's third-largest party in parliament. "The internationals helped shape the image of Vox, the rallies, the discourse, and gave it lots of messages to test, like anti-immigration," explains Jordi Vaquer of the Open Society Foundations.

Entering the mainstream also opens up new sources of funding. Vox first achieved electoral success at the regional level, in Andalusia in December 2018. Even though the party had previously criticized state funding for parties, it gladly accepted nearly 3 million Euros of such funding.[82] In Germany, meanwhile, political parties that make it into the Bundestag in consecutive elections become eligible for state funds to support their activities worldwide. The far-right Alternative für Deutschland (AfD) created a foundation, the Erasmus Stiftung, to tap into those funds when it becomes eligible. If the AfD is able to remain in the Bundestag in 2021, which is likely given its successes in the local and European parliament elections in 2019, the foundation could receive as much as 70 million Euros of taxpayer money per year.[83] Those funds will help establish Erasmus Stiftung offices in multiple countries with a mandate to support like-minded organizations and promote their international cooperation.

Once in power, the populist right attempts to transform the mainstream by suppressing oppositional civil society. In Brazil, for instance, "The Bolsonaro government has criminalized popular movements and political organizations," explains Tchenna Maso of La Via Campesina and Movement of People Affected by Dams in Latin America. "The government is focused on suppressing organizing on the left, shutting down marches and protests." Bolsonaro early on in his term issued a decree to "supervise, coordinate, monitor and accompany the activities and actions of international organizations and non-governmental organizations in the national territory."[84] A major focus of this heightened government control has been on environmental organizations, which the Brazilian president has even blamed for the intensification of fires in the Amazon.[85]

Suppressing progressive civil society organizations also involves restricting their access to funding. "When it comes to the European situation, if some of these parties take power, as happened in Austria, there's a lot more to lose in Europe than in the United States because civil society groups are tied to the state," adds Heidi Beirich. In Germany, for instance, the AfD is championing the removal of government support for precisely those civil society initiatives devoted to identifying and confronting the far right.[86]

This has already happened in Poland. "We are dealing with structural discrimination against civil society organizations including Krytyka Polityczna," explains Igor Stokfiszewski. "We have been cut off from any public funds. We have been attacked in the public media, on public TV, and pointed out as an enemy of the people." In Russia, the Putin government instituted a "foreign agent" law in 2012 that stigmatizes any NGO that accepts money from a foreign entity.[87] In Hungary, the parliament passed two laws in summer 2018, one criminalizing assistance to migrants and another that imposes a tax on any groups that advocate on behalf of the undocumented. Many organizations feel that if they "owned up to the fact that they were working on this subject, it would damage their overall reputation and their ability to fundraise among Hungarian citizens and attract volunteers," reports Márta Pardavi of the Hungarian Helsinki Committee.

The problem goes beyond the financing of civil society organizations. If the populist right manages to take control of government, it often engages in "state capture," using the mechanisms and resources of state power to strengthen the party and its affiliated organizations. In Hungary, for instance, the Fidesz government of Viktor Orbán has helped concentrate the media in the hands of its supporters and has even distributed something as relatively minor as licenses for cigarette sales to party loyalists.[88] If the Hungarian government renationalizes utilities or banks, it's not because of some fundamental belief that the state benefits from interfering in the economy in this way. Rather, Fidesz simply wants more power in its hands and more spoils to distribute. "The problem is not that they are privatizing the state for themselves," argues sociologist András Bozóki, who once served in the Hungarian government as a minister of culture.

They are nationalizing other people's private goods for the state and the state is equal to themselves. There is a privatization via nationalization because the state itself is privatized. Don't be misled when you hear that some private activities are nationalized. It just means that the larger mafia took over the smaller one.[89]

Such policies of state capture, alongside voter suppression and constitutional changes, help explain the persistence in power of such parties and politicians: Vladimir Putin in Russia (since 1999), Recep Tayyip Erdoğan in Turkey (since 2003), Daniel Ortega in Nicaragua (since 2007), Benjamin Netanyahu in Israel (since 2009), Viktor Orbán in Hungary (since 2010), and Narendra Modi in India (since 2014). Even Donald Trump, a septuagenarian in a country with a two-term limit on the presidency, "joked" on multiple occasions about becoming "president for life" and did his utmost to overturn the results of the 2020 election.[90] Despite his age and his unpopularity with much of the country, he has made noises about running again in 2024. His former strategist, Steve Bannon, has talked of Trump's base of support preparing for a governing majority for 50 years. "Trump is a transformative president and a historic figure," Bannon says. "He is going to be in your lives ten, twenty, and thirty years from now—that's a Kafkaesque novel, isn't it? It is."[91]

By systematically dismantling the guardrails of democracy, these political forces aspire to transform the electoral realm and end the more conventional oscillation of political passions. Bannon is being disingenuous when he talks of a governing majority. The new right does not just want to win at politics. It wants to end politics—as it is practiced in democratic societies.

A CHANGING PLAYBOOK

Three key elements facilitated the move of these political, economic, and cultural sentiments into the mainstream. The first was the end of the Cold War, which destroyed an anti-fascist consensus that joined together not only the United States and Soviet Union but also all mainstream political parties. The emergence in the 1990s of far-right politicians like Jörg Haider in Austria, Jean-Marie Le Pen in France, and Vladimir Zhirinovsky in Russia paved the way for future parties and movements to break the anti-fascist taboo more vigorously. Indeed, the new right went further by attempting to criminalize anti-fascist organizing by branding the "antifa" as a terrorist entity.[92]

The second element was the internet, which linked up niche groups. "Social media amplifies everything—that goes for veganism as well as the radical right," explains Matthew Feldman of the Centre for Analysis of the Radical Right in the UK.

> It's the medium that most speaks to the radical right: potentially international, potentially permanent, potentially anonymous—all the things that the radical right lacked going back many years. If you wanted to be involved in, let's say, Holocaust denial, you'd have to have known the groups beforehand, probably subscribe to some dodgy magazine of questionable quality. But now you or I could go on Twitter or Facebook, type in "Holocaust denial" and get materials not available even in the 1990s.

A third element has been the patient organizing of the new right; some of it copied directly from the left's playbook. The identitarian movement has borrowed various counter-cultural strategies and community organizing tactics.[93] It is active on campuses, for instance, where it projects a "cool" and "hip" aesthetic that appeals to young people. From Italian Marxist Antonio Gramsci, the new right has borrowed the idea of taking over the state through a "long march through the institutions" like political parties, trade unions, the military, and the police. It has overcome the extremist suspicion of electoral politics and political institutions more generally. The Tea Party, for instance, targeted the Republican Party as the first step to influencing U.S. politics. Within a year of its formation in 2009, it was grabbing low-level precinct leader positions within the Republican Party, 60 percent of which, out of 150,000 in all, were vacant at the time.[94]

After the EU parliament elections in 2009, when Hungary's far-right Jobbik party won three seats, Larry Olomoofe of the People of African Descent Resource Centre remembers seeing

> a cluster of people in Hero Square in Budapest around the Hungarian flag, and it turned out they were Jobbik members handing out leaflets and continuing their crusade. Even though they'd achieved

unprecedented results in the election three days prior, they were still out there doing this. While we were intellectualizing them away by saying, "look at these idiots," they took our political participation strategies, created a critical mass, and now they're setting the agenda.

These three factors—the disappearance of an anti-fascist consensus, the creation of extremist communities online, and the grassroots organizing of the far right—created the conditions within which a new, anti-liberal politics could thrive. This new right has marshaled its political, economic, and cultural arguments to consolidate power at a national level and simultaneously attack global elites. This attack goes beyond economic institutions (like the World Bank) to those of civil society (like human rights organizations) that campaign for the rights of minorities, refugees, or political prisoners against the presumed will of the majority.

This antipathy toward globalism, however, has not stopped the new right from pursuing a global project of its own, with its own peculiar version of universalism. The ultimate goal: to replace existing international institutions and agreements with what Larry Rosenthal, the chair of the Berkeley Center for Right-Wing Studies, calls "an approximation of the liberal order in illiberal terms."

2
Transnational organizing of the new right

Kaleb Cole is an extremist version of Steve Bannon—with guns.

Cole is the leader of the Atomwaffen Division (AWD) in Washington state. A white supremacist group with cells in 20 U.S. states, the AWD is dedicated to precipitating a global race war, drawing its inspiration from such sources as Nazism and cult leader Charles Manson.[1] In December 2018, Cole embarked on a 25-day tour of Europe. In Poland, he visited Auschwitz where he took a selfie with an Atomwaffen flag. In Ukraine, he attended a neo-Nazi music festival.

His trip was also focused on creating a global network of white supremacists. Thanks to Cole, the AWD has linked up with the fascist Azov Batallion in Ukraine, the white supremacist Sonnenkrieg Division in Europe, and the neo-Nazi Antipodean Resistance in Australia.[2] AWD aspires to be a paramilitary outfit, and it has been implicated in the murders of five people. Cole is an avowed "accelerationist," someone who cares little about electoral politics and only wants to hasten the collapse of the liberal system. In November 2019, police in Texas arrested Cole with one of his associates and seized guns, ammunition, and drugs from their car. The authorities charged Cole with threatening journalists. Pending a trial in 2021, he has been held without bail.

Kaleb Cole is just one of several white supremacists with global ambitions to recently come out of the woodwork.

Rinaldo Nazzaro, whose *nom de guerre* is Norman Spear, is similarly fixated on the downfall of the U.S. government. Unlike Cole, Nazzaro has avoided the reach of the FBI by relocating with his Russian wife to St. Petersburg. There he appears to work as a security consultant, with a working relationship with the Russian government. But his main preoccupation has been to run The Base, a paramilitary outfit that hopes one day to create a white homeland in the Pacific Northwest of the United States.³ Several days before a pro-gun rally in Virginia in January 2020, the FBI arrested three Base members on weapons charges and on suspicion of intending to foment violence at the rally.⁴ Nazzaro, however, remains beyond the FBI's grasp.

The attempted coup on January 6 in Washington, DC, attracted an even larger group of armed white nationalists. Although fixated on reversing Trump's 2020 electoral defeat, many of the organizers are global in their strategizing, their connections, and their aspirations. Unlike with AWD and The Base, however, the far right was able this time to piggyback on the organizing of more conventional conservative organizations. Groups like the Republican Attorneys General, Turning Point Action, and Tea Party Patriots planned the two days of rallies that preceded the storming of the Capitol.⁵ Militia members, QAnon fanatics, and Proud Boys mixed freely with Christian activists, former congressional staffers, and off-duty police officers.

The presence of ex-military among the ranks of the insurrectionists points to a higher level of organization than initially reported.⁶ In this sense, the insurrection was not an unplanned riot. The FBI was aware in advance of the plans to attack the Capitol Building.⁷ The FBI office in Norfolk, Virginia passed on a report of this planning to their counterparts in Washington, DC, which included this message picked up from an online discussion:

> Be ready to fight. Congress needs to hear glass breaking, doors being kicked in, and blood from their BLM and Pantifa slave soldiers being spilled. Get violent. Stop calling this a march, or rally, or a protest. Go there ready for war. We get our President or we die. NOTHING else will achieve this goal.

In the aftermath of the attack, the authorities arrested members of the Oath Keepers, an anti-government militia movement, who organized a group of well-trained insurrectionists, devised plans to make "citizens' arrests" of members of Congress, and coordinated their actions during the assault on the Capitol building.⁸

Cole, Nazzaro, and many of the January 6 insurrectionists are ardent white nationalists. They are equally fervent internationalists. This is not a contradiction. The Nazis, after all, also developed their own peculiar version of internationalism.

In the 1920s and 1930s, the Nazis defined racial purity in transnational terms—not German, but Aryan. To create their ideology, they drew on Norse mythology, Hindu symbolism, and U.S. race theories.[9] Indeed, racism trumped nationality. Some ardent German nationalists who failed to meet Nazi standards of racial purity, particularly those of Jewish descent, occupied a much lower status in Hitler's Germany than those of Scandinavian stock. Even Han Chinese and Japanese, whom the Nazis designated "honorary Aryans," ranked higher than German Jews or Roma.

For all their talk of Germany First and the need for an extended realm (*lebensraum*) for the German people, the Nazis were in fact globalists who forged close international ties with fascists in Italy and Spain as well as imperial royalists in Japan. Hitler went so far as to imagine that he could bring the entire Muslim world onto his side in his war against Jews and liberals. The Nazis recruited Muslim soldiers, allied with religious leaders to issue pro-Nazi fatwas, and even disseminated the notion that Hitler was the long-expected "twelfth imam."[10]

These attempts to woo Muslims, which were ultimately unsuccessful, didn't prevent Nazis from making overtures to Hindus as well. The radical Hindutva movement in India in turn looked to Hitler for inspiration. M.S. Golwalkar, a leader of the extremist Rashtriya Swayamsevak Sangh (RSS) movement, wrote in a 1939 book, "Germany shocked the world by her purging the country of the Semitic Races—the Jews ... a good lesson for us in Hindustan for us to learn and profit by." Another far-right leader, Bal Thackeray, told *Time* magazine in 1993, "If you take Mein Kampf and if you remove the word 'Jew' and put in the word 'Muslim,' that is what I believe in."[11] Thanks to Savitri Devi, a European neo-Nazi convert to Hinduism, some neo-Nazis even believe that Hitler is an avatar of Vishnu.[12]

In the 1960s, George Lincoln Rockwell, the founder of the American Nazi Party, translated this particular brand of Nazi internationalism into the American context. Aryan supremacy became, simply, white supremacy. Rockwell and other neo-Nazis, "always viewed their challenge as uniting white people in white countries around the cause of recovering, from their perspectives, their ethno-states," notes Heidi Beirich of the Global Project Against Hate and Extremism. Internationalism, the neo-Nazis demonstrated, need not be an inclusive project.

Rockwell was joined in this project by William Luther Pierce—the author of *The Turner Diaries*, a touchstone text for extremists—who established ties with the far right in Germany and Greece. Others in the movement promoted cross-border relations as well. "It's hard to understand the mythology of transnationalism within the white nationalist movement without going back to Francis Parker Yockey and Willis Carto—both now deceased but two highly influential white nationalists in the United States," points out Eric Ward of the Western States Center.

Yockey developed the idea of a far-right alliance between Russia and the United States that was then developed by folks like David Duke who toured Eastern Europe extensively. Willis Carto held international gatherings around Holocaust denial and promoted far-right internationalism in the pages of *Spotlight*, the weekly flagship of the white nationalist movement from the 1970s through the 1990s.

In the days before the internet, this transnationalism of white supremacy spread through books, magazines, and even music. Resistance Records sold white power music to neo-Nazis in North America and Europe, Ward points out, generating as much as a million dollars a year in sales.[13]

Today, thanks to the internationalism of their philosophy, neo-Nazis can be found in otherwise unlikely geographic locales. They show up at Poland's Independence Day, in Ukrainian military forces, and at the fringes of Russian politics, even though the Nazis considered Slavs to be subhuman. "When the Central America migrant crisis began," reports Manuel Perez-Rocha of the Institute for Policy Studies, "there were some small rallies of self-described neo-Nazis in central Mexico." The Malay heavy metal group, Boot Axe, subscribes to neo-Nazi ideology in its support of a "pure" Malay race,[14] and there are enough bands of similar persuasion to put together a festival in Malaysia.[15]

Given its frequent recourse to nationalist rhetoric, the new right often presents as nationalist. Its appeals to race or ideology, however, facilitates transnational solidarity. "One of the biggest misconceptions of the American left and left-of-center movements in Europe as well is the tendency to think of the far right as a nationalist movement," says Melissa Ryan, the editor of the Ctrl Alt-Right Delete newsletter.

"It's actually the opposite. They operate internationally. They share best practices; they share funding streams. They're internationalists claiming to be nationalists."

THE GREAT REPLACEMENT

The innovation of the new right has been to find a vehicle for white supremacy that can appeal to mainstream voters who would otherwise be uncomfortable with direct references to Hitler or neo-Nazism. This vehicle is a powerful new transnational narrative: the "great replacement" of white people by non-white people.

At first glance, the man who came up with the idea of the "great replacement" might not seem your usual suspect. Renaud Camus was a radical student demonstrator in Paris in 1968 and in 1981 voted for socialist Francois Mitterrand as president of France.[16] A noted poet and novelist, Camus published books on his gay identity that attracted accolades from the likes of intellectual Roland Barthes and poet Allen Ginsberg.[17] By the early 2000s, however, Camus had begun to outline a new philosophy that distinguished between "*faux*" or false French (immigrants or their children) and real French (those who had lived in the country for many generations).[18] In 2010, he published a book entitled *Le Grand Replacement* bemoaning the prospects of a France and Europe transformed by immigration.

Camus's work became the foundational text for a growing movement called Generation Identity, an updated version of white nationalism that has spread throughout Europe, influenced the alt-right in the United States, gained momentum on the internet, and become a global phenomenon out of all proportion to the relatively small number of actual adherents. The "identitarians" embraced Renaud Camus and spread his ideas in a virtual echo chamber. The philosophy of the great replacement has inspired violent extremists as well, showing up in the manifestos of mass shooters in Christchurch, New Zealand, in March 2019, and El Paso, Texas, in August 2019.

The great replacement doctrine is not just about keeping out immigrants but, through a policy of "remigration," expelling ones already in place. The platform of the German far-right party, Alternative für Deutschland (AfD), for instance, reads: "Germany and Europe must put in place remigration programs on the largest possible scale."[19]

France's National Rally and Austria's Freedom Party also reportedly back remigration, as do various identitarian groups and small far-right parties in Europe.[20]

Although white nationalists use the phrase "great replacement" in its explicitly racist meaning, more cautious conservatives transpose the phrase into the cultural context of a "civilization" under threat. This reformulation strikes a chord in Europe where conservative politicians frequently lament the erosion of "Western civilization" at the hands of multiculturalists. Thilo Sarrazin, the former German social-democratic politician, published an explosive bestseller in 2010—*Germany Abolishes Itself*—that translated the great replacement ideology into cultural terms that appealed to a broad audience. In the place of multiculturalism, the new right proposes "ethnopluralism" and "diversity in isolation"—maintaining cultural walls between different ethnic groups—as an alternative to the European Union's official motto of "united in diversity."[21] Thus, they turn identity politics on its head, asserting a "positive" identity for a privileged majority to counter the demands of minority communities for equal access and opportunity.

The cultural versions of the great replacement have significant appeal in the United States as well. Even after the election of Donald Trump as president in 2016, for instance, support for the alt-right remained relatively low: about 6 percent, according to a Reuters/Ipsos poll in 2017. But the message that the majority is under threat has broader political appeal. In the same 2017 poll, 39 percent of Americans agreed with the statement that "white people are currently under attack in this country."[22] In a 2019 poll, a roughly equivalent number believed that "immigrants are invading our country and replacing our cultural and ethnic background."[23] This percentage corresponds to the number of people who constitute Trump's base of unwavering supporters and who continue to voice approval of him despite his refusal to concede the 2020 election.[24]

Anti-immigrant ideas have long circulated across borders. "The promotion of *The Camp of the Saints*—the French xenophobic and racist novel that first mainstreamed the replacement theory that everyone is talking about—was highly promoted and distributed by Social Contract Press" in the United States, explains Eric Ward. "Through that kind of work, the idea of a Fortress America is built off what the new right was doing in Europe based on Fortress Europe—the idea of stopping all undocumented migration into the U.S."

This "Fortress" concept has spread even further. Far-right Hindu nationalists aim to create a Fortress India that expels all undocumented Muslims, including those who have lived in the country their whole lives.[25] Several moves by the Modi government—a National Register of Citizens that left 1.9 million mostly Muslim Indians stateless, followed by the Citizenship Amendment Act that fast-tracked citizenship for many undocumented migrants except Muslims—suggest that the prime minister is heading inexorably in that direction.[26] Impressed by this state-led Islamophobia, far-right activists and politicians in several countries have reached out to Hindu nationalists and lavished praise on Modi.[27]

Similarly, Benjamin Netanyahu pushed through a new citizenship law in Israel that effectively formalized second-class status for non-Jewish Israelis, saying that only Jews could exercise the right of self-determination and establishing Hebrew as the official language of the country. Bolsonaro is building a kind of "Fortress Brazil" by portraying refugees as a threat and calling them "scum of the earth."[28] In Myanmar, the expulsion of the predominantly Muslim Rohingya minority reinforced the government's efforts to create a more homogenously Buddhist country.

In the 1920s, the American far right attracted adherents by blaming all the ills of the nation on "degenerate races," an argument that united incipient fascists with conservatives like Calvin Coolidge.[29] With the great replacement narrative, this disturbing history of political consolidation on the right is repeating itself. "The demographic replacement is a similar master frame that can unite both clear extremists and conservatives who might be worried about demographic change," warns Matthew Feldman of CARR. "Once you add those two together you have potential majorities in many countries. They've found a winning formula. There's nothing that I've seen that comes remotely close to countering that formula."

THE FOCUS ON EUROPE

Steve Bannon's organizing focus, when he left the Trump administration, was Europe. The choice for the American alt-right to look across the Atlantic seemed obvious. The far right in Europe has capitalized politically on the refugee crisis aggravated by the wars in Afghanistan, Iraq, Syria, and elsewhere in the Middle East. It has taken advantage of Euroskepticism, the dissatisfaction with the institutions and policies of European integration. And it is operating in an explicitly transnational political space that generates opportunities for the new right to join hands across borders.

For many years, the European far right directed its ire against the European Union but couldn't prevent their countries from joining the regional body. Even after failing to block membership, these fringe political actors continued to champion withdrawal.

The victory in 2016 of the Brexit campaign initially provided momentum for such Euroskeptics eager to escort their own countries out of the EU: Frexit, Czexit, and the like. Nigel Farage, the architect of Brexit, became a leading force in the European new right, even as his project of pulling the UK out of the EU was initially proving to be such a political disaster for his country. In the space of two months in 2019, while one Brexit plan after another foundered, Farage rebuilt the fledging Brexit Party, blitzed the country with a social media campaign, and captured 31 percent of the UK vote in the European elections.[30] Farage and his Brexit Party were a mass of contradictions. Here was a right-wing party that explicitly rejected the European Union, led by a man who had served in the European parliament for two decades, and that was, briefly, the largest single party operating in that assembly. And Farage, an avowed nationalist, accomplished this feat in part by forging a transnational alliance. "He seriously went to school with the Five Star Movement in Italy," reports Larry Rosenthal. "He just backed up his truck and asked, 'How do you do this on-line thing?' And then he reproduced it."

With the final passage of Brexit legislation at the end of 2019, Farage finally bid farewell to the European parliament, where he'd been pulling down 100,000 pounds a year for his job as a termite eating away the foundations of the house into which he'd been invited.[31] "To be honest," he admitted, "we used the wherewithal provided by the European parliament to build a UK political movement."[32] Part of his time was also spent misspending funds, which forced the EU to dock his pay. His departure from the European parliament was of a piece with his undistinguished tenure as a parliamentarian. "I'm hoping this begins the end of this project," he crowed on his last day in the body as he waved his little Union Jack. "It's a bad project, it isn't just undemocratic, it's anti-democratic." The parliament's vice president, Mairead McGuinness, told him to sit down and put away his flag.[33]

Even before Farage bid farewell to Europe, however, the new right's strategy was changing. The European new right was no longer on the outside looking in. It was winning more and more seats in the European parliament. As Lorenzo Marsili of European Alternatives in Rome points out,

> They gave up attacking the EU and calling for an exit from the Euro and leaving the EU. Now the rhetoric is to take it over, to build the EU as a space of exclusion with stronger borders and looser fiscal policy. They have Europeanized their own rhetoric. They have a vision for Europe that's possibly more worked out than the center left or center right.

The new right, in other words, now wants to work its way through European institutions. It prefers "voice" rather than "exit," to use economist Albert O. Hirschman's famous formulation.[34] "There is quite a bit of potential for the better use of the new institutional power that the populists have been gaining in municipalities, in regions, in countries, and in EU institutions," Jordi Vaquer adds. "These parties have learned some of the games of international cooperation in the EU. They are increasingly sharing agendas, conspiracy theories, the media space."

It has long been a dream of the European far right to create a powerful, transnational organization. In 1997, Jean-Marie Le Pen created EuroNat, but it attracted mostly fringe groups from Eastern Europe. Only in 2015 was Le Pen's dream realized by his daughter Marine, who joined Geert Wilders in launching the parliamentary bloc known as the Europe of Nations and Freedom. Ironically, the formation was possible in part because Marine Le Pen had successfully maneuvered her father, a polarizing figure even within his own party, out of the National Front. Reflecting their new approach to working within the EU, the member parties of this bloc prefer to call themselves "sovereignist" rather than anti-European. In 2019, the bloc doubled in size as a result of the European parliament elections and renamed itself the Identity and Democracy Party. Representing nearly 10 percent of the parliament, the bloc encompasses Italy's Lega, France's National Rally, the German AfD, Austria's Freedom Party, the Finns Party, and several smaller parties. Despite its growing size, Identity and Liberty doesn't even represent the entire European new right as it doesn't include either of Hungary's far-right parties, Fidesz and Jobbik, Poland's Law and Justice Party (PiS), or Spain's Vox.

Steve Bannon wasn't the only political figure to eye the European new right as ripe for the influencing. Russia has been even more persistent in its outreach. Vladimir Putin's United Russia party has signed formal agreements with Italy's Lega and Austria's Freedom Party. The Kremlin has provided some financing for the European far right, either directly or through wealthy intermediaries like Konstantin Malofeev.[35] Media outlets like RT and Sputnik amplify certain Russian messages for their European audiences. Still, "it's not like the Fourth International, this time a right-wing one, with a secretariat in Moscow and every country has a national chapter," Jordi Vaquer cautions. "Each of these parties has deep national roots, and their overwhelming focus is on national politics."

Putin himself has sounded new right messages about the obsolescence of liberalism, the dangers of immigration and minority rights, and the virtues of traditional values.[36] Like his new right colleagues in Europe, Putin has emphasized the importance of Russian sovereignty above all, for instance, asserting in a 2020 amendment that the Russian constitution takes precedence over international law. Burnishing his reputation as a Russian nationalist, and obscuring his career origins as a Soviet apparatchik, he has fought for the rights of ethnic Russians in the near abroad and pushed back against NATO encroachment on his borders. His embrace of nationalism also coincides with souring engagement with the United States. "But in terms of rhetoric, Putin is not really a populist," explains Ilya Matveev. "Populism means this rhetoric of 'common people' versus the elite. Putin never attacks the elite in Russia. It is his own elite. He is a nationalist, not a populist. His rhetoric is about Russia as a nation versus other countries like the U.S. or the West in general."

Putin is not even opposed to the global elite.

"This type of rhetoric is quite instrumental," adds Ilya Budraitskis, a Moscow-based political theorist.

It doesn't mean that Putin has any clear long-term strategy to become a true leader of a new uprising against the liberal elites, that he really wants to become a leader of a right-wing populist international. He uses this kind of rhetoric as an element of a game for recognition that he's playing with the Western elite. He wants to become a full member of the international elite that he was expelled from after the annexation of Crimea in 2014.

As much as he can, however, Putin is committed to changing the ideological composition of this elite by supporting anti-liberal political forces throughout the world, whether on the right or the left.

Hungary, too, aspires to be a hub of coordination for the European new right. A number of extremists, like Swedish far-right businessman Daniel Friberg and his identitarian publishing house Arktos, have made their home in Budapest.[37] The Hungarian government wants to be "a leading force within the EU of the sovereignist versus the federalist camp," Márta Pardavi of the Hungarian Helsinki Committee in Budapest says. Prime Minister Viktor Orbán, in office since 2010, has frequently criticized liberals and liberal internationalism, and assailed the European Union for making "grave mistakes" on migration and economic policies.[38] His party's departure from European norms has pushed the EU to censure Hungary, the right-of-center European People's Party to suspend Fidesz's membership in the bloc, and Freedom House to revoke the country's democratic status in 2020.

Orbán doesn't seem to care. His critiques of the EU are greeted with enthusiasm by other sovereignist parties. Meanwhile, Orbán is building a transnational power basis in southeast Europe. "His political and business associates are buying media in Macedonia and Slovenia," Jordi Vaquer observes.

Orbán was the first European leader to welcome Milorad Dodik, the separatist leader from Republika Srpska who is now a member of the Bosnian presidency. He is close to the increasingly authoritarian Serbian President Aleksandar Vučić. He is hosting in Hungary the fugitive former Macedonian premier Nikola Gruevski, sentenced to two years in prison for corruption.

At the paramilitary level, Ukraine, too, has had an influence on the new right. The conflict in eastern Ukraine has served as a training ground for white supremacists and neo-Nazis from around the world who flocked to openly fascist units like the Azov Battalion. These foreign fighters have returned (or attempted to return) to their home countries to apply what they've learned. The Ukrainian government, for instance, arrested a member of the French far right fighting in the country who was plotting to attack several targets in France, including a synagogue and a mosque.[39] Former fighters from Italy smuggled into their country an air-to-air missile, rocket launchers, and machine guns, which the Italian authorities confiscated in a raid.[40] In September 2019, the FBI arrested a U.S. soldier in Kansas who planned to attack CNN. He'd been mentored by two American GIs who'd fought with a far-right Ukrainian paramilitary group.[41]

The European new right has done its share of exporting its ideas to like-minded groups in more distant countries that it considers outposts of European civilization. "The far right in Australia has been bringing in speakers from the far right globally," reports Phil Ireland, the chair of GetUp in Australia. "Nigel Farage is a darling of theirs. I understand that there have been interactions with Steve Bannon. Geert Wilders from the Netherlands has also been brought out to Australia."

A more complicated relationship connects the European far right with Israel. Neo-Nazi organizations for the most part want nothing to do with the country. But new right parties in Europe, like Austria's Freedom Party, have reached out to Israel, with party leader Heinz-Christian Strache visiting Israel in 2016.[42] Such connections "allow these parties in Europe to say that they're not anti-Semites because people see that they are working with Jews and supporting Israel," explains Ran Cohen of the Israeli Democratic Bloc. "It also allows them to exchange their anti-Semitism for Islamophobia in a very smooth way."

Israel has become a beacon for transnational right-wing activism in another way. "If you want to talk about refugees, you have to understand Israel and Palestine," explains Khury Petersen-Smith of IPS. "In the late 1990s, early 2000s, Israel said, 'We should just build a wall to keep out Palestinians.' At the time, it was out of bounds of what's acceptable in the international community. But Israel said, 'Well, we're doing it.' And now there are a lot of walls." Trump has frequently compared his proposed wall at the Mexican border to Israeli walls: "Do walls work?" he asked rhetorically in February 2017. "Just ask Israel. They work."[43] Trump administration officials have visited Israel to examine how Israel builds its walls.[44] In addition, Israeli firms have won contracts to supply technology at the U.S.–Mexico border.[45] And the Israeli government has also sent troops to Honduras to train the border patrol there.[46]

CLEAVAGES ON THE RIGHT

It's hard to imagine that nationalists all trying to make their countries "great again" could find much common ground. Populist right-wing governments can indeed all agree that their governments have exclusive and sovereign control within their borders. In practice, however, they have clashed over territory and trade. Differences in religion, ethnicity, and historical memory also divide the new right. Only a common threat—global institutions, immigrants, minority rights—provides coalitional cohesion across borders.

"At a time of deep nationalism, it's actually hard to get nationalists to agree on anything," observes Eric Ward. "That's why Yockey, Carto, and Pierce really pushed the idea of white identity. The European far right doesn't really coalesce until the *identitaire* movement takes off."

Despite ideological agreement about the identitarians' great replacement theory, the European far right is not on the same page on all issues, for instance, financial flows within the European Union. "Salvini is arguing for spending more money for Italy," points out Alex Demirovic, a senior scholar at the Rosa-Luxemburg-Stiftung in Germany. "But the German right-wing populists were founded on a criticism of the Euro policies and the European central bank policies after the crisis, so they are totally against any support for other European countries." The European new right in creditor countries like France and Germany has made a habit of criticizing the enormous monetary contributions their countries have made to the European Union budget. But the new right government in Poland, the largest recipient of Euro funds, does not sing in that particular chorus.

Russia is another divisive issue. Although a couple of far-right parties have signed association agreements with Putin's United Russia party, PiS in Poland hasn't followed suit. The head of PiS, Jarosław

Kaczyński, "would never say that he's an ally of Vladimir Putin," points out Bartosz Rydliński, a professor of political science in Warsaw.

A lot of PiS supporters still think Russia is responsible for the crash in Smolensk in 2010 [which killed Kaczyński's brother, President Lech Kaczyński, and much of his cabinet]. Also, in 2008 when Russia invaded Georgia, Lech Kaczyński went to Tbilisi with the presidents of Lithuania, Estonia, Ukraine, and other Central European countries to show solidarity with Mikheil Saakashvili. Kaczyński said, "Today, Georgia, tomorrow Ukraine, the next day the Baltics. And there might come a day when Poland faces a similar threat."

Although Bolsonaro and Orbán share a distaste for the LGBTQ movement, other far-right leaders like Geert Wilders have embraced same-sex marriage and decried Islamists for opposing gay rights.[47] Similarly, some elements of the far right are old school sexist, while others have updated their ideology to acknowledge women leaders like Alice Weidel of the Alternative für Deutschland and Pia Kjærsgaard of the Danish People's Party. In a perverse way, the anti-immigrant agenda has absorbed feminism. As Birgit Sauer points out, the more modern new right argues that "Western countries are gender equal while most of the migrants have traditional patriarchal gender relations." Some elements of the European far right have begun to support stronger measures to protect the environment—in part out of concerns that rising waters will produce more migrants—and craft a new kind of Green fascism.[48] Both Bolsonaro and Trump, however, remain firmly aligned with the fossil-fuel industry.

Racism and intolerance are also stumbling blocks for building a global new right. Nationalists tend to disparage minority rights unless the minority happens to be their ethnic brethren in another country. The Austrian far right sticks up for ethnic Germans in northern Italy, while the Italian far right pushes back against any mention of dual citizenship for the German minority.[49] In a world of rapidly changing demographics, meanwhile, white nationalism can only forge a wider consensus by redefining "white," much as the Irish and Italians became white in the United States in the nineteenth century and the Nazis expanded their definition of Aryan. Thus, the new right struggles over the acceptability of Jews in their movement: many white supremacists adhere to their historic anti-Semitism while the alt-right has opened its ranks to people of Jewish background, like top Trump advisor Stephen Miller.[50] Similarly, a number of prominent alt-right men in the United States have dated or married women of Asian descent[51]—echoing the racist sentiment that some Asians are "honorary whites"—and even white supremacist Dylann Roof wrote that "East Asian races ... are by nature very racist and could be great allies of the White race."[52]

CIVIL SOCIETY ON THE RIGHT

Transnational activism is not limited to politicians and political parties of the new right. As the internationalism of the neo-Nazis demonstrated, extremist civil society organizations have long been creating connections across borders. "The world of social conservatives in the United States is intensely involved internationally in every single place, pushing anti-LGBT and anti-abortion thinking," explains Heidi Beirich, formerly of the Southern Poverty Law Center. "They are very cognizant of the need to go beyond the nation-state to push their issues. You'd think that the most parochial movement, Christian conservatives in the U.S., wouldn't think that way. But they think bigger than we do."

The new right civil society has largely focused on pushing back against the human rights demands of minority populations: the LGBTQ community, people of color (in predominantly white countries), and Muslims (in majority Christian, Hindu, Buddhist, and Jewish countries). Such organizations challenge the social gains of progressives "from below" even as new right politicians attempt to deconstruct the progressive aspects of the administrative state from above. This "inside–outside" strategy recalls the very same successful civil rights campaigns that the new right is now trying to roll back.

The World Congress of Families (WCF), founded in 1997, promotes its religious-nationalist agenda through regular global gatherings. "Their convenings have increasingly been a site for cross-fertilization across political and religious movements, mostly within Christianity but also other faith traditions," reports Tarso Ramos of Political Research Associates. One year after meeting in Budapest in 2017, the WCF congratulated Viktor Orbán on his electoral victory:

your victory is also a beam of hope for Western Christian Civilization. Many nations in Europe have grown weary and seek little more than a childless decline and ultimate disappearance. In contrast, you have mobilized the Hungarian people toward rebuilding a family-centered, religiously grounded nation, as a contribution to the renewal of all Europe and the recovery of an authentic Christendom.[53]

Christian fundamentalists in the United States have poured $50 million in dark money contributions to a number of WCF partners in Europe.[54]

Another recipient of that funding, Alliance Defending Freedom International, has launched court cases in more than 50 countries against same-sex marriage and abortion.[55] With 3,200 affiliated lawyers and special consultative status at the United Nations, ADFI is the international wing of a combative Christian fundamentalist organization in the United States that has been involved in key legal cases, including defending the Christian baker in Colorado who refused to make a cake for a same-sex couple.[56] In Europe, the organization has worried about the impact of Islamophobia—not on Muslims but Christians. "Governments are using the Islam problem to also reduce the freedom of Christians within Europe," explains Roger Kiska, ADFI's senior counsel. "They will say we need to limit freedom of expression or freedom of religion because of Islamic terrorism, because of Islamic fundamentalism, and they have been using that also to cut back on the right of Christians to express themselves in the public square."[57]

The global right-wing petition organization CitizenGo, based in Spain, specializes in online activism among ultra-conservatives and thinks of itself as a right-wing version of the liberal MoveOn. It made its name by gathering nearly 1.9 million signatures for a Council of Europe petition against late-term abortion, the largest number of signatures for a citizens' initiative of that type in Europe.[58] CitizenGo has also promoted its anti-transsexual messages on buses around the world.[59]

Throughout Eastern Europe but also in some Western European countries, the Roma minority has been a particular target of far-right hostility. "The right wing and extremists always need to have an enemy: one day it can be Roma, another day it will be another group," explains Zeljko Jovanovic of the Open Society Roma Initiatives Office in Berlin. "Usually the most under-represented groups with the least political power to strike back are those who are attacked, minority groups in particular." Also responsible, he adds, are groups from the center left and center right that fail to see that the attacks on Roma represent a danger for democracy in general.

Given the dominant narrative of the great replacement within the new right, immigration has served as a major networking opportunity for civil society organizations like the Center for Immigration Studies and the Federation for American Immigration Reform. The Swedish Democrats, originally formed by neo-Nazis, have received a warm welcome from the U.S. new right, and Russian funding has helped spread the party's anti-immigration misinformation in Sweden.[60] Anti-immigrant organizations organized against the Global Compact on Migration, and new right politicians govern in the five countries that refused to ratify the compact (United States, Israel, Hungary, Poland, and the Czech Republic).

Although the great replacement remains a powerful narrative for the far right, a shift is now underway at the level of civil society— toward climate change. With the Adelphi Institute, German journalist Susanne Götze conducted research that determined that "nearly all the right-wing parties in Europe are linked to climate deniers."[61] The shift could be seen even before the COVID-19 pandemic closed borders. In the 2019 European parliament elections, for instance, the right wing showcased its new agenda of climate denial.

"Climate change was always a bit of a niche topic that the far right focused on, but this time it overtook the topic of migration, which has been huge in Europe and featured as the top theme among far-right activists for last few years," reports Julia Ebner of the Institute for Strategic Dialogue (ISD). "Now for the first time it has completely shifted toward a focus on climate change. There were also smear campaigns against Greta Thunberg as the face for pro-environmentalism. This strategy of putting a face on the topic was the same thing they did to George Soros on the migration topic."

For this new campaign of climate-change denialism, civil society organizations of the new right found a face for their side: Naomi Seibt. The 19-year-old climate skeptic from Germany hit the headlines in

2020 thanks to her sponsor, the Heartland Institute, a climate-denial thinktank based in the United States with strong links to Europe. Seibt has connections to the youth chapter of the Alternative für Deutschland, and her mother has done legal work for the party.[62] Although she has been coy about her political affiliations, the teenager has been quite clear in linking the older and newer preoccupations of the new right: "I've always been skeptical of the ideas of white nationalism, of identitarianism and white identity," she told a reporter. "However, I am an empiricist, and I could not help but notice that I could have peaceful, free, easy, civilized, and safe discussions in what is essentially an all-white country."[63] It was an indirect way of suggesting that multicultural countries are full of strife and danger, that they are not free, and that they are not civilized—all classic racist tropes. After her short tenure in the media spotlight, Seibt has attempted to maintain her notoriety by abandoning her empiricism and embracing the QAnon conspiracy theory.[64]

Civil society organizations are also active in the diaspora, where they funnel money back to right-wing parties and politicians back home. "In the case of the Philippines for instance, many of the Filipinos who support Trump in the United States also support [Philippine President Rodrigo] Duterte," says Walden Bello. A global network of Diehard Duterte Supporters (DDS) holds meetings in various countries and aggressively criticize Duterte opponents on the internet.[65] The often-violent rhetoric becomes even more ominous for those who recognize that DDS also stands for Davao Death Squad, the paramilitaries linked to Duterte when he was mayor of Davao City.

The 28-million strong Indian diaspora is a key constituency for Modi's BJP—and a source of fundraising as well.[66] Donald Trump's appearance at a Modi rally in Houston in mid-September 2019 underscores the importance of diaspora politics in the electoral imagination of both leaders.[67] Right-wing Jewish donors in the United States provide financing for the non-profits, political parties, and settlement activities of Israeli extremists.[68] Meanwhile, the diaspora can also be a source of support for the far right's push for regime change abroad, as is the case with a group of Chinese living in America who translate Trump's tweets into Chinese in the hopes of undermining the Communist Party in Beijing.[69]

DIGITAL ORGANIZING

The far right has proven to be not only early adopters when it comes to digital technology, but adept at constructing its own alternative platforms when barred from access to mainstream outlets.

"Stormfront went up on the Web in 1995, and that was the first place where all of the sudden you had global thinking around white supremacy," says Heidi Beirich.

> More recently, they've been able to forge the bonds of white pride worldwide, and the Web just made it easier. So, now you can have American white supremacists funding identitarians in places like Italy and Austria to fund a boat to go out and round up immigrants. This coordination factor didn't use to exist.

The far right early on realized the potential of the internet. Established in 1984, Liberty Net was the first message board to link white nationalists for the purposes of planning and recruitment. Its creator, Aryan Nations activist Louis Beam, was able to use the network to get around border controls to send hate literature to other countries.[70] Later, when the World Wide Web debuted in 1989, the far right quickly understood the key to viral content, which was to harness what *Atlantic* writer Derek Thompson calls "the natural tendency of web content to veer toward high-arousal emotions, such as outrage and paranoia, to attract attention and promote social sharing."[71] The far right used new platforms like the website Infowars (started in 1999) and the Breitbart network (2007) to spread their ideologies through memes and conspiracy theories.

The bulletin board 4chan, set up in 2003, fed the preoccupations of a young, mostly male generation of "Anons" devoted to ridiculing "normies" just for laughs, as they did when they mounted digital attacks on Tom Cruise and the Church of Scientology. Those preoccupations became explicitly political in the 2010s as the Anons veered to the far right by going after women and feminists, particularly in the Gamergate affair, which boiled down to an opportunity for misogynists to spread hate against women and feminists in the gaming community. The banning of discussion about Gamergate in 4chan led to the creation of 8chan and a more serious fusion of far-right politics with the counter-cultural spirit of the early digital jesters. Coordinated attacks on Scientology gave way to the birther movement—which questioned Barack Obama's U.S. citizenship—and conspiracy theories involving a child pornography ring in the basement of the Comet Ping Pong pizzeria in Washington, DC (which derived from something as incidental as the initials "CP" that link the two).[72] The "alt-lite" community of disaffected young men began to merge with the alt-right.[73]

In the Trump era, 4Chan produced perhaps the wildest right-wing conspiracy theory of all: QAnon. Even though the Comet Ping Pong charge was baseless, an anonymous 4Chan poster took this nonsense to another level by alleging in October 2017 that Hollywood actors and liberal politicians were part of an international child trafficking network, and that these Satan-worshiping pedophiles in fact run the world. As in some superhero action film, only Donald Trump and his allies could save the day.[74] It would be easy to dismiss QAnon as truly beyond the fringe except that some Republican politicians actually believe in it. Marjorie Taylor Greene, a new Republican member of Congress from Georgia, described QAnon as "a once-in-a-lifetime opportunity to take this global cabal of Satan-worshiping pedophiles out."[75]

The new right's digital activism is not confined to conspiracy theories and lame jokes. "There's absolutely evidence that the far right has found ways to create compelling content," Ethan Zuckerman adds. "A lot of that content is in plain sight. Their most powerful tool is exploiting YouTube's recommendation algorithm. If you spend enough time on a topic, you tend to go down these rabbit holes of extremism." Canada's Jordan Peterson, for instance, might seem like just another self-help guru. But if you start watching his videos on YouTube, his references to race, masculinity, or incel culture (involuntary celibates) could very well lead you to more extreme content, thanks to YouTube's suggested links.[76]

Even when the far right is "deplatformed"—which removes promoters of hate speech from mainstream social media like Twitter or Reddit—it continues to distribute its content through 8chan (now 8kun), the chat app Discord, the Twitter substitute Parler, or platforms like Gab, which has attracted nearly a million registered users with its extremist content, alt-right celebrity posters, and sophisticated user interface.[77] Live-streaming extreme content through sites like Twitch, whether it's a Trump rally or a gunman killing two people outside a synagogue in Halle in October 2019, provides the far right nearly unfettered access to a global audience.[78]

"These movements are not necessarily transnational in the sense of someone in a castle in Austria leading the movements of all the neo-Nazis," Zuckerman continues. Rather, they are transnational in their storytelling. "These movements are always trying to get you to reject standard narratives and believe that there's a suppressed narrative out there, and that once you unlock that suppressed narrative, you will understand the secret truth of the world." That's where Bannon and Breitbart come in: to upcycle alternative narratives, like the great replacement, into the mainstream.

These transnational connections form a three-way collaboration. "On the one hand you have extreme right groups trying to push their narrative, dictate the political agenda, and also dictate what's reported in the news," Julia Ebner explains.

> These are often coordinated campaigns involving troll armies and social media fake accounts. The second part of the triangle is the alternative media outlets: a whole new empire of alternative blogs and hyper-biased information that the far right has built across Europe in different languages and often linked to American media outlets like Breitbart or Rebel Media in Canada. Once the disinformation spreads across one platform it spreads across the other platforms, so it's hyper-networked in this sense. The third part of the triangle are the far-right populist parties.

These parties benefit from these campaigns, share the biased articles, and piggyback on the hashtags within an extremist echo chamber. At times, far-right activists launch unbranded social media campaigns in which they try to obscure their fingerprints to give an appearance of neutrality, much as Russian trolls tried to influence the U.S. presidential election in 2016 through a set of fake Facebook avatars and groups.

This sharing takes place most visibly across the Atlantic. But traces can even be found in China. For instance, the Chinese website Zhihu sponsored a "Q&A" after the New Zealand mosque attack in 2019. "A lot of people cheered for [the attack] and expressed support for the shooter," researcher Chenchen Zhang says. "Those were top voted comments." Although the website ultimately removed those comments, other racist and Islamophobic content remains uncensored in China because, from the point of view of the government, it highlights the failures of Western liberalism and shows the strength of the Chinese system.[79]

The new right expected that digital organizing would serve as the prelude to real-world action: demonstrations, political mobilizations, policy implementation. After the failure to spark mass mobilizations at the time of the Charlottesville Unite the Right gathering in 2017, however, a certain disconnect appeared between the most extreme exhortations online and the capacity to rally boots on the ground.[80] While digital organizing retained its centrality in new right thinking, other methods of influencing the mainstream acquired greater salience.

Moreover, other opportunities presented themselves for the new right's global organizing—such as the coronavirus pandemic of 2020.

3
The new right's pandemic pivot

Not long after the outbreak of the coronavirus in Europe in early 2020, the former liberal and current prime minister of Hungary Viktor Orbán quickly displayed his skills as a political opportunist. As cases started to multiply in nearby Italy, Orbán moved to take advantage of the crisis to advance his own political agenda. Since becoming prime minister for the second time in 2010, he'd been steadily remaking Hungary, a small Central European nation with a population of 10 million, into a more homogenous, more illiberal, and more vertically organized country. He'd defied the European Union on several occasions, all in the interests of bolstering his authority within the borders of his country.

From the beginning of his tenure, Orbán has been fixated on keeping immigrants out of Hungary. He has built walls along the country's southern borders with Serbia and Croatia and illegally held asylum seekers in legal limbo.[1] He has refused to accept his country's quota of the 160,000 refugees that the European Union agreed to resettle throughout the region—because, he said, he wanted "to keep Europe Christian."[2] He even made it a crime for organizations within Hungary to advocate on behalf of undocumented immigrants and refugees.[3]

It was no surprise, then, that on March 1, 2020, Orbán's chief advisor on domestic safety announced that Hungary would no longer accept refugees into transit camps along the Serbian border because "there is a certain connection between the coronavirus epidemic and illegal migration."[4] Later that month, Orbán would echo that sentiment when he said that "we are fighting a two-front war. One front is called migration and the other one belongs to the coronavirus. There is a logical connection between the two as both spread with movement."[5]

Further anti-immigration measures during the coronavirus crisis became unnecessary as Hungary effectively walled itself off and the EU closed its external borders. But Orbán wanted to put the pandemic to even greater uses. At the end of March, with the help of the supermajority his party enjoys in the Hungarian parliament, he pushed through an "enabling act" that gave him nearly unlimited power to rule by decree for an unlimited period of time. The act provided Orbán with new tools to attack his critics. Spreading "false information" about the coronavirus, for instance, became punishable by up to five years in prison. This measure "is nearly indistinguishable from a similar measure in Saudi Arabia," writes long-time Hungarian activist Laszlo Bruszt. "In effect, the enabling act minimises the remaining room for Hungary's independent media."[6]

Orbán was determined to permanently weaken an already marginalized political opposition. "In the two weeks since the law passed," writes Zack Beauchamp in Vox, Orbán "has seized funding provided to opposing political parties for their campaigns and re-appropriated it in the name of stimulus. He has taken advantage of the loss in coronavirus advertising revenue to buy up one of the few remaining independent media outlets in Hungary."[7] With his disgust for independent journalism exceeded only by his dislike of minorities, Orbán has also pushed through legislation withdrawing gender recognition of trans citizens and banning same-sex adoption. Freedom House's decision, in its 2020 report, to label Hungary as "not free" put additional pressure on the European Union to act against a member that had clearly departed from the rules and conditions of membership.[8]

The terrible irony of the enabling act was its irrelevance given the supermajority that Orbán's party enjoyed in parliament. When faced with judicial opposition to one policy or another, he has used that supermajority to amend the constitution—eight times by 2020. During his decade of rule, he has declared Hungary an "illiberal state," kicked out the Central European University, and worked behind the scenes to close the major independent daily newspaper, *Népszabadság*.[9] "With the exception of a short period after a by-election in 2015," writes historian Eva Balogh, "he has ruled without any domestic constraints for the last ten years."[10]

Autocrats, however, thrive on self-aggrandizement. Orbán doesn't just want to exercise power through other actors; he wants that power to be visibly invested in him as a pseudo-monarch. "Orbán wants to show that he is on the winning side, that he's managing the crisis well," reports Márta Pardavi. Even when he ended the enabling act in June, he retained the right to declare a medical state of emergency at any point. "It's hard to let go of these powers once they have been put in place," she adds.

Orbán's politics all along have been based on fear: a fear of immigrants, a fear of non-Christians and non-heterosexuals, a fear of Brussels, a fear of globalists. The coronavirus produced an entirely new fear that Orbán could leverage. He was not alone in exploiting the coronavirus in this way. The new right—whether the extreme, radical, or populist right—similarly thrives on fear. It, too, moved quickly to use the coronavirus pandemic, which generated widespread panic, to advance its own agenda. All the hallmarks of the far right came into play during the COVID-19 crisis. It pushed to close borders. It demonized foreigners and particularly border crossers. It spread a variety of conspiracy theories. And where it was in power—Hungary, Israel—it moved to increase that power through emergency measures.

On the other hand, the fact that the top four countries where the pandemic spread out of control—the United States, Brazil, Russia, and India—were governed by right-wing leaders may well set back the new right's cause. COVID-19 has dramatically exposed the sheer incompetence of the new right in many countries, with Donald Trump's 2020 electoral loss, for instance, far more a function of his bungling of the pandemic response than any of his other failings. Moreover, the scale of the COVID-19 threat has put on the table the kind of large-scale transformative policies supported by progressive activists that hitherto circulated only on the margins.

COVID-19 will inevitably contribute to a transformation of governance. But it's still unclear which way the political pendulum will swing.

PANDEMICS AND POLITICS

Most diseases require only medical interventions. Epidemics of infectious diseases, as they go global, often require political responses as well. As they cross communities and borders, pandemics threaten national and global economies, push governments to declare states of emergency, and trigger urgent debates over rapid-response resource allocation.

A pandemic's mortality rate alone can have profound political consequences. The Black Death in the fourteenth century created labor shortages in England that eroded the foundations of feudalism, while the genocide of indigenous peoples by diseases Europeans brought to the New World in the fifteenth and sixteenth centuries helped create a huge surge in the African slave trade to provide laborers for mining and agriculture.[11] In the modern era, epidemics have often left in their wake profound reorganizations of society. The cholera outbreak in London in the 1850s, for instance, focused attention on public health and led to the modernization of the city's sewage system.[12]

COVID-19's rapid spread in 2020 starkly revealed the strengths and weaknesses of different political systems. China responded to the initial outbreak as it would a manifestation of dissent: with censorship and political containment, followed by a more general social quarantine.[13] In South Korea and Taiwan, competent and centralized democratic leadership—combined with sophisticated technology, the means to ramp up national production and distribution of critical resources, and a public spirit of compliance—helped contain the pandemic without resort to a full social lockdown. The U.S. failure to respond in a timely and efficient manner—to devise a national strategy or put in place consistent testing, contact tracing, and quarantine mechanisms—revealed how a weak federalism ensures different outcomes for different states and populations.

To address COVID-19, even democracies felt the need to suspend normal political operations. Over 80 countries declared some kind of state of emergency during the pandemic.[14] These temporary mandates permitted authorities to impose quarantines of individuals, close businesses and public gathering spaces, and otherwise ensure physical distancing among the population.[15] In some cases, this authority has extended to the equivalent of wartime requisitioning. Even those leaders who brazenly ignored the pandemic resorted to extreme measures: Gurbanguly Berdimukhammedov of Turkmenistan forbade anyone in his country from uttering the word "coronavirus."[16] Other undemocratic leaders took advantage of the coronavirus to put greater pressure on their favorite targets: immigrants, dissidents, and journalists.[17]

In liberal and illiberal countries alike, the spread of COVID-19 was accompanied by an increase of surveillance, ostensibly to monitor compliance with the rules of quarantine and trace the contact trails of the infected. Singapore introduced an app, TraceTogether, that citizens voluntarily download and that accesses their phones' Bluetooth data. The government promised not to collect any data except phone numbers.[18] South Korea gathered information on the movement of infected persons via cell phone data, credit card records, and closed-circuit television but also shared some of that information publicly.[19] In a number of countries, authorities used drones to warn people to stay at home.

Although much of the data collection and surveillance has been consensual—citizens have participated in the system to feel safer—some countries are engaged in systematic violations of privacy. Israel passed legislation allowing its spy agency to use data collected for counter-terrorism purposes in the coronavirus fight.[20] Thanks to the coronavirus, China has refined and ramped up many of its intrusive surveillance techniques, from facial-recognition software to smartphone apps that restrict travel. More sophisticated bio-surveillance, powered by advanced AI, have been put into place at many borders, ostensibly to track the potentially infected, but it will be difficult to roll back this technology when the pandemic recedes.[21]

Pandemics can promote greater international cooperation to prevent cross-border infection. After the eruption of SARS in 2003, the World Health Organization took on greater responsibility to coordinate global responses to pandemics. But especially in the initial panic, pandemics often encourage a turn inward as countries close borders. In 2020, for instance, the countries that vested the WHO with new authority after SARS largely ignored the revised protocols, particularly around notifications and travel restrictions.[22] Countries imposed follow-the-pandemic travel bans. To deflect attention from his own failures to respond adequately to the coronavirus, Donald Trump escalated his attacks on the WHO, withdrawing U.S funding and ultimately quitting the organization altogether.

Pandemics have long been associated with the movement of traders and soldiers, the agents of globalization. With its critique of globalization, the new right has been well positioned to advance its agenda in the new COVID-19 era.

OPPORTUNITY FOR NEW RIGHT LEADERS

For some new right leaders, the pandemic was an opportunity to display the same kind of denialism that they'd expressed about climate change.

Donald Trump, for instance, dismissed the novel coronavirus as nothing more serious than a seasonal flu, and, as he said in a February 26 press briefing, "we'll essentially have a flu shot for this in a fairly quick manner."[23] In January and February, he insisted that his administration had the situation "totally under control."[24] He would later claim that he hadn't received any reason to believe otherwise even though the World Health Organization on January 23 released all the information about COVID-19 that was necessary to understand its potential global impact. Some members of the Trump administration, like Health Secretary Alex Azar, tried to push the president to take the threat seriously. But others, like Commerce Secretary Wilbur Ross, saw an opportunity in the epidemic gathering force in China. "I think it will help accelerate the return of jobs to North America," Ross told the press that January.[25]

During this critical period, Trump viewed the pandemic as a political tool that Democrats and the expert class were using to undermine his administration's policies. Trump supporters rallied around this notion that COVID-19 was a hoax to undermine the Trump presidency. On February 24, for instance, Rush Limbaugh told his radio audience that "the coronavirus is being weaponized as yet another element to bring down Donald Trump. Now, I want to tell you the truth about the coronavirus ... I'm dead right on this. The coronavirus is the common cold, folks."[26] In mid-March, influential right-wing Congressman Devin Nunes (R-Ca) was still dismissing fears of infection by saying, "it's a great time to just go out, go to a local restaurant."[27]

In all, Trump wasted 70 days before he finally began to take the pandemic seriously.[28] According to two epidemiologists writing in *The New York Times*, this delay was responsible for 90 percent of U.S. deaths.[29] Even after finally supporting various quarantine restrictions, Trump chafed at the economic losses and supported governors, invariably conservative, who more aggressively pushed for their states to reopen, with the predictable result of a resurgence in cases throughout the country at the beginning of summer 2020 and a much more serious upsurge the following November.

For all his initial indifference to COVID-19, however, Trump didn't miss the political opportunity that the pandemic presented to push through parts of his cherished economic agenda, like further tax cuts and deregulation by fiat.[30] He implemented a 60-day moratorium on accepting new immigrants. Despite the huge costs of the stimulus packages and the drop in government tax revenues, he pushed forward with his plan to build a wall along the border with Mexico and spend an additional half a billion dollars painting the structure black.[31] Even after he was voted out of office in November, Trump used his lame-duck period to sign a raft of executive orders undermining environmental standards, rushing through last-minute appointments, and pardoning his cronies.

Jair Bolsonaro largely followed the same script as Trump by downplaying the risk of the pandemic. On March 15, despite having been in close contact with several members of his administration who'd already contracted the disease, Bolsonaro joined a demonstration of his supporters where he touched a reported 272 people, claiming that his own tests came back negative.[32] Even as the infection rate was climbing dangerously in Brazil, Bolsonaro continued to argue that the crisis was little more than a media conspiracy.[33] By May, his right-wing supporters were calling for the return of military rule and an end to the lockdown that state governors had put into place. Bolsonaro, like Trump, encouraged his followers to ignore the recommendations of policymakers and health experts to maintain a social quarantine, and Brazil quickly became the epicenter of the virus in the Global South. After firing members of his team for their perceived disloyalty, Bolsonaro faced an approval rate of only 33 percent by the end of April.[34] Only a massive payout of benefits to low-income Brazilians prevented his popularity from plummeting further. By July, he himself had come down with the disease, as Trump would do as well in October.

Boris Johnson, the UK prime minister, also took an exceptionally cavalier attitude. "I can tell you I am shaking hands continuously," he told reporters at one point. "I was at a hospital the other night where I think there were actually a few coronavirus patients and I shook hands with everybody."[35] Then, of course, Johnson became the first world leader to contract the disease and nearly died. He changed his view of the pandemic accordingly, but not before his country posted the highest death toll in Europe.

In the Philippines, President Rodrigo Duterte initially dismissed the pandemic as late as mid-March, mocking those who were scared of the coronavirus. He moved slowly on travel restrictions and on limiting his own personal interactions.[36] Then, when the threat became unavoidable, he pivoted to his default position of strongman, acquiring emergency powers to address the pandemic. He pushed a "shoot to kill" strategy to police what would become one of the world's longest and strictest lockdowns. He shuttered a major TV station that was occasionally critical of his policies and prosecuted the editor of Rappler, an independent internet news site.[37] In July, he implemented a new national security law that provided him with even greater powers to go after his opponents.

Other new right leaders immediately understood how to capitalize on the situation to advance their agendas. Benjamin Netanyahu used the pandemic to suspend court proceedings, which not coincidentally delayed his own corruption trial, and then exploited the crisis to push for a new coalition government that temporarily saved his political career.[38] In Italy, far-right leader Matteo Salvini used the pandemic to push his "closed ports" policy. In February, even as the outbreak was gathering steam in his country, Salvini declared that "allowing the migrants to land from Africa, where the presence of the virus was confirmed, is irresponsible." At the time, there was only one reported case on the whole continent, in Egypt.[39]

Perhaps the most aggressive power grabs came from the leaders of Russia and China. Russian President Vladimir Putin pushed through a referendum that required an up-or-down vote on over 200 amendments to the constitution, including one that declares marriage as only between a man and a woman and another that allows Putin to serve two more terms as the leader of the country. The public approved the changes in a vote marked by workplaces pressuring their employees to participate, the government offering lottery prizes to lucky voters, and some outright fraud as well. The vote wasn't even strictly necessary, since the Russian parliament had already approved the changes.[40] But Putin has always worked hard to demonstrate that his Russia is democratic, if only formally so.

Xi Jinping, meanwhile, didn't feel the need to playact. He'd already made himself leader for life in 2018, when the National People's Congress simply removed the two-term limit on the presidency. So, in the same week that Putin was securing his future, Xi focused instead on securing China's future as an integrated, politically homogeneous entity. To put an end to the street protests that had been roiling Hong Kong for several years, Xi implemented a new national security law in the territory that threatened demonstrators with long prison sentences on four potential charges: secession, subversion, terrorism, and collusion with foreign forces.[41] Some authoritarian leaders used the coronavirus to consolidate more power; Xi was more interested in consolidating control over territory while the world was distracted by the pandemic.

Outside of government, new right political movements were also advancing an anti-immigration platform. In Germany, the identitarian movement hung banners proclaiming "Defend Our Borders" on the Brandenburg Gate, once a potent symbol of the erased border between East and West Germany.[42] Together with other extremists and the ultra-right AfD, the identitarian movement infiltrated a series of protests against the German government's quarantine policies. The protests, which sprang up in dozens of German cities, highlighted many of the conspiracy theories associated with the coronavirus, blaming the pandemic on Jews, globalists, China, the pharmaceutical industry, and tech companies. "What unites people is the hatred of the political elite and public broadcasting," said Matthias Quent, a right-wing extremism researcher.[43]

Throughout Europe, far-right parties were retooling their "great replacement" narrative—that immigrants are poised to overwhelm majority populations—to incorporate the coronavirus.[44] It wasn't just Orbán and Salvini. Shutting borders, enacting travel bans, and restricting immigration all became the new conventional wisdom. The threat that outsiders supposedly pose to the health of nations has long been a singular obsession of fascists.

The new right was also busy implementing its favorite strategy: hijacking existing movements and pushing them in an explicitly ideological direction. As the pandemic spread, the alt-right seized on the anti-vaccine movement as a vehicle to challenge both liberal policymakers and the scientific establishment. In the United States, organizations like Medical Freedom Patriots ("pro-God, anti-vaccine, QAnon friendly") largely displaced the anti-vaxxers of the libertarian and hippy left.[45] What started as an attack on medical and economic measures to contain the virus shifted into high gear once vaccines became available in late 2020, even in places where new right leaders like Trump were celebrating the arrival of the new drugs.[46] A similar alliance between the far right and anti-vaxxers in Europe has taken advantage of an even deeper mistrust of the science of vaccines.[47]

In Europe, at least, far-right parties in opposition did not benefit politically from the coronavirus crisis. The Alternative für Deutschland witnessed a drop in public support from 15 percent to 9 percent, the far right in Italy suffered a comparable loss in support, the National Rally in France saw its control of council seats slip from 1,438 to 840 between the 2014 municipal elections and those that took place in June 2020, and the far right in Spain experienced at best a flatlining in public opinion polls.[48] With borders closed, these parties couldn't stoke fears of immigration. And European leaders—Angela Merkel, Emmanuel Macron, Giuseppe Conte, Pedro Sánchez—were largely successful in dealing with COVID-19. Where the new right was in power—Poland, Austria—it could take advantage of a rally-around-the-rally effect. Thus, while the new right in opposition was successful in spreading conspiracy theories, it was unable to translate this into concrete political advantage.[49]

New right civil society organizations have largely taken their cues from new right political leaders during the pandemic. Organizations like the Center for Immigration Studies presented seminars on institutionalizing Trump administration policies on immigration, such as stripping asylum seekers, refugees, and immigrants of all rights. The organization CitizenGo launched a petition to defund the World Health Organization, echoing the sentiments of Trump and his allies. And the World Congress of Families and the Alliance Defending Freedom International vigorously pushed their anti-abortion and anti-LGBT agendas during the pandemic, making notable advances in Poland, Hungary, and Ghana.

CENTER VS. PERIPHERY

Analysts of the new authoritarian wave that has swept across the world over the last few years have largely focused on power grabs in capitals. Leaders like Donald Trump, Vladimir Putin, and Xi Jinping have attempted to reduce the influence of legislative and judicial bodies in favor of their own executive power. They have targeted civil society and media, and used the coronavirus crisis to consolidate their control.

An equally important feature of this new authoritarianism is its intolerance for regional or local power bases that lie beyond executive reach. For countries with federal structures, this means a conscious effort to strengthen the federal center at the expense of the regions. It's part of the remaking of the nation-state in the twenty-first century, a reversal of the two-edged trend to devolve power to local authorities and delegate authority to international institutions. These nationalists don't just hate globalists. They hate anybody who stands in their way, including just about any potential counterforce taking shape on the periphery of their own countries.

Autocrats fear the periphery because it's where dissent can germinate beyond the prying eye of the panoptical state. East Germany's revolution in 1989, for instance, began with demonstrations every Monday in the southern city of Leipzig. The Romanian revolution a few months later was sparked by the Hungarian minority in Timisoara. The overthrow of Slobodan Milosevic in Serbia in 2000 began with protests by miners in Kolubara, an hour's drive from Belgrade.

Federal states face a continual tension between center and periphery, which occasionally breaks the country apart (as with Yugoslavia and the Soviet Union). The Spanish government cracked down on Catalan moves toward independence in 2017, imposing direct rule for a time. Ukraine, Moldova, and Georgia all faced secession movements that resulted in autonomous regions claiming statehood. Occasionally, breakaway regions achieve international recognition as states—Bangladesh, East Timor, South Sudan.

The autocrat fears secession as well as anti-government protest. The first attacks the unitary power of the nation-state, the second challenges the unitary power of the ruler. It's one and the same thing for the authoritarian nationalist.

As the pandemic transformed the United States into the world's leading hotspot, Trump and his strategists were desperate to deflect responsibility and distract attention from their mismanaged response. One tactic was to consciously pit states against each other in a replay of the pre-Civil War conflict over federal authority. Trump and his allies in predominantly red states pushed to reopen the U.S. economy and at the same time preserve the "freedom" of Americans to refuse to wear protective masks in public.[50] This strategy echoed the arguments of southern states in the late 1850s to maintain their economic system without federal interference, and to have the "freedom" to own slaves. Trump also precipitated a showdown over reopening public schools by ordering students to return in person for the upcoming school year, even threatening to withdraw federal funding from schools that didn't reopen.

Trump did not have a unified federal government behind him. A number of public health officials, including the director of the National Institute of Allergy and Infectious Diseases Anthony Fauci, counseled caution about reopening the economy and forcing students to return to school. The military balked at the president's plan to send soldiers out onto the streets to suppress public protest.[51] But the president discovered that he still controlled the security forces attached to other federal agencies. He deployed the National Guard in DC to tamp down protests in June, prompting the mayor of the nation's capital to demand that the president withdraw the forces. Agents from both Immigration and Customs Enforcement and Customs and Border Protection were also used to police demonstrations in the wake of the killing of George Floyd.

But then Trump tried something different. He sent federal agents into Portland, Oregon, to crack down on anti-racism protests. They beat up peaceful protesters and fired impact munitions at demonstrators, seriously injuring one of them. They drove around the city in unmarked vans pulling people off the street. Oregon officials at every level—the city, the state, and congressional representatives—demanded that these agents of the Department of Homeland Security, the U.S. Marshals Service, and other federal authorities leave Portland immediately. The state filed suit against these federal agencies, and the ACLU called it a constitutional crisis.[52]

Rather than back down, President Trump doubled down, claiming the paramilitaries were there to restore order and that he was prepared to send them next to Chicago, with other major cities on a list of future deployments. "Look at what's going on—all run by Democrats, all run by very liberal Democrats. All run, really, by the radical left," Trump said. "If Biden got in, that would be true for the country. The whole country would go to hell. And we're not going to let it go to hell."[53]

By claiming that areas of the country under Democratic Party control were in fact swamps of anti-Americanism, Trump enlisted the classic vocabulary associated with dehumanizing America's putative enemies prior to attack. Trump's use of federal paramilitaries, moreover, was a classic tactic of autocrats to test how far they can push their authority and what forces they can count on in an emergency. The Black Lives Matter protests inadvertently provided Trump with that opportunity. In the event of a conflict between the federal government and the states escalating into civil war, Trump would know which guns are on his side. After his electoral loss in November, Trump attempted to overturn the results through legal suit and direct pressure, and even contemplated a federal declaration of martial law to remain in office.

Trump was not the only leader to strengthen the federal center at the expense of the regions. Halfway around the world, the Russian authorities arrested Sergei Furgal, the governor of the far eastern city of Khabarovsk, on charges that he orchestrated the murder of two men 15 years ago. Tens of thousands of people demonstrated on the streets of Khabarovsk in July 2020, demanding the release of this leader of the opposition. Furgal and his supporters argued that the arrest was politically motivated.[54] The protests continued into 2021.

In Hong Kong, authorities used a new national security law criminalizing many forms of protest to arrest several pro-democracy advocates, who were promptly jailed. Others decided to abandon the city. A dozen dissidents who failed to reach Taiwan by boat were captured and charged with illegal border crossing. The Chinese Communist Party has cracked down on any challenges to its authority from the periphery, whether in Hong Kong, Xinjiang, or Tibet.

In Turkey, meanwhile, Recep Tayyip Erdoğan replaced the mayors of cities affiliated with the People's Democratic Party—the pro-Kurdish opposition party—concentrated in the country's southeast region, and put pressure on the party through financial audits and attacks by the government-affiliated press.[55] Narendra Modi has made it more difficult for state governments, particularly those led by the political opposition, to raise revenue.[56] Jair Bolsonaro clashed with the governors of Brazil's states over their respective handling of the coronavirus.

The new nationalists have defined "the people" in very specific ways to exclude portions of the population based on ethnicity, religion, or politics. They are transforming the federal government into a tool to reward only those who support the ruler in the capital. They are attacking democracy, yes, but also reducing faith in governance more generally. What better way "to deconstruct the administrative state," as alt-right guru Steve Bannon likes to say, than to turn government into a body with no power or legitimacy beyond its military and police.

MORE EXTREME RESPONSES

While the radical right has focused on immigration, the extreme right has taken a very different approach. In their attempts to change the existing order step by step, advocates of restricted immigration and closed borders are ameliorationist. The extreme right, on the other hand, supports accelerationism: speeding the collapse of the existing order. For these more apocalyptic activists, the pandemic created precisely the kind of conditions—panic, widespread fear and skepticism, economic volatility, heightened belief in survivalism—that could precipitate a wholesale rejection of the liberal order.

Although they represent only a small fraction of the new right, these extremists have attempted to expand their influence during the pandemic by urging racist attacks on minorities and foreigners. The United States emerged as an epicenter of this epidemic of hate. Anti-Asian attacks and harassment, motivated by the mistaken belief that China and the Chinese were deliberately spreading the coronavirus, spiked in the United States, with one monitoring initiative recording 1,500 incidents in one month.[57] On March 24, the FBI shot and killed a white supremacist who was planning a car bomb attack on a hospital in Missouri.[58] Another white supremacist was arrested the following month for planning an attack on a Jewish assisted-living facility in Massachusetts.[59]

In some cases, these accelerationists simply urged their followers to add to the chaos. For instance, according to the New Jersey Office of Homeland Security and Preparedness, one neo-Nazi group recommended that its supporters "incite panic while people are practicing social isolation during the COVID-19 outbreak, which includes discharging firearms in cities and putting bullet-sized holes into car windows."[60] More ominously, accelerationists raised the possibility online of using the coronavirus as a bioweapon. According to one law enforcement agency report in February 2020, "extremists discussed a number of methods for coronavirus attacks, such as spending time in public with perceived enemies, leaving 'saliva on door handles' at local

FBI offices, spitting on elevator buttons and spreading coronavirus germs in 'nonwhite neighborhoods.'"[61]

Some elements of the new right, including neo-Nazis and armed militia members, also participated in the movement to pressure U.S. governors to reopen the economy in their states. "The protests, which have been supported by conservative megadonors, have ties to a host of darker internet subcultures," according to *The Washington Post*, "people who oppose vaccination, the self-identified Western-chauvinist Proud Boys group, anti-government conspiracy theorists known as QAnon, and people touting a coming civil war."[62] The prospect of a "coming civil war" attracted the "Boogaloo Bois," armed men who believe that the lockdown is the first step by the police and other authorities to take away their weapons.[63] What was remarkable about these anti-government protests was the support they received from President Trump, presumably the head of government.

The organizing of these militia movements was on full display in Michigan, where in May 2020 hundreds of demonstrators, some armed, tried to force their way onto the floor of the Senate chamber in the State House in Lansing. Later, 14 far-right activists planned to snatch the governor from her vacation home and put her on trial for "treason." Thanks to an FBI infiltrator, they were arrested in early October. The governor in turn blamed Trump for inciting these kinds of actions by, among other actions, tweeting "LIBERATE MICHIGAN" during the coronavirus lockdown in that state. The president had tweeted the same about Virginia, and the conspirators in fact considered kidnapping the governor there as well.[64]

In 2021, the militia movements shifted into high gear in a last-ditch attempt to keep Donald Trump in power. The assault on the U.S. capital looked much like what happened in Michigan in May, but with a much larger force that overwhelmed the unprepared security in DC. Some of that far-right organizing may have been aided by a $500,000 Bitcoin bequest from a French computer programmer just before he committed suicide. Half the money went to far-right media personality Nick Fuentes, who was present at the January 6 insurrection in Washington, DC.[65] These efforts attracted international support from a motley collection of groups: QAnon believers throughout Europe, the Happy Science cult in Japan, Falun Gong practitioners in Taiwan.[66] Emboldened by the publicity it received and the martyrs it lost during this attempted coup, the far right planned various follow-ups to disrupt the inauguration of the new administration, which did not come to pass because of heightened security measures.

In the United States, the most extreme component of the "Stop the Steal" coalition has been the "accelerationists" who hope to spur on a race war. To that end, some showed up at the Black Lives Matter protests in the wake of the police killing of George Floyd in Minneapolis. Several were arrested for fomenting violence at these rallies, one for shooting a protester in Albuquerque and two more for a pair of murders in California. There have been at least 50 cases of cars ramming into demonstrators; the vast majority driven by extremists inspired by the accelerationist meme "all lives splatter."[67]

The new right has devoted considerable time and energy to spreading disinformation across the internet. It has touted conspiracy theories involving China—for instance, that the coronavirus was engineered in a biolab in Wuhan—which have been taken up by conservative media outlets and promoted by Trump and the Republican Party. In the run-up to the 2020 elections, Republican congressional candidates ran ads that blamed China for "the Wuhan epidemic," promised to "make China pay" for "the lies they told and the jobs they stole," and warned, "To stop China, you have to stop Joe Biden."[68] Republican congressional candidate Joanne Wright in Los Angeles, like many of her tribe, asserted that China manufactured the disease but added the twist that Bill Gates financed the plot.[69]

Far-right conspiracy theorists take a special interest in maligning "globalists" like billionaire philanthropist Bill Gates, but they also attacked George Soros, infectious disease expert Anthony Fauci, and WHO head Tedros Adhanom. They've also added an anti-Semitic spin by accusing Jews of creating the coronavirus and conspiring to undermine the world economy.[70] Alternatively, Muslims have come under attack, particularly in India where the government blamed the outbreak in the country on a religious gathering of Muslim missionaries in New Delhi in March 2020. In the aftermath of that incident, Deutsche Welle reported, "a Muslim man was beaten up by a mob in Delhi, vendors were refused entry into localities, people refused to buy from Muslims, and a hospital reportedly segregated coronavirus patients by their religion."[71]

Beyond offering an excuse to vent online spleen and spread conspiracy theories, the pandemic has presented a digital recruitment opportunity. According to a study by the Institute for Strategic Dialogue, the far right used its coronavirus conspiracy theories to bring new members into the movement. One Telegram channel devoted to white supremacy and COVID-19, for instance, grew nine-fold from 300 viewers to 2,700 in one month.[72] In the United States, the average number of daily searches related to white supremacy rose dramatically as the lockdowns spread.[73]

THE EUROPEAN UNION

Prior to the outbreak of the coronavirus pandemic, the European Union was already being stretched to breaking point. The United Kingdom left the EU in early 2020 and formalized its exit at the end of the year. Hungary and several other East European countries were heading in a distinctly authoritarian direction. Italy was flirting with right-wing populism. Widening economic disparities hadn't helped. Germany remained a powerhouse, but Greece had not made up the ground it lost in the 2009 crisis, and the countries of Eastern Europe had not yet closed the gap with the western half of the continent. Thus, the pandemic was a timely tool for the new right to make use of in impeding and rolling back European integration.

The EU is the only regional structure in the world to have dismantled many of its internal borders. In 1995, seven European nations created the Schengen Area, abolishing their internal border controls and visa requirements. Eventually becoming subject to European Union law, the area expanded to include 26 states. Until the pandemic hit, citizens of EU member states could move and work virtually anywhere within the bloc. But opposition to this freedom of movement, given that it challenges the state's undisputed control over its own borders, has been a major rallying cry of the far right. It has argued that Schengen makes the control of immigrants more difficult (as with the influx of Tunisians into Italy in 2011) and compromises anti-terrorist policing (in the wake of a terrorism suspect's flight from Germany to Italy in 2016).[74] Still, Schengen survived.

What the far right had been trying and failing to achieve for years, the coronavirus managed in a matter of weeks. Some members re-established internal border controls without notifying the EU Commission, as required by the Schengen Border Code.[75] These moves prompted the EU to declare in mid-March a temporary closure of all internal borders. Europe was supposed to celebrate the 25th anniversary of Schengen's abolition of border controls at the end of March 2020. Instead, there were new gates and road barriers where not long before travelers could pass between countries without even knowing it.

Then, by imposing even more restrictions on migrants still desperate to get into Europe, European governments implemented another key plank in the new right's platform. In mid-March, after Greece sent troops to its border with Turkey to stop refugees from crossing over by land, the EU closed its external borders to non-nationals. The desperate continued to attempt to reach Europe by sea. Of the 800 who left Libya in March 2020, 43 made it to Italy and 155 landed in Malta.[76] The Libyan coast guard gathered up the rest and returned them to Libya.

Not all European countries took such a hardline stance. Portugal boldly gave all migrants and asylum seekers full citizenship rights on a temporary basis so that they could access health care during the pandemic.[77] A number of countries, including Spain and Belgium, suspended deportations. Beyond that, however, migrants suffered disproportionately from the pandemic. In one German refugee camp, nearly half the 600 residents came down with the disease.[78]

The pandemic also deepened already existing cleavages in the EU, for instance, between Italy and everyone else.

Italy was the first hotspot to emerge in the European Union. Within a few days of the first reported case of infection in Lombardy on February 20, COVID-19 was putting an enormous strain on the hospitals of northern Italy. The EU's response was largely bureaucratic—more consultations. When it came to concrete assistance, the EU had little to offer Italy.

On March 10, only a couple of weeks after the appearance of its first case, Italy's permanent representative to the European Union Maurizio Massari wrote in no uncertain terms in *Politico*, "Italy has already asked to activate the European Union Mechanism of Civil Protection for the supply of medical equipment for individual protection. But, unfortunately, not a single EU country responded to the Commission's call. Only China responded bilaterally. Certainly, this is not a good sign of European solidarity."[79]

Worse, a number of European countries, including like France and Germany, actually imposed export limits on critical medical supplies for fear that they would need them in the coming days.[80] Though the eventual intervention of the European Commission to impose region-wide export restrictions in exchange for EU members rescinding their national bans may have alleviated shortages within the bloc, it was at the expense of poorer countries outside of it.[81]

For many Italians, the failure of European solidarity was nothing new. Writes Luigi Scazzeri at the Centre for European Reform:

> Over the past decade, Italy has gone from being one of the most enthusiastic supporters of greater European integration to one of the most eurosceptic member-states. Many Italians felt that Italy did not receive much European solidarity during the eurozone crisis, and that the Union served as an enforcer of damaging austerity policies. The damage to Italians' view of the EU was then compounded by the bloc's response to the migration crisis. Italy took in 650,000 migrants between 2014 and 2018, and efforts to distribute these among other EU countries were largely symbolic ...[82]

Hungary's authoritarianism, Portugal's generosity, Italy's call for solidarity, Germany's tightfistedness: European responses to the current crisis are literally all over the map. As Nathalie Tocci, a former advisor to the EU foreign policy chief, told *The Guardian*: "This is definitely a make-it-or-break-it moment for the European project. If it goes badly, this really risks being the end of the union. It fuels all the nationalist-populism."[83]

In July 2020, however, the EU stepped away from the brink by achieving a consensus on a $2.1 trillion bailout package that directed significant funds to the countries—Italy, Spain, Greece—hardest hit by the pandemic. Much of the nearly $900 million targeted at the countries most affected by the lockdowns came in the form of grants so did not add to the debt problems of the southern tier. And despite the usual rift between the "frugal" and the "needy" countries, and some intemperate rhetoric at the summit, a spirit of solidarity prevailed. "We showed collective responsibility and solidarity and we also show our belief in our common future," concluded summit chairman Charles Michel.[84]

THE LEVIATHAN PROBLEM

In the 1970s, political scientist William Ophuls argued that overwhelming environmental problems—pollution, overpopulation, the energy crisis—required a Leviathan, a "government with major coercive powers" that could ram through necessary measures to safeguard the ecosystem and save humanity from extinction.[85] This argument has resurfaced during the more recent climate-change debate, in the form of either an authoritarian state like China or a world government providing the coercive power necessary to reduce carbon emissions over the objections of sectoral interests like the fossil-fuel industry.[86]

Because it poses an urgent short-term threat, COVID-19 has turned a largely academic question into a viable policy choice, as even liberal societies have adopted more coercive measures to protect public health. "It's very difficult for an emancipatory movement to find a genuinely democratic way to change people's behavior, to find consensus among interests," notes Wolfram Schaffar.

In the absence of robust international institutions—and the new right is determined to keep them weak—the Leviathan option necessarily relies on strong states. As such, COVID-19 is strengthening the sovereignist backlash against what had hitherto seemed to be an inexorable multilateralism. In addition to border closures and travel bans, a number of countries introduced export restrictions to ensure access to critical resources, including medical supplies and food.[87] These measures were billed as temporary, provisional, and situational. Nevertheless, because they intersect with the agendas of far-right political movements, they may ultimately encourage the growing anti-globalist, anti-immigrant, anti-multicultural trend in world politics.

In theory, the new right is skeptical of a strong state, which runs counter to notions of individual liberty. In practice, however, the new right expands the power of the state when it is in power, as Viktor Orbán has done in Hungary. The new right generally favors a strong military, the suppression of political opposition, and an economic patronage system that rewards political followers. The pandemic has exposed the new right's allergy to transparency, its penchant for executive authority, and its preference to compel rather than solicit compliance. The new right favors a Leviathan state, but to maintain control within borders rather than to tackle cross-border problems.

But the pandemic has also exposed significant vulnerabilities that the new right is not well positioned to address. Dealing with an infectious disease requires competent governance, which many new right leaders did not exercise before or during the crisis. In revealing enormous gaps in health care, COVID-19 may yet instigate the overhaul of public health infrastructure—hospitals, national disease control, public insurance—for which earlier cholera epidemics laid the groundwork, but that has been conspicuously absent from the platforms of the new right. The failures of the intelligence and national security apparatus, meanwhile, have undermined the argument that only a strong military can protect the lives of the population.[88] Even as liberal and illiberal countries have called on their militaries to play a larger role in battling COVID-19, the pandemic may well prompt a thorough reconceptualization of national security at the level of doctrine, budget priorities, and international cooperation.[89] A national security system predicated largely on large military budgets and military deterrence, so frequently a preoccupation of the new right, is fast becoming anachronistic. A tank, in the end, is useless against a virus (not to mention climate change, economic inequality, or any of the other threats to human security).

Despite various coronavirus power grabs, COVID-19 doesn't spell the end of democracy. Open societies are generally more flexible and capable of responding to seismic shocks of this nature than non-democratic societies. "Leaders who portray themselves as saviors are more exposed to blame if the death toll soars," writes Declan Walsh, and there is even evidence that democratic societies suffer lower mortality in pandemics than undemocratic ones.[90] But all societies will have to address the defects in governance that the pandemic has laid bare, from an inability to respond to urgent threats in a timely manner to failures in addressing the underlying economic and social inequalities amplified by the virus.

The pandemic has proven to be a political stress test. There will be more to come.

4

Responding to the new right

The Christchurch shootings shocked the world. On March 15, 2019, a white supremacist originally from New South Wales in Australia opened fire in two mosques in New Zealand's second-most populous city, killing 51 people and injuring 49. He signaled his solidarity with the global new right by titling his manifesto "The Great Replacement," which he sent to various places prior to the attacks, including the prime minister's office.

The Christchurch attacks were a surprise to many inside and outside of New Zealand. "This is an incredibly tolerant, multicultural country," says Paul Spoonley of Massey University in Auckland. "In an international value study, the proportion of New Zealanders who see immigrants as contributing positively to the country is probably two to four times higher than countries in mainland Europe. To be anti-immigrant or against a particular religion is politically damaging."[1]

New Zealand's current reputation for tolerance—by 2011, the country was ranked third in the industrialized world for its tolerance of minorities[2]—belies its history of discrimination. The indigenous Maori community dealt with an apartheid system well into the twentieth century, and Chinese immigrants weren't able to become citizens until the 1950s. The country has also been home to a small but globally connected far-right community, which was implicated in several murders and over a hundred incidents of racist violence between 2005 and 2013.[3] The largest of these groups, the League of Rights, boasted a membership of a thousand people. A strain of anti-immigrant sentiment has thrived on the margins and even in mainstream parties like New Zealand First, the junior partner in a coalition government with the Labor Party.

Prior to 2019, the Muslim community repeatedly complained that the New Zealand authorities weren't properly addressing Islamophobic threats.[4] "It was taken quite lightly because we always believed that New Zealand was the safest place on earth, that things like that happen somewhere else," observes Ikhlaq Kashkari, the president of the Muslim Association of New Zealand. "We were living with a false sense of security even though we were getting more news every day from around the world about the promotion of Islamophobia."[5]

Christchurch itself was not immune to these trends. "When Christchurch emerged as having a problem, the defenses went up and local representatives said, 'we're not a racist city,'" reports Rawiri Taonui, New Zealand's first professor of indigenous studies. "There have been more racist incidents in Christchurch than pretty much anywhere in the country."[6]

Despite rising Islamophobia and a history of far-right organizing, the New Zealand authorities were not primed to look for a white man like the Christchurch shooter. "After 9/11, a number of people here suddenly labelled all the Muslim people of New Zealand who were living peacefully in the country as terrorists," points out Meng Foon, New Zealand's commissioner of race relations. "The New Zealand secret service targeted them more and, unfortunately, missed the shooter last year in Christchurch. They dropped the ball in terms of monitoring white supremacists."[7]

The Christchurch shootings were not surprising in another, more global sense. Far-right violence had intensified leading up to 2019, with attacks inspired by racism, Islamophobia, and anti-Semitism taking place in Pittsburgh and El Paso, Munich and Hanau in Germany, Macerata in Italy, and Baerum in Norway. Many of these shooters saw themselves as part of a larger movement and their acts as paying tribute to their predecessors, particularly Anders Breivik, a far-right crusader who killed 77 people in Norway in 2011.[8]

Matt Nipert of the *New Zealand Herald* has written a study showing the connections between these gunmen and Brenton Tarrant, the Christchurch shooter. These extremists cited many of the same sources, shared the same rhetoric, and didn't think of themselves as lone wolves even when acting alone. Tarrant, he says, "didn't throw a dart on a map and it landed in New Zealand. There are strong ties between the far right in New Zealand and Australia." Tarrant also went to New Zealand because of its lax gun laws. Once there, he cast around for targets. "He said in his manifesto that he chose New Zealand because he wanted to show that no place is safe for Muslims," Nipert adds, "but really it was just a cover for his own laziness. He could do it without leaving the country again."[9]

New Zealand's failures before March 15, 2019, were on par with the performance of other countries. Their policing didn't take seriously the prospect that digital connections, narratives like the great replacement, and cross-border organizing would translate into homicidal actions.

But New Zealand's response after March 15 was something altogether different. Squarely addressing its failures, the government of Jacinda Ardern immediately and unequivocally responded to the Christchurch killings with an unusual combination of empathy for the victims and zero tolerance for the culture that nurtured the perpetrator's hatred, all the while recognizing the need for cross-border coordination. As it turned out, that's exactly the kind of policy approach that paid off a year later when the coronavirus hit.

After March 15, Ardern demonstrated what leadership looks like. Following the lead of the mayor of Christchurch, she called the action "terrorism." She donned a hijab and reached out to the Muslim community, refused to speak the name of the perpetrator, and introduced sweeping gun-control measures.[10] She even went to the island of Fiji to console family members of those killed that day in Christchurch.

Unlike in the United States, where repeated mass shootings have not led to substantial gun control, New Zealand outlawed automatic weapons "with widespread public support and universal parliamentary support (119 out of 120 MPs voted in favor)," Paul Spoonley notes. "There was some grumbling among those who go hunting that the ban had gone too far or was actioned too rapidly. Also, illegal weapons are not subject to registration and restrictions on sales. But we're light-years away from the United States."

The government moved more forcefully to pre-empt right-wing violence, launching dozens of investigations into extremist groups and individuals, jailing a neo-Nazi who shared a video of the Christchurch killings, and arresting a Defense Force soldier with links to the far right. It also pushed forward with a new effort to amend existing laws to outlaw hate speech.[11] "If all the New Zealand government does is extend the Human Rights Act and the Harmful Digital Communications Act, it will safely avoid curtailing free speech," concludes Martin Cocker of Netsafe. Although such prohibitions against hate speech set New Zealand apart from countries like the United States, the state has to be careful not to simply ban unpopular opinions. "It's very difficult to combat the kind of things we're seeing online without creating measures that could very easily impinge on free speech," he adds.[12]

Perhaps Ardern's most ambitious project was the Christchurch Call, "a commitment by Governments and tech companies to eliminate terrorist and violent extremist content online."[13] Only two months after the shootings, New Zealand joined France in pushing for change at the international level. "They knew that they were unlikely to drive global change on social media as a country of five million people far away from the main political centers in the U.S. and Europe," observes Matthew Feldman of the Centre for the Analysis of the Right Wing. "They put white nationalism very squarely on the UN General Assembly agenda."

The big players—Facebook, Twitter, Google, Microsoft, and Amazon—all signed onto the Call, committing to develop algorithms and AI tools to quickly identify and remove hateful content from their platforms.[14] Any Kiwi who views extremist content online is now automatically directed to websites that help people leave hate groups.[15] The Call also inspired Australia to pass a law criminalizing social media companies that don't expeditiously remove "abhorrent violent material."[16] That's all to the good, but it hasn't yet detoxified the internet. The impact of the Call, which is nonbinding, has been limited due to the "lack of alignment among countries and a lack of consistent pressure on multinationals," Martin Cocker points out. "If the Christchurch Call moved to the point of achieving consistency among countries in terms of what they demand from industry, it could continue to have some influence."

When the shooter pleaded guilty in late March 2020, New Zealand was saved from the spectacle of a very public trial. "His guilty plea will likely reduce the priority of efforts to curb the far right," Matt Nipert says.

> My concern is that New Zealand still views him as a lone wolf, as one deranged individual, that it's not our problem, that an Australian came here to do it. That's true, but the problem is global. These

groups operate cross borders and see themselves as a brotherhood not as citizens of a country. Someone did an analysis of who logs onto 8chan. You can't see their identities but you can see where they log on from, and New Zealand was very highly ranked.

Meanwhile, the Ardern government has had to face other major problems, chief among them the coronavirus pandemic. Demonstrating the same kind of firmness, managerial competence, and empathy applied after the March 15 tragedy, the prime minister led a successful effort to radically reduce the infection rate far faster than her European or North American counterparts. In both cases—one a political epidemic, the other a medical pandemic—it showed zero tolerance by jailing right-wing extremists after March 15 and, during the first week of the COVID-19 lockdown, demoting the health minister, who blithely visited a beach.[17]

Although the COVID-19 response has been more top-down, both efforts received overwhelming domestic support. Ardern's approval rating rose to 51 percent a month after the Christchurch killings and soared to 65 percent during the coronavirus crisis.[18]

According to Meng Foon, the New Zealand government also learned from its initial mistake of ignoring the threat of white extremism, and was determined to ensure that its response to the coronavirus was fully inclusive. As a result, the virus did not have a disproportionate impact on people of color so evident in the United States. "I don't think any person of color has died of COVID-19," he notes. "Only about 4 percent of the total of those who contracted COVID-19 are Maori and Pacific Islander."

For Ikhlaq Kashkari, the key commonality has been the quality of the social response. He chokes up when he remembers how many people came out to support mosques in the days after the shootings. "People have gone out of their way to help each other as they did on March 15," he says. "Our slogan here is: Stay home, stay safe, and be kind. Those three things explain it all."

While other governments—Vietnam, South Korea, and Slovakia—responded successfully to the coronavirus pandemic, none did so after learning valuable lessons from a successful battle against the global epidemic of right-wing violence.

BANNING HATE

As soon as an individual or group commits a crime, the authorities can apply all the tools of law enforcement to bring the culprits to justice. Shooters are charged with murder. Vandals who paint swastikas on synagogues are arrested. Groups that run afoul of financial laws can be sanctioned.

A more complex challenge is to prevent such crimes from happening in the first place. It's by no means self-evident, even in countries with hate speech laws, that an expression of ugly sentiments—racist, sexist, xenophobic—is prosecutable as incitement or permissible as free speech. The extreme right, and its violent disregard for law, is easier to go after. Those who plot violent acts can be stopped, as the FBI did with the men who planned to kidnap the governor of Michigan. But what if someone praises the "great replacement," which mass shooters and the radical right both embrace? The blurring of distinctions between these two categories, as in the creation of the new right, poses a whole new set of challenges to states, from the national level down to the municipality, as well as to social media companies.

Consider, for example, any effort to flag and remove hate speech from a platform like Twitter. It's one thing for Twitter to identify memes that glorify the Islamic State. It's not likely that someone in the mainstream, Muslim or not, is going to praise the would-be caliphate. But white supremacist language has migrated, via the new right, into mainstream discourse. According to an account of a discussion at a Twitter staff meeting, one employee explained that "on a technical level, content from Republican politicians could get swept up by algorithms aggressively removing white supremacist material. Banning politicians wouldn't be accepted by society as a trade-off for flagging all of the white supremacist propaganda."[19]

Of course, European countries have occasionally done just that: banned parties and politicians. "If the key objective is to minimize the direct impact of far-right groups, nothing is more effective than a ban," writes Cas Mudde. "Banning far-right parties is also the best way to prevent them from winning votes, and consequently influencing other parties, and potentially policies."[20] After his incitement to insurrection, social media platforms decided that Donald Trump had crossed a line and banned him. Based on this precedent, Twitter suspended Rep. Marjorie Taylor Greene (R-GA) for spreading election fraud misinformation.

Some countries, like the United Kingdom, banned the Nazi and fascist parties that emerged in the 1930s and 1940s. Other countries banned the neo-Nazi parties that regrouped after World War II, such as the Socialist Reich Party that Germany's constitutional court outlawed in 1952. The tactic is not used so frequently in Europe today, though Finland recently banned the Nordic Resistance Movement. Even in Germany, where the prohibition against Nazism is perhaps the strongest, the constitutional court refused in 2017 to ban the National Democratic Party, a longstanding extremist faction. Rather, as noted in Chapter 1, mainstream political parties have grimly tolerated the presence of far-right groups but refused to partner with them to form governments. In some countries, like Austria, even this informal agreement has evaporated, as the Freedom Party joined governments in 2000 and 2017. Once banned, some extremist parties reemerge under different names, like the neo-Nazi Workers Party in the Czech Republic that became, after its ban in 2010, the Workers' Party of Social Justice.

Germany has been more willing to enforce its bans on extremist organizations than to shut down extremist political parties. In early 2020, for instance, Germany outlawed Combat 18, an extremist organization founded in the UK. But it did so only after the group was tied to the assassination of Walter Lübcke, a Christian Democratic politician in Hesse. Moreover, as researcher Michael Zeller has pointed out, Germany tends to ban organizations like Combat 18 only in reaction to upsurges in extremist violence and the resulting public outrage rather than after an assessment that the group's rhetoric or actions violate the pertinent section of the constitution, namely that associations "whose aims or activities contravene the criminal laws or that are directed against the constitutional order or the concept of international understanding shall be prohibited."[21]

Some countries, like Austria, have criminalized Holocaust denial. Austria has also banned the Nazi flag, as has France, Russia, Poland, Ukraine, Lithuania, and Latvia. Germany has imposed perhaps the most restrictions on Nazi-associated language and objects. In Germany, you can't wave a sign with a swastika on it or make a Nazi salute in public. In 2012, members of the National Democratic Party were even kicked out of the Saxony parliament for wearing Thor Steinar clothing, a manufacturer that deliberately markets to neo-Nazis.[22]

Yet, such prohibitions against Nazi symbolism, for instance, in schools, have been difficult to impose, as sociologist Cynthia Miller-Idriss points out. Determined designers and students devise clever workarounds. If schools ban students from wearing t-shirts that proclaim 88—"h" is the eighth letter of the alphabet, so "hh" or 88 has come to represent "heil Hitler"—then they'll just wear shirts with the equation "100 – 12." Although Germany bans people from wearing clothes that celebrate the Nazi Party—Nationalsozialistische Deutsche Arbeiterpartei or NSDAP—neo-Nazis figured out that they could buy Lonsdale shirts with the British clothing manufacturer's name across the chest. Then, donning a bomber jacket and leaving it half-unzipped, they can proudly display the middle four letters of the brand name: NSDA.[23]

Where federal authorities have been unable or unwilling to ban the far right, localities have sometimes stepped into the vacuum. In Poland, for instance, the conservative Law and Justice Party (PiS) occasionally sided with the extreme right. But Warsaw, the capital of the country, remains quite liberal politically. So, even though PiS and the Catholic Church have promoted various forms of homophobia, the Warsaw mayor signed a 12-point declaration strongly defending LGBT rights in 2019.[24] The year before, he banned a far-right march despite its nominal purpose of celebrating the country's hundredth anniversary of independence (the constitutional court subsequently overturned the ban). With these and other moves, the municipality has pushed back against a national trend.

In the United States, states have occasionally taken the lead in combating the far right. Most states have some type of hate crime law on the books (with several exceptions, such as Arkansas, Georgia, South Carolina, and Wyoming). Georgia even banned masks in public to reduce the influence of the Ku Klux Klan (suspended during the coronavirus pandemic).[25] Unlike a number of other countries, however, the United States has no hate speech laws, owing to constitutional protections of speech and assembly. Every state has provisions in their constitutions or statutory prohibitions against paramilitary forces, which several municipalities have used against the far right.[26] Several

Democratic governors indirectly targeted the far right by mobilizing against Trump administration policies and vigorously pushing back against the president's attempts to send federal paramilitaries into cities to suppress dissent under cover of "fighting crime."

Despite the strength of civil liberty arguments that have made bans at the federal or state level quite rare, the space has been open for U.S. citizens themselves to band together against the far right. One famous example is the community response in Billings, Montana, which inspired a PBS documentary, *Not In Our Town*. In December 1992, when a rock was thrown through the window of a Jewish family displaying a menorah, the local newspaper printed a menorah that nearly 10,000 citizens put up in their windows. Later, when skinheads disrupted a church service, members of different faiths appeared in the pews to convey a sense of security and solidarity. The police chief of Billings strongly supported this civic response, which provided important official validation. The Billings example inspired similar local movements around the United States and even elsewhere in the world.[27]

Schools throughout the United States and the world have used the *Not In Our Town* video as part of the curriculum, and education is indeed a powerful against the far right. Some countries have mandated instruction in the schools on hate crimes, racism, tolerance, and multiculturalism. Other civic institutions—religious, cultural, and labor unions—have followed suit.

More recently, new civic movements have arisen to fight the new right. The Sardines came together to urge voters to reject right-wing populism in the Emilia-Romagna region of Italy. "We are anti-fascist, pro-equality, against intolerance, against homophobia," one of the founders described the movement.[28] Their protests spread to 90 cities in late 2019 and early 2020. In the pandemic era, the Sardines have been at the forefront of the migrant rights and Black Lives Matter movement in Italy. In Brazil, meanwhile, *Movimento Estamos Juntos* (We're In This Together Movement) has brought together both left and right in defense of democracy and against Jair Bolsonaro's authoritarianism. Drawing inspiration from the civic movements that brought an end to the country's military rule, the new movement hopes to unite all the disparate anti-Bolsonaro forces.[29]

NAMING AND SHAMING

When Jair Bolsonaro received a Man of the Year award from the Brazilian–U.S. Chamber of Commerce in 2019, activists from both countries raised such a stink that New York venues declined to host the May ceremony. In the end, Bolsonaro had to go to Texas to accept his award (where he faced further protests).[30]

Similarly, anti-Trump groups in England, with their threats of mass protests, prompted the U.S. president to cancel his trip to London in early 2018.[31] When he made his first presidential visit to the UK later that year, the appearance of the infamous Baby Trump balloon led the president to steer clear of London. "I guess when they put out blimps to make me feel unwelcome, no reason for me to go to London," Trump said.[32]

At the Hindu World Congress in Chicago in September 2018, several activists from Chicago South Asians for Justice managed to gain access to a plenary session packed with 1,000 people and featuring the head of the far-right RSS, Mohan Bhagwat. "We stood up and chanted 'RSS turn around, we don't want you in our town,'" reports Mansi Kathuria, one of the protesters.

> The response was pretty terrifying. The folks attending the conference immediately turned on us, pushing and grabbing. We were standing on chairs to have better visibility, and they pulled the chairs from underneath us. A man was choking one of my friends who was part of the disruption. The crowd took our banner and pushed us out of the hotel altogether into the parking lot.

But the protest attracted a lot of media coverage, including in India.[33]

Naming and shaming has a long tradition in the human rights movement. By exposing the wrongful actions of a government and organizing a pressure campaign to force the government to change its policies, activists threaten the reputation of the country, which in turn puts its trade deals and tourism earnings at risk. It can be a powerful tool for non-state actors to use against oppressive states.

Even if the target of the "name and shame" strategy shrugs off the reputational damage, it's important to pursue the campaigns nonetheless. Herbert Pell, who was instrumental in bringing war crime charges against the Nazis during and after World War II, saw "how Confederate veterans in the South had created for themselves a misty-eyed mythology about the US Civil War and was determined that the Nazis would not do the same," writes Dan Plesch in his study of international war crimes tribunals.

> Pell's motivation was to prevent postwar nostalgia for the Nazis breeding more war: "In a small German village, the local member of the Gestapo will be the hero ... He will tell young boys ... of the fun of shooting Jews in Poland, or the profit of looting France ... Presently will come someone hopeful of succeeding Hitler."[34]

Naming and shaming can effectively sever that link between the horrors of the past and a revival of such horrors in the future.

In the United States, the Southern Poverty Law Center (SPLC) is devoted to identifying extremist organizations and exposing their noxious policies, as is Hope Not Hate in the UK. Other countries, however, lack such an authoritative list of hate groups, so it is more difficult for civil society organizations to pressure outfits like Facebook to ban extremist organizations. "There's no equivalent of ADL or SPLC in most European countries that puts up something that says, 'here are the bad guys and here's what they think,'" says Heidi Beirich, formerly of SPLC. "I've been asked repeatedly by Facebook and others, 'Who can we talk to in these other spaces. Who can give us a list of bad actors in Germany.' The answer is basically nobody." This gap inspired her to create a new organization, the Global Project Against Hate and Extremism.

Naming-and-shaming tactics, by focusing on prominent individuals of the new right, can effectively push these leaders to the margins. Richard Spencer, who spent much of the 2010s traveling between the United States and Europe to strengthen the transatlantic far right, came to national prominence as the organizer of the Unite the Right rally in Charlottesville in 2017. But his failures to bring large numbers of people out onto the street, the cancelation under public pressure of his campus speeches, his banishment from social media, and his court troubles all contributed to his demotion within the alt-right.[35] The same applies to Milo Yiannopoulos, the far-right provocateur and former Breitbart editor, who was also booted from social media, had his book contract with Simon & Schuster canceled, and was driven into millions of dollars of debt.[36]

Name-and-shame tactics can apply as well to groups as well as individuals. Whenever the far right appears in the real world—a speech, a demonstration, a conference—a counterforce of anti-fascist protesters are there to wave signs, chant slogans, and even disrupt the event. At the Unite the Right march in 2017, the mostly young white men of the far right were met by determined students, clergy, and city residents. For a gathering in Washington, DC, to mark the one-year anniversary of the march, only two dozen white nationalists showed their faces—in contrast to the thousands of counter-protesters.[37]

The far right, however, has used the theater of protest and counter-protest to attract greater media attention, which means that anti-fascist activists sometimes unwittingly give the far right greater visibility. One German town figured out a way to subvert this dynamic of demonstration. In 2014, in the town of Wunsiedel, the organization Right against Right set up an "involuntary walkathon." The 250 neo-Nazi marchers, unbeknownst to them, were registered for this walkathon: the further they walked along the parade route, the more money they raised for EXIT Deutschland, which helps people leave far-right organizations. In the end, the neo-Nazis raised over $10,000 for an organization devoted to destroying their base.[38] Inspired by Right against Right, the Jewish Bar Association of San Francisco came up with an "adopt a Nazi" campaign, by which donors pledged an amount of money for each extremist who showed up at a "Freedom Rally" in the Bay Area. The extremists got the message and canceled the event.[39]

Naming and shaming plays a public role in delegitimizing far-right organizations and individuals. A somewhat different process, naming and turning, has moved individuals out of white nationalism. A number of YouTubers have set out to debunk the claims of the new right and succeeded in transforming the perspectives of "formers" like Caleb Crain.[40] There are also professional organizations devoted to deradicalization, such as the German Institute for Radicalization and De-Radicalization Studies, which serves as a network for practitioners.

The German government has been a trailblazer in this regard, establishing its Exit to Enter program in 2009. Participants in the right-wing scene are identified, often at a workplace, and then gradually weaned off their dependency on the far right through discussion, training, apprenticeship, additional education, and cash incentives. Every person gets involved with the far right for their own complex reasons, so each case of exit is tailored to the needs of the individual.[41] But such programs can only function within a larger social-welfare ecosystem and even then can only reach a small percentage of extremists. As Kristina Nauditt and Gerd Wermerskirch point out, "many right-wing extremists are neither young nor unemployed, whereas labor-market integration is primarily focused on young adults who either have tired of the far-right scene or are looking to integrate into society after serving jail sentences for crimes they have committed."[42]

DIGITAL PUSHBACK

The far right has long organized transnationally in the digital realm, while the left seems to be a few steps behind. "The playing field is not level," says Julia Ebner of ISD. The far right "has a big advantage in terms of algorithms of social media favorable for spreading conspiracy theories and potentially harmful and inciting content."

One place to begin leveling the playing field has been to monitor the far right's digital footprint, tracking how far-right ideas and memes move through the internet and social media. ISD has produced just such a report that tracked the phrase "great replacement" and the associated term "remigration" in three languages across Twitter.[43] Another tactic has been to deploy AI to identify key words and images that suggest impending violence and alert the police accordingly.

Then there's turning the far right's digital tactics against the extremists. With "doxxing," far-right activists compile personal information about their adversaries on the left in order to release private information about them on the Web, initiate trolling campaigns against them, or harass them at their home or place of work. In extreme cases, doxxers phone in "terrorism" tips that bring SWAT teams to surround the victim's house. Sleuths have done the same to right-wing extremists, often exposing the true identities behind their anonymous avatars. "I'm interested in raising the cost of being a white nationalist," one such sleuth told *The Washington Post*, "raising the cost of being a Nazi, raising the cost of making these threats anonymously online, and making it clear that these people are not as hard to find as they think they are."[44]

But perhaps the most controversial and potentially successful technique for challenging the far right on the digital turf has been deplatforming. Providing information about how the far right breaks the rules of the social media platform and applying pressure to hosting companies like Facebook and Twitter to remove organizations associated with hate have substantially reduced the potential audience for far-right organizations and individuals.

Consider the example of Infowars. For years, the conspiracy theorist behind Infowars, Alex Jones, had been disseminating misinformation, false rumors, and hate-filled rants across multiple platforms. He said, for instance, that "Hillary Clinton has personally murdered and chopped up and raped [children]," that FEMA has plans to incarcerate all Americans in concentration camps, that the mass shooting at Sandy Hook Elementary in Newton, Connecticut never happened. Across his websites, podcasts, and videos, he was regularly reaching more people than the *National Review, Newsweek,* or *The Economist*.[45]

After the parents of Sandy Hook victims took Jones to court, public pressure to deplatform him rose significantly. In early August 2018, Apple dropped his podcasts. Facebook, YouTube, Spotify, Twitter, and eventually PayPal followed suit.[46] Jones claimed that the publicity associated with the bans would only give him a larger platform. But, according to *The New York Times*,

> In the three weeks before the August 6 bans, Infowars had a daily average of nearly 1.4 million visits to its website and views of videos posted by its main YouTube and Facebook pages, according to a *New York Times* analysis of data from the web data firms Tubular Labs and SimilarWeb. In the three weeks afterward, its audience fell by roughly half, to about 715,000 site visits and video views, according to the analysis.[47]

Unfortunately, although the major social media platforms dropped to around two percent of the traffic to the site, several conservative and libertarian sites—the Drudge Report, The Liberty Daily—have continued to drive people to Infowars.[48] Meanwhile, the coronavirus pandemic boosted sales of Jones' survivalist products. Deplatforming, in other words, cannot by itself silence a noxious voice.

Deplatforming faces other challenges. Once kicked off of platforms like Twitter, controversial figures start popping up in more like-minded places like Gab where it can be more difficult to monitor their rhetoric and proposed actions. "The argument has been that deplatforming will force a lot of the stuff into the shadows," notes Matt Nipert. "But it's already happening in the shadows. It won't remove the problem but it will make recruitment difficult, will prevent the jump to the mainstream. When the far right complains about it, you know you've done a good thing."[49]

And the right has complained. "I lost 4 million fans in the last round of bans," Milo Yiannopoulos has said. "I spent years growing and developing and investing in my fan base and they just took it away in a flash." He tried to set up on other platforms, like Telegram and Gab, but "none of them have audiences who buy or commit to anything." Joe Mulhall of Hope Not Hate thus concludes that the "failure to transfer their audiences from major to minor platforms is a perennial problem of the deplatformed."[50]

The impact goes beyond the narrowing of the audience. The deplatforming of Donald Trump in early 2021, for instance, had an immediate impact on the level of disinformation available in social media. "Online misinformation about election fraud plunged 73 percent after several social media sites suspended President Trump and key allies last week, research firm Zignal Labs has found, underscoring the power of tech companies to limit the falsehoods poisoning public debate when they act aggressively," report Elizabeth Dwoskin and Craig Timberg in *The Washington Post*.[51]

Deplatforming can resemble a game of whack-a-mole. As soon as extremists are identified and removed from one social media niche, another set arises to take their place. In 2020, for instance, prompted by the threat of a boycott from sponsors like Starbucks and Ford, Facebook upped its fight against the far right by deplatforming hundreds of accounts associated with the Boogaloo Bois.[52] It followed this up by purging QAnon accounts in October 2020 and "Stop the Steal" content in January 2021. These movements, too, migrated to other platforms, which led to efforts to shut down the alternative platforms, as when Amazon, Apple, and Google pulled the plug on Parler, which had pitched itself as an alternative social media platform.

The real threat to the far right, however, has been to attack its source of funding. However, even when deplatforming involves cutting off these sources—for instance, when PayPal canceled accounts for extremist organizations in the wake of the Charlottesville march in 2017—the new right has established alternative e-commerce sites (1776.shop), crowd-sourcing platforms (Hatreon), and ways of transferring money (with cryptocurrencies like Bitcoin).[53]

When it comes to organizations, the success of deplatforming depends in part on the target. "If an organization is in the growth phase, then deplatforming is effective—you are removing their ability to do what they want to do," argues Martin Cocker. "Once organizations are fully developed, deplatforming increases the complexity of combatting them and their issues."[54]

Deplatforming also goes both ways. Authoritarian governments are skilled at removing critical voices from the public sphere by ensuring that they have no platform at all. For illiberal governments that operate in a semblance of democracy, the tactics can be more sophisticated. In Russia, for instance, news aggregators are liable for the content that appears on their sites if they have more than a million daily users—unless they draw their news only from officially approved media.[55] This tactic ensures that views challenging the government's narrative remain on the margins.

Progressives are well aware of the opportunities that digital organizing presents. "We're in an age when there's more instantaneous communication than at any point in human history," points out Kumi Naidoo, the South Africa-born human rights activist.

> There's a constant flow of information but very little coordination on a transnational level in a broad sense. There are lots of reasons: resources, language, access. But we have to figure that piece out: how and who to resource that. We have a five-year window to make some serious strides or we're going to be in trouble.

One organization that has sought to fill the gap on transnational coordination is the Online Progressive Engagement Network (OPEN), which links up citizen advocacy groups like MoveOn throughout the world. In the last six years, it has brought together 19 such organizations, including Zazim in Israel, GetUp in Australia, and Skiftet in

Sweden. The network can mobilize its members rapidly on key transnational issues, such as corporate tax havens or the construction of a new coal mine by a TNC. OPEN has set up online forums where members can communicate and has also provided open-source platforms that are cheaper and more accessible. Now, it's pushing to expand into the Global South. "Our members are mostly white and heavily European, so we have to figure out how to diversify," explains Giovanna Alvarez-Negretti of OPEN who is based in Barcelona. "In order to reach out to people in countries with a lot of poverty and inequality, mobilizing people will have to expand to mobile phones and accessible technology."

Deplatforming can play a role in marginalizing the most hateful voices. In the end, though, progressives have to bring more people into the digital realm and fill it with factual information and positive opportunities for transnational cooperation.

5
Transnational progressive organizing

The World Social Forum began when 12,000 people converged on Porto Alegre in Brazil in January 2001 under the banner of "another world is possible." Across two decades of convenings, the WSF has represented a high point in progressive, multi-issue global organizing. Its successes and shortcomings provide an important reference point for current efforts to challenge the transnational right.

An extraordinary combination of political debate, strategy session, and carnival, the World Social Forum united two distinct trajectories in transnational organizing.

At the UN level, it was the culmination of a series of gatherings—such as the Earth Summit in Rio de Janeiro in 1992 and the World Conference on Women in Beijing in 1995—that brought together representatives of states and civil society. "The first transnational mobilization was of the ecological movements to create the Earth Summit and to create legally binding treaties for biodiversity and climate change," recalls activist author Vandana Shiva. "That legal infrastructure is what the one percent and the so-called populists are attacking right now."

The second strand consisted of grassroots protests against the institutions and mechanisms of economic globalization. Environmentalists, trade unionists, and farmers met in Seattle in 1999, temporarily shutting down the World Trade Organization meeting and blocking what former director-general Renato Ruggiero called the "constitution of a single global economy."[1] These activists created what has been called the anti-globalization movement. "I found that very ironic because the so-called anti-globalization movement was a very global movement," observes Kumi Naidoo, formerly the head of Amnesty International. "It was using some of the tools of transnational connectivity and the internet and online ways of connecting. We should call it instead a global justice movement or a gender justice movement or an economic justice movement."

This global justice movement accelerated after 1999, through the protests against the World Economic Forum in Davos in January 2001 and the G8 summit in Genoa in July 2001. But then it collided with the events of September 11, 2001. "The next big mobilization was set for October 2001, two or three weeks after the 9/11 attacks," recalls Phyllis Bennis of IPS.

> First, every airport in the world was shut down. And people just realized that we just can't keep going as if nothing had changed (because George W. Bush made sure of that). So, that meeting never happened, and even though the global justice movement continued to do really important work, organizationally it never really recovered from that blow.

As the union of these two trajectories—the top-down gatherings and the bottom-up protests—the World Social Forum provided a people's alternative to the World Economic Forum meeting at Davos. Even as the September 11 attacks interrupted the momentum of the post-Seattle mobilization against the WTO and free trade, the WSF only grew larger, spawning regional forums and creating innumerable joint enterprises.

"All the demos against the war in Iraq were coordinated in those spaces," Fiona Dove of the Transnational Institute remembers. "Some of the big trade campaigns, the movement against corporate impunity, also began there." Sarita Gupta, formerly of Jobs with Justice, says that the organization's relationship to "the New Trade Union initiative in India—which seeded the Asia Floor Wage Campaign but is now taking on gender-based violence in the garment sector—happened 100 percent because of the WSF process."

Kali Akuno connects the work of his organization, Cooperation Jackson in Mississippi, to the meetings, delegations, and conversations around the WSF, particularly participatory budgeting, a more inclusive mechanism for determining spending priorities that began in Brazil. "In the early 2000s, me and several others took a couple of different popular education courses on participatory budgeting," he remembers. "A number of political forces here in Mississippi committed ourselves to bringing participatory budgeting here and implementing it after that."

The forum was also noteworthy for being driven by groups from the Global South. The meetings took place in Brazil, India, Senegal, Tunisia, Kenya, Mali, and Venezuela. The WSF did not take place in the Global North—in Montreal—until its 15th edition in 2016.

In the wake of the 2008 financial crisis, other global movements intersected with the WSF. The Occupy Movement in the United States, the indignados in Spain, and the Arab Spring embraced a parallel spirit of social justice. These spontaneous uprisings achieved certain victories—the Occupy Movement "for the first time put inequality at the top of the global agenda," argues Srećko Horvat, the Croatian philosopher and author of *Poetry from the Future*—and helped sustain the energy of the World Social Forum. But they didn't produce a durable transnational movement.

Particularly after 2008, many participants grumbled about the forum's refusal to take political positions and its overall skepticism toward vertical organizing. "The Social Forum was the last truly global response to a failing globalization, a response on the scale of the problem," argues Lorenzo Marsili.

> It was an incredibly rich space for cross-fertilization, for the exchange of best practices. But it failed to make the transition from a pure Habermasian discursive space, a forum for debate, to something more political—not necessarily a political party but a global political movement that would act as a movement, taking a stand on specific questions and trying to influence the debate with a global critical mass.

Kali Akuno agrees, "Instead of being a movement of movements, which is how it billed itself, there needed to be conversations about how to develop a coordinated international political strategy for maximum impact for our social movements," he points out. "Unfortunately, a certain level of rehashing of the ideological debates of the twentieth century reemerged. Some forces didn't want to repeat the centralized politics of the left of that period."

For Oded Grajew, one of the founders of the World Social Forum, the institution was always political in the sense of trying to influence policy. But the forum was also careful to be an open space that welcomed a wide variety of organizations. When some people wanted the WSF to make a declaration in support of Brazilian leader Dilma Rousseff, for instance, Grajew encouraged them to put one out in the name of the organizations that agreed, but not in the name of everyone. "Others wanted to make a declaration that the most important thing to do is to fight climate change," he says. "But others say that the most important thing is gender inequality or social inequality. You must respect everyone who has different positions and priorities."

Although the 2018 Social Forum mobilized 80,000 people, the process no longer has the same momentum it did in the 2000s. The Workers Party in Brazil, which supported the WSF in its early years, lost power, and its leader Lula was imprisoned. The pink tide of left-leaning governments in Latin America ebbed. The sheer expense and carbon footprint of such gatherings were also challenges. "I always said that in periods of declining resources, we should conserve every bit of our energy and meet once every decade," Vandana Shiva notes. "We bathe every day—but in India we have a cycle of 12 years before we go to bathe in the Ganges for the Kumbh, the fair of creation."

As it neared its twentieth anniversary, the World Social Forum began to shift away from multi-issue gatherings to thematic issues such as the migration crisis (Mexico in 2018), the fight against the extraction economy (South Africa in 2018), and the focus on transformative economies (virtually in 2020). Although the thematic forums allow for more focused networking and organizing, activists still speak fondly of the larger, multi-issue gatherings. "If there's a moment when we need a WSF-like space, it's right now," observes Sarita Gupta, currently the director of the Ford Foundation's Future of Work(ers) program. May Boeve points out that "looking at issues with a cross-sectional analysis is all the rage now but we were doing that a long time ago—with the climate crisis, the wars, the debt crisis, bringing all those issues together. Those spaces are not happening now." Ethan Earle adds, "Just because something has completed its life cycle doesn't mean it can't be reborn. So, another iteration of the World Social Forum or something similar could again be useful one day."

The regional forums are no longer taking place. But one of the organizers of the U.S. Social Forum, Grassroots Global Justice, is preparing to launch a national convening of 10,000 people in the United

States for 2021 that will attempt to take this kind of organizing to the next level, providing space for multi-issue discussions and building between different sectors with a more political focus. "We learned a lot of lessons from the U.S. Social Forum," says GGJ's Cindy Wiesner. "We're thinking long-term about how to create a new independent political vehicle that's so desperately needed and that brings us together beyond our nonprofit organizations or activist collectives so that we can contend for power."

In the wake of the coronavirus, WSF alumni pulled together a new effort on Zoom called the Global Dialogue for Systemic Change.[2] But as with many progressive actions, it has consisted primarily of education rather than organizing. Other activists have focused on issuing manifestos, like the COVID-19 Global Solidarity Manifesto.[3] Energized by progressive organizing in Europe and the partial success of Bernie Sanders in the 2016 and 2020 Democratic Party primaries, a new Progressive International launched in May 2020. It has issued an open call, set up a progressive wire service, and launched several campaigns on international debt, the Green New Deal, and tenant organizing.

All of this is promising. But nothing yet approaches the size, breadth, or spirit of the World Social Forum.

LOCUS OF ACTIVISM

Much of the multi-issue transnational activism of the left has shadowed official international gatherings. The World Social Forum was a response to the World Economic Forum in Davos. The mobilizations against free-trade agreements often took place alongside WTO meetings, G-7 gatherings or meetings around particular agreements like the Trans-Pacific Partnership or the North American Free Trade Agreement. During the 1990s and into the 2000s, the Helsinki Citizens Assembly created a civil society equivalent to the Conference on Security and Cooperation in Europe while the ASEAN People's Forum attempted something similar with the Association of South-East Asian Nations. High-profile meetings of government officials provide a time and a date as well as a news hook for potential media coverage of the civil society shadow events.

"It does make it easier when you have clearly defined institutions and their gatherings to go up against," observes Kavita N. Ramdas. "When those institutions, however flawed, now seem the last resort of sanity, however, it makes you wonder whether we should be going up against the World Bank when Trump is ripping up any kind of interactions with anyone in the world." Other potential targets of protest and pressure include the headquarters of transnational corporations, international weapons shows, and global banks.

One obvious locus of activism for progressives is the United Nations, an institution that has embodied internationalism since its founding in the wake of World War II. Its human rights conventions, institutions devoted to refugees and climate change, specialized agencies like the International Labor Organization (ILO), and commitment to peacekeeping all embody progressive transnational ideals. And indeed activists view the UN as one of the places open to enacting policy with global reach.

Workplace justice organizers, for instance, scored a victory in June 2019 when the ILO established a new global standard to end violence and sexual harassment at work.[4] "Across the world, campaigns are happening now to ratify the treaty and implement the framework at the national and local levels," reports Cathy Feingold of the AFL-CIO. The Global Campaign to Reclaim People's Sovereignty, Dismantle Corporate Power, and Stop Corporate Impunity is a multi-sectoral network of over 250 social movements, trade unions, and affected communities focused on reining in the power of transnational corporations. One of its principal campaigns is to push a binding treaty to regulate TNCs through the UN. "This global campaign brings together diverse movements that feel unified in the struggle against corporate power," says Kumi Naidoo.

However, Kavita N. Ramdas of Open Society continues, "The UN has lost so much legitimacy. Through 9/11, the bombing of Afghanistan and Iraq, the interventions to destabilize the Middle East, the rest of the world has lost confidence that the UN is anything but a mouthpiece for the United States and for the Global North." Another criticism—from those pushing for immigration reform or fighting climate change—is that the UN is "all talk, no action," that it produces lots of paper and holds plenty of conferences, but moves at a snail's pace. Moreover, as Phyllis Bennis, argues, "From the vantage point of the far right, the UN is already irrelevant. The far right is not focused primarily on challenging the UN because they don't see it as a viable instrument of the globalists. They're more focused on the international financial institutions."

One exception, because of the coronavirus pandemic, is the World Health Organization. Its very effectiveness made it a target of the new right, with Donald Trump leading the attack. In response, foundations, cultural figures like Lady Gaga, and progressive organizations moved quickly in 2020 to throw their financial and moral support behind the WHO. It remains an institution that embodies the spirit of transnational solidarity and cooperation based on professional and technical expertise—these very qualities make it the object of the new right's scorn.

Other institutions of liberal internationalism remain viable. Activists can rely on legal mechanisms at the International Criminal Court. The Organization of Security and Cooperation in Europe, whose members also include the United States and Russia, has a structure in which NGOs can speak directly to governments as part of the reviews of country performances on democracy and human rights. Within Europe, activists can also take their concerns to the European Court of Human Rights, the European Commission, and several other bodies. Indeed, when it comes to transnational activism, Europeans have several mechanisms for influencing policy across borders.

REGIONAL ORGANIZING

Multi-issue transnational organizing at the global level, via the World Social Forum, has subsided to a certain extent over the last few years. But transnational organizing at a regional level remains robust.

Europe, for instance, is a natural locus for such organizing because, as Lorenzo Marsili points out, it is an economically and politically integrated continent with "a transnational government in the form of the European Commission and the European Parliament and a very sophisticated system of interdependencies among member states. So, it provides fertile ground for building a genuine transnational counterpower within the space that EU provides." One such effort, Europe for the Many, is working transnationally to strengthen the "remain and reform" movement within the European Union in the face of Brexit and other manifestations of Euroskepticism.

An example of successful European transnational activism was the campaign against the Anti-Counterfeiting Trade Agreement (ACTA), which generated demonstrations in cities across Europe and involved young people, in particular.[5] Widespread concern that ACTA would infringe on freedom of expression eventually prompted the European Parliament to kill the measure in 2012. "Because ACTA was transnational and about to affect transnational space, only transnational mobilization was able to stop it," Igor Stokfiszewski of Krytyka Polityczna points out. "It became a pattern for coordinated transnational action of social movements and political parties to resist those kinds of political solutions." But, he cautioned, with the exception of climate change and a few other issues, most of the problems facing Europe do not lend themselves to transnational solutions.

In Africa, too, a number of continental initiatives have taken root. Africans Rising for Peace, Justice, and Dignity involves over 370 organizations across the continent. On May 25 every year, Africans Rising sponsors events focusing on a different issue. In 2019, the focus was on slavery and human trafficking, with more than 130 events across the continent and in the diaspora as well. Coumba Touré of Africans Rising explains, "The issues we're struggling with here are the same that Africans are struggling with in Brazil or the United States or Europe. By being Africans, some of our issues are automatically transnational."

In Latin America in 2015, ten years after the defeat of the Free Trade Agreement of the Americas, social movements came together to create La Jornada Continental, the Continental Meeting for Democracy and against Neoliberalism. "We decided that the social movements of the continent needed to come together to strengthen the struggle against neoliberalism, corporate power, and free-trade agreements and stop the takeover of democracy by right-wing and authoritarian forces," explains Karin Nansen of Friends of the Earth International in Uruguay. "But we are also integrating cross-cutting issues such as environmental justice and feminist perspectives, which are fundamental to expose and confront the root causes of the systemic crisis we face."

Women, too, are organizing across Latin America. "The women's movement is old but what we are seeing is a new wave of this movement, a new generation of young women, many of them really radical not just on access to abortion but against all the inequalities of the patriarchy," reports Luciana Ghiotto, who teaches political economy at Universidad Nacional de San Martín in Buenos Aires. The Movement of People Affected by Dams in Latin America (MAB) is drawing social movements together in the region and hopes to spread the organizing to Africa and Asia as well. Meanwhile, in North America, the groups behind the tri-national initiative to oppose NAFTA are hoping to revive the process in 2020, in part to challenge NAFTA 2.0 but also "to make the case that environmental and social concerns should be concerns for labor unions," says Manuel Perez-Rocha of IPS.

In Asia, Women Cross DMZ has brought together women from the two Koreas, the United States, Europe, and elsewhere to advance peace and reunification on the Korean peninsula. "The Trump administration has been upending traditional approaches to U.S. foreign policy," notes one of the driving forces behind the movement, Christine Ahn from Hawai'i. "For better or worse, it has created some strategic opportunities. As a peace movement and a feminist movement, we have to seize the moment to create peace on the Korean peninsula." Toward that same end, Cheong Wooksik of the Peace Network in Seoul is part of a regional movement "pushing an agenda of creating a nuclear-weapons-free zone on the Korean Peninsula as a prior step to the creation of a NWFZ in Northeast Asia."

One of the most successful regional organizing efforts in Asia is constantly on the move. Founded in 1983 as a "floating peace village," Peace Boat brings together hundreds of passengers from countries all around the world for two long peace tours in Asia every year (and three global tours). "Having people go beyond national borders is the very foundation of building peace," explains Peace Boat's Akira Kawasaki in Tokyo.

> When you look at the current intergovernmental disputes—for example, between Japan and South Korea or Japan and China—they're a symptom of people very much trapped in narrowly defined nationalism. Cultivating a sense of global citizenship or an identity as Asians rather than Japanese, Chinese, or Korean through our Asia voyages—a change in mindset—is the basic methodology Peace Boat has employed since its founding in 1983.

In Northeast Asia, Peace Boat brought together groups from the two Koreas, Japan, and China for a meeting in Ulan Bator, Mongolia, to discuss concrete steps toward peace and denuclearization in the region.

Largely absent from regional organizing, at least on an activist level, is China. This poses a challenge to the progressive movement, which has praised the government in Beijing for its efforts on sustainable energy and criticized it for human rights abuses. Although Chinese environmental activists have collaborated with their regional counterparts, civil society on the mainland remains relatively weak and isolated. "We can't have a movement that calls itself global or a discourse that calls itself planetary that shuts out not only 1 billion people but the 1 billion people who through their political organization will shape the next decades in quite a significant way," observes Lorenzo Marsili. Peace Boat has been perhaps most successful in engaging ordinary Chinese citizens. According to Akira Kawasaki, so many participants in the voyages are now Chinese that the workshops onboard are conducted in Chinese, not only Japanese and English.

There have also been cross-regional initiatives. The Asia-Europe People's Forum, for instance, has provided a progressive alternative to the Asia-Europe Meeting since 1996. A number of transatlantic progressive efforts have flourished over the years, but the rise of the right has complicated matters. "We used to appeal to the Europeans to be the voice of reason that's been more willing to challenge the U.S. government," reports Medea Benjamin of Code Pink. "Because of the growth of the far right in Europe, the groups we work with tend to be weaker."

TRANSLOCAL ORGANIZING

Outside of a few countries—South Korea, Spain—left parties are not in power. "I don't see much light at the national level," says the AFL-CIO's Cathy Feingold, "except for the smaller countries like New Zealand and its wellbeing budget or Iceland and geothermal energy and feminism."

Given this record, it is no surprise that some on the left are refocusing away from national politics. "This right-wing hasn't come from nowhere," Fiona Dove of TNI points out. "They've been building this for quite a while. So, transnationally, we need to root politics locally, bring politics back closer to the people. In Europe at any rate, we're quite excited by this new municipalism."

Rooting politics locally and working transnationally is not a contradiction. In Spain in 2015, after winning power in several major Spanish cities, the left immediately realized "that the challenges of the current moment are transnational—climate change, unaccountable financial flows, the corporate capture of democratic institutions, the right to migrate and the protection of refugees, the arms trade—that had to be addressed through transnational cooperation," Sol Trumbo Vila of TNI explains. "So, there was a strong effort to connect nationally and transnationally with similar projects in Italy, in Latin America, and also with Cooperation Jackson in Mississippi and Richmond Progressive Alliance in California." Thus was born the Fearless Cities campaign.

Through the Fearless Cities campaign, Spanish cities worked with their counterparts across Europe to press for regulation of transnational corporations like Airbnb. It's difficult to fight Airbnb locally, explains Laura Roth of Barcelona En Comú, "but if cities join efforts they are much stronger than companies in some cases. Cities are more willing to do these things compared to states or national political parties." In Spain, she adds, "When the refugee crisis started, cities basically pressured the state to accept many more refugees because they were willing to put the resources into receiving all those people."

In Poland, the populist right is in control of national politics and most government structures. But the country is rather decentralized. "Because of this decentralization, it is possible to resist many of the tendencies that the government is trying to introduce at the level of cities," including its anti-LGBT actions, Igor Stokfiszewski of Krytyka Polityczna explains. "One of the first actions of the Warsaw mayor was to sign an 'LGBT charter' that secures the wellbeing of the LGBT community at a city level." The progressive mayor of Seoul, Park Won-Soon, made similar efforts to transform the city even as politics at the national level drifted further to the right (under the eventually impeached President Park Geun-hye).[6] California and other states have mounted challenges to the Trump administration's regressive climate and immigration policies.

Translocal organizing is not just municipal. In Europe, renewable energy cooperatives are linking up to enable consumers to create a new energy model. As Jason Nardi explains, these new linkages are facilitated by blockchain technology and cryptocurrencies that avoid the speculation and environmental problems of Bitcoin. Local currencies—for instance, the léman in Geneva, Switzerland—can also help with relocalizing supply chains.[7] "The whole supply chain for craft beer production is relocalized," Nardi reports. "It is using the léman to substitute for the Swiss franc in exchanges with all the suppliers up to the bar or restaurant that sells the beer, from who produces the crop to who transforms it—even to mushroom producers using the residual 'waste' to nurture their cultivation."

Nor is the translocalism restricted to cities. "The groups that we fund—peasant movements, indigenous people's movements, women's movements working in rural areas—there is transnational movement building," observes Nikhil Aziz of the American Jewish World Service. "A lot of it is still localized, still responding to immediate assaults in terms of land grabs or the impact of climate change." The Inter-Island Solidarity for Peace group, meanwhile, brings together activists from a number of Asian islands burdened by military bases and militarization—Jeju, Okinawa, Taiwan, Guam, Hawai'i.

LINKING ISSUES

The World Social Forum was transnational and multi-issue. Although such big tent organizing is difficult and expensive, there are plenty of more modest transnational efforts that connect two or more issues.

The environmental movement, for instance, has brought together concerns over sustainability with economic justice, feminism, and issues of war and peace. "The #FridaysforFuture strikes: that is international organizing through solidarity," Vandana Shiva points out. "That is today's World Social Forum." At Standing Rock in 2016, indigenous activists and environmentalists joined hands to block a proposed energy pipeline slated to cross reservation territory. And in Okinawa, environmentalists and peace activists have worked together to stop the construction of a new U.S. military facility, arguing that the base would disrupt the fragile ecosystem along the coast.

Labor and environmental activists have found common cause in such organizations as the Climate Justice Alliance, Labor Network for Sustainability, and Trade Unions for Energy Democracy. One opportunity for transnational linkage on these issues involves challenging corporations that use the investor-state dispute settlement (ISDS) mechanism in free-trade agreements to file suits against countries that have tried to implement responsible environmental policies or regulations.[8] Manuel Perez-Rocha has compiled a database of all the suits filed by extractive industries against countries, which he plans to share with climate change activists "so that they understand the perils of ISDS in their fights against the fossil-fuel industries. Countries can make very nice declarations, but it doesn't matter if they can't meet those commitments because they might be sued by corporations."

Arms trade activists have linked arms with human rights campaigners to stop the flow of weapons to places like Saudi Arabia, Egypt, and Israel. Sustainable farming advocates work with indigenous communities and environmentalists. Anti-corruption forces cooperate with economic justice advocates pushing for greater regulation of global financial institutions. #MeToo activists have taken on structural racism.

There is no shortage of cross-linkages in progressive transnational organizing. The challenge, as Cindy Wiesner points out, is to aim not for the lowest common denominator politics but to cohere at a higher level: "To be honest, this is the kind of work that doesn't get acknowledged by funders or by other movement counterparts—the work of bringing people together despite differences around shared interests."

The left faces some tensions in its overall agenda. Activists square off over the relative importance of pocketbook issues vs. identity politics. Environmental concerns do not always play well among traditional working-class constituencies, particularly those whose livelihoods depend on polluting industries. So, cross-linkages can also lead to cross-purposes.

But these are not the only challenges facing progressive transnational organizing.

The rapid spread of the new right has thrown progressives onto the defensive in country after country. One immediate response has been to refocus attention on the national rather than transnational level. Ran Cohen observes,

> Each and every organization or party is really busy with what's happening at home—in Hungary, in Israel, in Greece—without giving much attention to how anti-democratic forces are rising around the

world and whether or not we should be looking at it as a global emergency that requires global solutions.

At a time of heightened threats, the other tendency has been to refocus on one issue to the exclusion of others. When Metta Spencer of Canada's *Peace Magazine* approaches people to work on multi-issue efforts these days,

> Almost everyone would say: I'm working my butt off on climate change or on chemical weapons and I can only do so much. You're asking me to diffuse my efforts. You have too broad a scope. Just take one thing and work on that. But by doing just that one thing, we don't see how we're connected to other people working on other issues.

Then there's the problem of agenda creep. With the new right eager to undermine the status quo, the left often ends up fighting for what had previously been taken for granted by liberal mainstream society such as independent media or free and fair elections. For a left determined to promote transformational change, it can be a challenge to pivot to defending the building blocks of an embattled status quo.

The commonplace challenges of transnational movement-building—the urgency of defending gains at a national level, the compartmentalization of activism, the tension between transformational and incremental change—have only been accentuated by the rise of the new right.

THE CENTRALITY OF DEMOCRACY

The new right is not just attacking liberalism, both domestically and internationally. "What's in danger here is democracy itself not just liberalism," argues Jan-Werner Mueller. "We can't leave the term 'democracy' to the populists, unless you want to say that we have democracy as long as the governing party doesn't stuff ballot boxes on election day. Orbán, Erdoğan, and other populist leaders damage democracy as such when they undermine fundamental political rights."

If the new right is challenging democracy, a natural response should be to strengthen democracy. "In order to address the crisis, we need more and more democracy, deeper democracy," argues Karin Nansen of FOEI Uruguay, "in which people have a say, where they can reclaim the political arena and take politics into their hands, and make fundamental decisions like how we should produce our food, how to distribute it, how to change the economic and energy systems."

"The answer to attacks on democracy is more democracy," agrees Eric Ward. "It is not the white nationalist movement that is threatening American democracy. What is threatening American democracy is our inability to put forward an alternative to white nationalism that is grounded and inclusive of American voices."

An inclusive, pro-democracy approach, however, can be either partisan or non-partisan. Annabel Park, who started the Coffee Party in 2010 in response to the right-wing Tea Party in the U.S., thinks that a non-partisan approach would have more traction, at least in the United States. "For a lot of Americans, democracy is a calling, almost a religion," she says. "Give them the right opportunity, they'll drop everything." But, she added, "They don't want to do something that's partisan. They don't want to spend their time just supporting a party or a candidate—because they are either conflict-averse or they reject the two-party system."

Political parties are, for the most part, national. So, it is rather difficult to promote a transnational partisan approach. In Europe, however, where members have been directly elected to the European Parliament since 1979, transnational politicking is increasingly an option, not only through linked parties—such as the various Green Parties—but through new transnational efforts like DiEM 25 and Volt.

As the co-founder of DiEM25, a relatively new trans-European movement with an electoral component, Srećko Horvat has no doubt that the left must organize transnational political parties to combat the far right. Although DiEM25 did not manage to enter the European Parliament after the 2019 elections, it received 130,000 votes in Germany with a budget of only 35,000 Euros. "130,000 votes in Germany is something we have to capitalize," Horvat says. "Even if we get 10 percent of these people to become active, that's already a step further." The party subsequently won nine seats in the recent Greek legislative elections.

Even in Europe, however, where European integration makes cross-border electioneering possible, the challenges are enormous, beginning with the EU's 24 official languages. "It's very difficult to persuade national parties that it's in their interest to establish transnational coordination and relinquish some sovereignty," says Lorenzo Marsili, author of *Citizens of Nowhere*. "I've talked to dozens of party leaders across Europe. They think nationally, their strategic campaigning is done nationally, and they think they won't have much to gain in investing in transnational structures, with the Greens being something of an exception."

For Mary Kaldor, the future of partisan campaigning within the European Union is "less a question of creating trans-European parties and more about building up coalitions that already exist." She cites the same anti-political sentiment in Europe that Annabel Park has observed in the United States. After all, voters have witnessed what happens when progressive parties take power. Progressive leaders in Latin America transformed mainstream politics by, for instance, introducing family payments in Brazil to reduce poverty and helping to end political impunity in Chile. But progressive parties have succumbed to some of the same problems that have afflicted liberal and conservative parties, such as corruption. Also, the electoral success of progressive parties has created a certain dependency, particularly as these governments co-opted social movements. "This weakened social movements and civil society, which lost their critical role, for instance, on the corruption issue," points out Oded Grajew.

One way of splitting the difference between partisan and non-partisan organizing is to embrace a platform transnationally—such as the Green New Deal (GND). Alexandria Ocasio-Cortez (AOC), the outspoken democratic socialist elected to Congress in 2016 who has promoted the GND, "has been an enormous inspiration for people in Europe, even for the Democratic Left Alliance in Poland," reports Bartosz Rydliński. "We are copying the argument of the Green New Deal." In Europe, most member countries of the European Union now back a call to put the Green New Deal at the heart of the economic response to the pandemic, with the European Commission's vice president pledging that every Euro of recovery funding "must flow into a new economy rather than old structures."

The inspiration goes beyond Europe. In South Korea, the Green New Deal was a major element of the ruling party's platform in its 2020 election victory. "People in the Global South are in fact inspired by AOC," Walden Bello concurs, "and are looking very carefully at the strategizing and approaches that she and other new women representatives in the House are providing."

Another strategy is to break down the traditional separation between groups that work on electoral politics and those that work across borders. "These are both important parts of the movement," argues Tobita Chow of Justice Is Global out of Chicago. "A big part of what we are trying to accomplish is to bridge that gap." The new group has brought together U.S. workers with laborers from other countries to make the case for global economic justice at presidential forums in early primary states in fall 2019.

THE STRUCTURE OF ORGANIZING

Right-wing movements are notoriously hierarchical, often organized around a single man (or, very rarely, woman). Outside of Communist parties and movements, which also tend to be hierarchical, the left has been suspicious of too much verticality. Consider the Occupy Movement, which avoided leaders and structures. The left, points out Ethan Earle, takes pains to make sure that its structures are "at least somewhat democratic and respectful of human rights. The far right doesn't share these values. It wants to win and that's all. It'll figure everything else out afterwards."

Laura Roth sees virtues in more horizontal organizing. "The left has traditionally tried to organize in ways that are not different from the right—and sometimes even worse in hierarchical, centralized ways—and that hasn't been successful," she points out. "I'd like to think that more horizontal and decentralized ways have the advantage of making the efforts less vulnerable to attack. A network is harder to attack compared to a visible structure."

"There is a suspicion of hierarchy, I accept that," counters Francine Mestrum of Global Social Justice in Belgium. "But a hierarchy can be made democratic. Trade unions are hierarchical, but they are democratic." Elsewhere, she writes, "the attachment to horizontality has now become a cover for hiding the really existing power relations. There is no structure, no one has any responsibility, and hence there is no accountability. There is no transparency, let alone democracy."

Srećko Horvat agrees: "The problems from the future are actually so big that you need more verticality in the sense of efficient decision-making process and global cooperation. For instance, if you have hundreds of millions of climate refugees, you really need a strong plan and infrastructure to handle this."

A related tension in transnational organizing has been between social movements and NGOs. At the World Social Forum, those who favor direct action against structures of power and those who favor engagement to reform structures of power have often been at odds. Although the Social Movements Assembly met during the forum to formulate consensus positions, Shalmali Guttal believes that the WSF "was much more a space for middle-class organizations. The class character of the organizers and participants was not that of the majority who are living in very dire straits today and who might be capable of organizing on the ground." Fiona Dove agrees: "The big World Social Forums at one point got very NGOized. Who got to go were other NGOs, not necessarily movements, and those with access to donors who could pay their way. At some point there was a sense that they were no longer representative."

One way of squaring this particular circle is the "inside-outside" strategy. NGOs attempt to influence policymakers on the inside with more-or-less quiet diplomacy. Meanwhile, on the outside, social movements make noise in the streets and otherwise mobilize people power in support of more radical change. If the two work at cross-purposes, they can cancel each other out. But if they cooperate, they can become more than the sum of their parts.

AGENTS OF CHANGE

Activism requires activists. The challenge for transnational activism is the lack of international institutions that can employ or otherwise support such activists. "Transnational organizing in the traditional sense is very difficult at this point without an institutional base," Gar Alperovitz points out.

One such institutional base remains the union movement. "Despite the challenges unions face, we're still the largest global force," Cathy Feingold says. The International Trade Union Confederation, where Feingold is the deputy president, represents over 200 million workers in over 300 affiliates. In terms of transnational activism, she points to new organizing in the informal economy, to a recently opened Just Transition Center to address the common interests of workers and a sustainable economy, and to the role that unions have played in democratization, like the Tunisian General Trade Union that shared the Nobel Prize in 2015 and continues to represent the "glue for the inclusive democracy" in that country.

Unions and workers organizations are taking on new transnational corporations like Amazon. In 2018, for instance, Amazon workers in Germany and Spain went on strike—and Polish workers conducted a work slowdown—in a coordinated push for better wages and working conditions. Although many Western European companies have set up in Eastern Europe to take advantage of cheaper labor—Poland has special economic zones just like China and Mexico—"Amazon is the first example where we have an intensive connection with workers abroad," reports labor activist Magda Malinowska of Inicjatywa Pracownika in Poznań. "They want to work with us because they now need us."

Organizing among domestic workers around the world has increased dramatically through the efforts of the National Domestic Workers Alliance, Jobs with Justice, and, beginning in 2013, the International Domestic Workers Federation, which represents 500,000 domestic workers around the world. With continued job loss in manufacturing and agriculture, health care remains a growing field. "The lack of care infrastructure around the world is very real," Sarita Gupta observes.

> It calls into question a much larger set of questions around caregiving and specifically around what people can depend on from their governments in terms of social programs. There's an opportunity to create 50–85 million more jobs in the health care sector in the global economy. How we shape that is a huge opportunity.

A growing challenge for the economic justice movement has been a "precariat" of temporary workers, part-time workers, workers without contracts, student workers, and so on. "In the Netherlands, only one in five people has permanent contracts: 80 percent of people are in precarious labor," notes Fiona Dove. "We need to rethink what we consider labor. Is it only those with permanent contracts in blue-collar jobs, or can we consider it working people in a much bigger sense?"

Economic precariousness is behind a good part of the new right's electoral success. So, there's an urgent political need to reach out to this constituency. "We need to counter the skillful use of identity politics by nationalists with the ability to reach out to not only the moveable middle but also to the groups that feel threatened by political and economic change," argues Jordi Vaquer. "This has to do with blue-collar workers, of course, but also with small homeowners, the lower middle class. They and their children are getting employment that pays less well, that's much more precarious. The inability to articulate narratives to reach these groups makes them vulnerable to the populist arguments."

Another way of conceptualizing agency in this regard is to bring together all those fighting against economic inequality, which would unite workers with farmers, indigenous communities, the unemployed, and the otherwise marginalized.

Fight Inequality Alliance, a global network founded in 2017, unites trade unions, social movements, and NGOs. "We have good strong policy recommendations on all the biggest policy levers to reduce inequality, many of them from our members and within the movement," explains Fight Inequality Alliance's Jenny Ricks, who is based in South Africa. "But we lack the countervailing grassroots people power to fight for a different future and a different type of system and society. We need to build power from below. It's not about having polite advocacy conversations in corridors in capital cities." Every January, Fight Inequality Alliance sponsors a week of action that coincides with the World Economic Forum in Davos. The Kenya chapter, for instance, held its alternative summit in 2018 at the Dandora landfill, a garbage mountain in Nairobi, which combined performances with discussions about inequality to create a microcosm of an alternative and equal society.

Similarly, in the United States, the Poor People's Campaign has revived Martin Luther King Jr.'s final effort to unite the economically marginalized of all backgrounds. "The Poor People's Campaign has managed to put together issues of war, environment, and economic justice," relates Edgardo Lander. "This offers a possibility of inclusion that's not seen as extremely radical or impossible but as common sense."

Another tactic to fight economic inequality has been the campaign Attac has organized globally advocating the levying of a tax on financial transactions in order to slow down the rapid flow of capital in and out of countries, and to raise money for various purposes. The network is active in 40 countries where the tax is part of a larger effort to construct alternatives to neoliberalism, strengthen food sovereignty, or promote, as in Austria, a "good life for all."

Intellectuals, too, have played key roles in social movements around the world, including the changes in Eastern Europe in 1989 (Václav Havel), the anti-apartheid movement in South Africa (Desmond Tutu), the democratization of South Korea (Kim Dae-Jung), and the rollback of authoritarianism in Latin America (Michelle Bachelet). Today, Edgardo Lander points out, the right has been effective in taking its culture war into the university, where it seeks to suppress the left and promote philosophies like climate-change denial. "There's an anti-intellectual version of the left that considers it not critical because it's not working class," he observes.

Particularly when it comes to the environmental movement, young people are an important vector of change. "I'm inspired by voices of young people," says Kumi Naidoo. "They're the main stakeholders of the future. High school students in particular have stepped forward in creative, powerful ways. The voices of young people might move CEOs and heads of state who have children and grandchildren."

May Boeve started out a decade ago as part of the group of young people who launched 350.org. "People have always understood climate change as an issue where young people are particularly vulnerable," she explains. "To have very young people publicly shaming political leaders for doing nothing has struck a moral chord now that's really quite powerful." This new generation—through #FridaysforFuture and Extinction Rebellion—has many allies providing assistance (for instance, 350.org's training director wrote a guide with them on how to organize climate strikes). In fall 2019, during the week of September 20–27, people all over the world walked out of their jobs to join students on their climate strike.

"This movement inspires me because millennials are playing an important role in their own future," says Tunisian youth activist Salma

Belhassine. "The symbol is also inspiring because older generations judge millennials as nonchalant and internet-obsessed. But they are showing that they, too, can take the future into their own hands."

Women have also led the opposition to the far right. The women's marches in Washington, DC, were a very visible signal of popular resistance to the Trump administration. The World March of Women has done the same thing on a global scale. "These right-wing movements are so misogynistic and intent on rolling back the gains of the women's movement that women's rights and women's issues have to be at the forefront of the response to the right," says Walden Bello. "At the same time, in pushing this issue especially in the Global South, we have to address some of the concerns about security that have moved many women to embrace right-wing parties that have emphasized personal security."

Similarly, because the far right has targeted them, ethnic, racial, and religious minorities occupy an important place in any progressive response. "Black Lives Matter, which emerged in the U.S. of course, has been taken up by African migrants in France and among Afro-Brazilians," notes Khury Petersen-Smith. "Black Lives Matter has also been a vehicle for talking about other issues. In the U.S., it has involved critiques of gender and heteronormativity, and there have been efforts to center an analysis around the leadership of black women and queer black folks." In 2020, the protests against the police killing of George Floyd in Minneapolis spread not only throughout the United States, in big cities and small, but also internationally. Anger over racism and police brutality brought 20,000 into the streets in Paris, 10,000 demonstrators in Amsterdam, tens of thousands in Auckland, thousands in London and Berlin and throughout Australia.

Migrants, too, have received the brunt of right-wing fury. The Transnational Migrant Platform—Europe (TMP-E) has served to amplify migrant and refugee voices. The Permanent Peoples' Tribunal devoted two sessions (in Palermo in 2017 and in Barcelona in 2018) to the violation of the human rights of migrants, which also featured testimony from migrant representatives, and concluded that current EU immigration policy is guilty of systemic abuses amounting to a kind of "necropolitics."[9] "It would be really useful right now to have the leadership of immigrant and refugee leaders, particularly those who have come from totalitarian-leaning societies," argues Eric Ward. "And because they are connected to another society, they would naturally be able to draw on support from those other places. That would give us a jumpstart on building transnational relationships."

But migrants and refugees are also wary of the limelight. "They tend to be the ones who want to keep their heads down because society is already hostile to them," explains Larry Olomoofe of PADLINK. "Even though we encourage them to fight for their rights, they'd rather deal with the situation as it is rather than escalate it."

One community often absent from the left's list are the very people who voted for the new right. "True activism is going into spaces where people have very different views and winning them over," maintains Kumi Naidoo. "Talking to ourselves about how bad the system: That's not broadening the people's camp."

6
Conclusion

The left has engaged in a tremendous amount of transnational activism: within regions, translocally, on an issue-by-issue basis. But with a few exceptions, like the Black Lives Matter protests in 2020, this effort is not making headlines. Nor is it precipitating a wave of new progressive governance at the level of nation-states.

Moreover, progressives are on the defensive in the face of well-funded and vigorous efforts by the new right to roll back the gains made by social movements over the last century of patient organizing. The internet, once a utopian dream of free speech and creative potential, has been overwhelmed by right-wing trolls, conspiracy theorists, and hatemongers. On top of this, a pall of despair has settled on people everywhere as they witness the effects of climate change, the corruption of public officials, and the ever-widening gap between rich and poor.

The coronavirus pandemic represents yet another challenge. The new right has capitalized on the changes that the pandemic has accelerated—with respect to the global economy, borders, and governance—to advance its racist, xenophobic, and illiberal agenda both domestically and internationally. By riding a third wave of authoritarian rule—following the rise of fascism in the early twentieth century and the spread of autocratic rule throughout the Global South in the 1960s and 1970s—the new right threatens to remake the rules of politics so that it can remain in power indefinitely and reshape society accordingly.[1]

The new right has not been irreversibly successful. Rather, it created a sense of momentum through a few critical wins: the Brexit referendum in the UK in 2016, Trump's election that year, Bolsonaro's victory in Brazil in 2018. A few big wins at the national level could do the same for the global left.

If Orbán or Erdoğan loses an election, that will have a domino effect," Ran Cohen points out. "Orbán and Erdoğan will claim that foreign forces are intervening in the elections, but they claim that anyway! So, let's work together on a global scale to make sure that authoritarian leaders go home.

Donald Trump's 2020 loss demonstrates that, despite his concerted effort to undermine democratic institutions, the electoral process, the court system, and impassioned community organizing continued to serve as a brake against autocracy. But 74 million Americans voted for Trump in the 2020 election. The Republican Party, ever more committed to an agenda of xenophobia and illiberalism, has a powerful bloc in Congress and controls a majority of state houses. Nationalist populism remains a winning strategy in many countries around the world. And yet, after November 2020, some of the air has leaked from the new right's balloon. "Without Trump, who's going to lead this? Brazil, Poland, and Hungary?" observes Eliane Cantanhêde, a Brazilian political commentator. "The party's over ... No one was taking this seriously anyway—but now without Trump, they'll just laugh."[2]

Civil society triumphs at the global level can be as inspiring as electoral victories. El Salvador's blanket ban on metal mining, instituted in 2017, was the result of a transnational effort.[3] "It was a concerted campaign going on for years built around the front-line communities who faced mining taking place in their backyards," Ethan Earle notes. "The tipping point in the campaign was when the archbishop of El Salvador, who'd been wavering, read the Pope's encyclical on climate change, changed his position, and came out in favor of the campaign."

Patrick Bond of the University of the Witwatersrand in Johannesburg points to other key transnational victories, such as the Montreal Protocol in 1987 to restrict CFCs affecting the ozone. "The single greatest victory was the movement to secure anti-retroviral medicines for free," he argues, "thanks to ActUp and African civil society led by the Treatment Action Campaign in South Africa working together to reverse [former President Thabo] Mbeki's opposition. This victory raised life expectancy in South Africa from 52 years at birth in 2005 to 64 in 2019." The UN Global Fund to Fight AIDS, Tuberculosis, and Malaria was vital to ensuring treatment access across the world, he adds.

Similar victories by the left in the future could have a catalyzing effect. The problem at the moment, however, is that in addition to several key wins under its belt, the new right has a vision of the future it wants. This vision is intolerant, exclusionary, and backward-looking, but it is a clear alternative to the current more-or-less liberal status quo. The left is still casting around for a similarly clear vision of an alternative to this status quo.

"Marxism so monopolized thinking on the left for 100 years in terms of social classes, bourgeoisie, proletariat and so forth," Larry Rosenthal points out. "It was effective in many ways but it ran dry and nothing has replaced it. What is necessary is some synthetic vision and its success somewhere." Fiona Dove also recalls when the left had a theoretical consensus around an understanding of the world. "I find it difficult to think of how to move forward without a common framework within which you build a political identity," she concludes.

"We have a crisis of alternatives," laments Luciana Ghiotto, coordinator of the Continental Platform Latin America Better without Free Trade Agreement.

> The World Social Forum showed its limits: the limits of only getting together to talk about how much we hate neoliberalism. But we need to be moving forward with alternatives. We also have a new wave of global social movements from what we had 20 years ago centered around two dynamic movements: climate action movements and the feminist movement.

It is easy to become pessimistic given the urgent threats and the failure, so far, of the left to come up with a popular, integrated political platform in the face of ascendant authoritarianism. One option is to step back, to hibernate in the equivalent of modern monasteries. "We could rather think about where to retreat, where to organize non-authoritarian pockets, self-organized communities where we can save and further develop the knowledge about humanism, human rights, and solidarity," Wolfram Schaffar says. "We may have to go through a difficult time until we can reconstruct what we now take for granted as civilization."

Another option is to ignore the new right, particularly if the movements are simply making a lot of noise and are not in control of key institutions. "Right-wing populists attack institutions and, because of that, they are not governing. Therefore, they can't produce results," points out Jan Nederveen Pieterse. "By criticizing, attacking, and targeting them, you may make them appear stronger than they are." The identitarians, for instance, have a limited following that doesn't even add up to a movement. And new right figures like Steve Bannon often exaggerate their own global clout. Deprived of the fuel of media attention, they will eventually run out of gas.

Preparing for battle is a third option. "We need to be prepared when the next crisis hits. Sooner or later, something will break, whether it's financial, climatic, or geopolitical in a way that will speed up the reorganization of the global system. The last time this happened in 2008, we were not prepared," Lorenzo Marsili points out.

When it hits, we'll need a few clear ideas of what needs to be changed, notably in the international system, and sufficiently worked out alliances between movements and parties across the world to use that window of opportunity that a crisis gives you to change the global structures. It will be a race: who will best manage the coming crisis. We are not winning this race.

But, he adds, "That's how all the beautiful movies begin. You have to be lagging behind in order to catch up and win. Otherwise it's not fun and no one watches it."

The next crisis, which hit after I spoke to Marsili, indeed revealed progressives to be still unprepared and still in the underdog position. But has the coronavirus pandemic also provided an opportunity for progressives to turn the crisis to their advantage?

It is often said that the Chinese character for crisis (*wei-ji*) translates into danger (*wei-xian*) plus opportunity (*ji-hui*). The reality is a bit more complex. Rather than opportunity, explains Sinologist Victor Mair, the second element of the crisis character really translates into either "incipient moment" or "resourcefulness" or "machine." "Any would-be guru who advocates opportunism in the face of crisis should be run out of town on a rail, for his/her advice will only compound the danger of the crisis," Mair adds.[4]

Following Mair's analysis of the critical phoneme *ji*, the current coronavirus crisis is not danger plus opportunity but a time of danger and a moment for technological resourcefulness. In other words, digging into the word "resourcefulness," it's a time to deploy scientific know-how to put available resources to more efficient or ingenious use.

Progressives, by offering the Green New Deal, are proposing just that: deploying scientific know-how to put available resources to more efficient or ingenious use. A "Global" Green New Deal, meanwhile, offers the kind of internationalist framework that could revive transnational cooperation at all levels: among international organizations, nation-states, civil society, and local initiatives.

THE GLOBAL GREEN NEW DEAL

Despite its political successes, the new right has an Achilles' heel. It has no credible response to the most urgent threat facing the planet: the current climate crisis.

For the last couple of years, new right leaders like Donald Trump and Brazil's Jair Bolsonaro have ignored climate change and boosted support for extractive industries like oil and coal. Thanks to Trump, the United States was the only country to pull out of the Paris climate deal. Bolsonaro, meanwhile, reneged on Brazil's offer to host the climate confab in 2019, which wrapped up in Madrid instead. Despite these ostrich moves by Trump and Bolsonaro, the climate crisis hasn't gone away. In fact, it's gotten worse.

Prior to the pandemic, the world utterly failed to restrain carbon emissions despite dire warnings from the scientific community. In 2020, despite a dip in emissions due to the economic downturn caused by COVID-19, the world again registered an all-time high in carbon dioxide concentration in the atmosphere.[5] The radical right doesn't have a plan to reduce carbon emissions. One wing of the movement continues to deny that there even is a crisis. The other wing is focused on dealing with only the demographic effects of the climate crisis—by proposing higher walls to keep out a future wave of climate refugees.[6]

The new right is unable to rise to this challenge. It has no effective response to the climate emergency other than to pretend that it doesn't exist. "I think that the right will go into a profound crisis on these questions," argues Tom Athanasiou of EcoEquity in Berkeley. "At this point, climate denialism, as a movement with any sort of legitimacy, is over. It's just a zombie phenomenon with billionaire funders propping up the sock puppets."

The Green New Deal, meanwhile, offers an inclusive response. The GND is not just about marshaling national (and eventually international resources) to combat climate change. It is intersectionality *par excellence*. The policy initiative, in the admittedly sketchy form introduced in the U.S. Congress, involves many of the infrastructure financing, job retraining, and targeted subsidies for green industries that the left has championed as a way to win back voters disillusioned by neoliberalism. It can also serve as a power strip that other movements can plug into: immigrant rights, the women's movement, anti-racism activists.

Although U.S. journalist Thomas Friedman coined the phrase Green New Deal, the concept is not an American invention. The Green New Deal Group began in the UK in 2007. South Korea launched something similar in 2009. That same year, the UN proposed taking it global.[7] So, it is no surprise that the Green New Deal has already established (or re-established) a transnational following. Yanis Varoufakis, the former Greek finance minister who co-founded DiEM25, calls the Green New Deal the "glue and cement" that can hold together a political alliance of greens, leftists, and liberals and serve as "both the inheritor of and a radical improvement on" the Juncker Plan of 2015, otherwise known as the European Fund for Strategic Investments.[8] In Asia, a GND could push China's Belt and Road Initiative toward greater sustainability.[9] For Africa, a GND could provide an opportunity for countries to leapfrog over existing technologies and achieve parity with the Global North at far less cost to the environment.

The Global Green New Deal cannot be solely an initiative of the rich. Tom Athanasiou argues,

> If the wealthy countries were to come to a vision of the global GND that involved real public finance for the international burden-sharing mechanisms devised under the umbrella of the Paris agreement—and which have to be animated if we're to have any hope of holding to the two-degree line, let alone 1.5C—that would certainly get the attention of people in the developing world.[10]

The World Social Forum served a convening function. Ultimately, many activists felt that it failed to produce strategic coordination, which involves the more political act of determining priorities and proposing collective action at all levels. The Green New Deal, meanwhile, can serve as the vehicle for strategic coordination. "The climate crisis and complete environmental breakdown is our window of opportunity," argues Srećko Horvat. "This is the first time in human history that there is a single issue on which all of humanity can agree."

Setting up GNDs in every country, coordinating among them, and establishing new international institutions to finance the effort will be an enormous challenge. "The challenge is comparable to the one after World War II, when a set of new multilateral institutions were spun out," Athanasiou concludes.

Prior to the outbreak of the coronavirus, governments and mainstream political parties routinely protested that there was neither political will nor sufficient resources to launch a vast, government-led initiative like the Green New Deal. The trillions of dollars spent on bailouts refute this argument. Unfortunately, much of that money went to shoring up a carbon-intensive status quo with money for extractive industries, airlines, and financial institutions.[11] But the climate crisis is an even larger existential threat to humanity, so progressives in every country must use the COVID-19 precedent to push for an even larger sum devoted to creating sustainable national economies and restructuring the global economy.

A Global Green New Deal is not a quick fix. It is a transformative framework that will require an enormous commitment of time, organizing energy, and finances. But that's what progressives need right now.

"One of the things that the right has been fantastically successful at is having a long-term project," observes Jenny Ricks. Indeed, Gar Alperovitz sees the reversal of the right's ascendance as a 30-year fight, comparable to the social movements of the past. "The environmental movement was nothing in the 1960s," he recalls. "There were conservationists, not many environmentalists. Yet somehow a movement was built around a set of ideas and moral themes that has become potentially transformative on the climate change issue. The same thing can be said of feminism."

LEFT POPULISM?

One variant of the Green New Deal is entirely reformist. It seeks to accommodate the existing structures of capitalism by relying on market-based solutions—like carbon taxes and cap-and-trade mechanisms.

Thomas Friedman, *The New York Times* columnist who originated the phrase, prefers to emphasize one aspect of the "New Deal" connection, which was FDR's effort to save capitalism rather than institute an alternative.[12] In this version of market-based environmentalism, the Green New Deal represents a more technocratic than political solution to the climate crisis.

But many progressives prefer to understand the GND as a way to build political support by pitting the corporate one percent that benefits from the current order—the fossil-fuel company executives, the small number of businesses that produce the largest amount of emissions, the wealthiest individuals with the largest carbon footprint—against the 99 percent of people with modest means who bear the brunt of the consequences of climate change.

In other words, the Green New Deal has been a battleground between those hoping to tweak the status quo and those aiming for a more substantial transformation of political economy. For those who support the latter, does the GND require a different kind of politics to confront the new right's populism?

The theorist Chantal Mouffe has been perhaps the most vocal proponent of left populism. She distinguishes between the tradition of political liberalism (rule of law, separation of powers, individual freedoms) and the tradition of democracy (equality, popular sovereignty). By emphasizing popular sovereignty over the technocratic emphasis on experts managing the political realm, she argues for an anti-establishment politics that rallies the people against the political elite, the underdogs against those in power. A political party that effectively uses such a left populism, as Podemos has done in Spain, can potentially win back many of the working-class and middle-class voters that supported the new right populists because they were articulating the only class politics in town.[13]

Mouffe also anticipates critics who charge that populists, whether left or right, have a poor record of dealing with minorities and movements that reflect identity politics. She foresees an ever-evolving coordination between working-class interests and those of "new movements" to create a "common will." In this way, progressives don't choose between class politics and identity politics but are constantly articulating a "99 percent" category that includes both. In this way, progressives maintain a rainbow cosmopolitanism and a coalition politics based on economic solidarity.

As a political strategy, this left populism has much to recommend it. The rise of the new right speaks to the utter rejection of conventional political strategies of the "third way," triangulation, and corrupt patronage. Progressives have to offer something new but at the same time something sufficiently familiar to voters that they see it as viable. Thus, Bernie Sanders managed to create an effective coalition by bringing his left populism within the Democratic Party. By contrast, the Green Party in the United States has not met with similar success.

The ruling coalition in New Zealand offers another successful variant of this kind of politics. Jacinda Ardern's Labour Party reflects a synthesis of traditional social-democratic politics with a more recent overlay of identity politics. A second junior partner is the Green Party, which provides a sustainable spin on the usual Labour politics. But what made the New Zealand case so unusual is the presence of a third partner in the ruling coalition: New Zealand First. Led by a number of prominent Maori politicians, New Zealand First is a strong advocate for the indigenous community. Its economic positions also overlap with Labour's. But New Zealand First has also maintained an anti-immigration platform that overlaps with the agenda of new right populist parties in Europe and Trump's Republican Party in the United States.

New Zealand First occupied a number of key ministerial positions in the Ardern government: foreign affairs, defense, and regional economic development. The party's leader, Winston Peters, served as the minister of foreign affairs, which put him in the interesting position of defending New Zealand's support of such pacts as the UN Migration Agreement. At the same time, the Labour Party couldn't get too far out in front on immigration questions without alienating its junior partner and by extension the constituency that supports it. The New Zealand example shows how progressives can incorporate David Goodhart's "decent populism," which represents the views of those who have a very local identity, without foreswearing entirely a cosmopolitan "anywhere" identity.[14]

In the general election in October 2020, Labour won enough seats to form a majority government but nevertheless chose to bring the Greens back on board. It didn't even have to contemplate reaching out to its third coalition partner. In a crushing loss, New Zealand First lost all its parliamentary seats. The pandemic largely removed the immigration issue from the equation. But inviting the populists inside the tent also deprived the party of its outsider status and thus its political distinctiveness.

A GEOPOLITICAL SHIFT

The new right has articulated a rather old-fashioned view of geopolitics in which nation-states are like billiard balls whose external borders are hard and impermeable. These sovereignists have pushed back against giving greater authority to international institutions. They have also resisted the continuing efforts of progressive civil society to expand minority rights and protections, as well as to champion human rights internationally.

At first blush, it seems that the coronavirus pandemic only strengthens the new right's backlash against globalism. Given the short-term responses to COVID-19—strengthening of borders, imposition of states of emergency, demonization of minorities—the political future of the globe is likely to be less democratic, less internationalist, and more intrusive. Additionally, the pandemic has aggravated social divisions, for instance, between those able to work remotely and the "essential workers" who expose themselves to the virus by picking up garbage, delivering mail, and staffing slaughterhouses and supermarkets. It has concentrated economic power in the businesses best positioned to ride out quarantines and apply for government stimulus funds. And by making hundreds of billions of dollars available in these funds, frequently without appropriate oversight, the pandemic has also accentuated government corruption.[15] But such pandemic trends fail to capture other dynamics of the crisis.

Despite the largely national (and nationalist) responses to COVID-19, for instance, there is still a recognition in most quarters that a global pandemic requires global cooperation and a global solution. While Donald Trump has withdrawn the United States from the WHO amid criticism of the organization's uncritical stance toward China, the organization has elicited praise for mounting a rapid response on a miniscule budget.[16] A beggar-thy-neighborism is to be expected in the first flush of a global panic. But the pandemic has also strengthened the international network of scientists, doctors, and policy professionals pushing for a more effective set of global rules for addressing these health threats, along with the requisite funding and authority to enforce them, as happened after the SARS outbreak in 2003.

The new right is not only concerned about the preservation of national sovereignty. It has a certain vested interest in the balance of power at the geopolitical level. It supported Donald Trump not simply as a putatively charismatic leader but for his version of U.S. hegemony, in which the United States allowed its junior partners full authority within their borders. Donald Trump only cared about human rights in U.S. adversaries like China or Venezuela or Cuba, a position that aligned with the concerns of repressive U.S. allies like Saudi Arabia and Egypt. A similar commitment to non-interference initially attracted many authoritarian leaders to China, which has also been strictly sovereignist in its orientation, one of several ideological overlaps with the new right. Although Joe Biden promises to reprioritize democracy and human rights in U.S. foreign policy, Trump did much to undermine U.S. authority on these issues. Having observed U.S. politics whipsaw from Obama to Trump to Biden, the international community will be wary of investing too much faith in American claims to be a beacon of liberal internationalism.

With the European new right on the ascendant, the European Union too cannot unequivocally champion liberal internationalism. The pandemic has, alas, not presented an opportunity for the international community to come together to tackle a common problem. Nor does the Leviathan option, with its emphasis on coercion to solve major global problems like climate change, preserve any space for the traditional concerns for human rights.

Progressives can and should offer a new internationalism that rejects both U.S. and Chinese hegemony in favor of a more equitable and democratic distribution of power. Such an internationalism must also reject nineteenth-century notions of inviolable national sovereignty as the nation-state is incapable of unilaterally addressing climate change, pandemics, or global supply chains. Pandemics do not recognize borders or the distinction between Global North and Global South. Rising oceans and superstorms will impact everyone. These global problems have remade the map of the world. Geopolitics hasn't yet caught up to that fact.

LOOKING AHEAD

The new right has hijacked much of the agenda and even some of the tactics of the left. And now it is hijacking the internationalism of the left as well. These forces are increasingly networked at the government and party level, through civil society interactions, and in cyberspace. They have developed a compelling narrative of "make [insert country name] great again" that plays on anxieties over a demographic, economic, and political "replacement" by those of a different ethnicity or religion.

Although the new right has disparaged the "administrative state," once it takes power at a national level, it often finds the levers of state power to be useful for the realization of such goals as border control or the promulgation of "family values." The same applies at a regional level. The new right discovered that rather than destroying the European Union it might be better served taking over the institutional apparatus. Despite broadsides against "globalists," the new right may well come to the same conclusion about international authorities if it gets closer to taking charge of institutions like the World Bank.

The left has not abandoned transnationalism. Environmental, economic justice, and peace groups are perhaps better networked now than ever before. Groups are organizing within regions and across widely dispersed localities. Awareness of the linkages among issues has never been greater.

And yet, the left seems a few steps behind on three fronts. It has not mobilized an effective global response to the far right. It has not woven together a popular and more strategically political successor to the World Social Forum—a large-scale, multi-issue campaign that addresses urgent global threats such as climate change, economic inequality, and endemic military conflict. And it has not come up with a positive alternative narrative that combines messages of hope and urgency while mobilizing people of different backgrounds under a common banner.

Above all, progressives need a quantum leap in transnational networking to counter what the new right is setting up. The left does not need another global network simply for the purposes of communication or one "based on old myths of unity and the effacement of internal inequalities among its participants," as Gadi Algazi points out. "Superficial international coalitions cannot address local complexity."

What is needed is strategic coordination. That coordination is particularly critical given the urgency of the situation. This is not 1975 or 1999. "While I have great faith in multi-issue organizing all over the world, I think that time will not allow them to stop the machinery of destruction," observes Edgardo Lander. "How do you construct another possible world and be effective in stopping this massive machinery of destruction which is threatening life on earth?"

The challenge, then, is to figure out how to combine the horizontality of organizing that respects local differences with the verticality of politics that the scale of the global problems demands. The Global Green New Deal addresses the urgency of climate change while also addressing the widespread discontent with neoliberal globalization that has provided a significant base of support for the populist right. With a "thousand flowers bloom" approach, many local initiatives can coordinate a decentralized campaign against the new right through monitoring, amplifying, and storytelling—within or at least near to the larger frame of the Global Green New Deal.

But for the various Green New Deals to move from paper to policy, a more vertically organized campaign is indispensable. That requires cooperation among political parties across borders. It requires sustained NGO campaigns at the UN and through other international agencies. It requires social movements providing the "street heat" necessary at critical junctures to provide inside players with the power they need. It requires, in short, strategic coordination.

Avoiding a climate catastrophe will also require a certain amount of coercion even more intrusive than the measures dictating face mask use and social distancing during the coronavirus crisis. At a national level, if voters support a Green New Deal, parliaments will still have to coerce a range of powerful interests (coal companies, oil and gas corporations, auto manufacturers, the military) to fall into line. And for any global pact that implements something similar, an international authority like the UN would have to coerce recalcitrant or non-compliant countries to do the same. This indispensability of coercion is the lesson progressives need to learn from the Leviathan problem.

For such coercion to be democratic, a Global Green New Deal requires progressive internationalism: to create a structure that allows for both horizontal and vertical organizing, that employs a coordinated "inside–outside" strategy, and that provides a truly democratic alternative to the authoritarian movements of the right, left, and center.

Another world is still possible, a world that is neither neoliberal nor hyper-nationalist. But it will require progressives to turn weaknesses into strengths, apathy into engagement, and frustration with the status quo into support for transformation.

In this way, the best can regain their conviction to stem what Yeats, 100 years ago, chillingly predicted would be a "blood-dimmed tide." In this way, progressives can win the battle for another world.

Notes

INTRODUCTION

1. Philip Rucker and Carol Leonig, *A Very Stable Genius* (New York: Random House, 2020), Kindle edition, p. 15.
2. Peter Baker and Maggie Haberman, "Trump Breaks With Bannon, Saying He Has 'Lost His Mind,'" *The New York Times*, January 3, 2018; www.nytimes.com/2018/01/03/us/politics/trump-bannon.html
3. Daniel Lippman, "Steve Bannon Launches Radio Show and Podcast on Impeachment," *Politico*, October 22, 2019; www.politico.com/news/2019/10/22/steve-bannon-radio-show-podcast-impeachment-055167
4. Jane Mayer, "New Evidence Emerges of Steve Bannon and Cambridge Analytica's Role in Brexit," *The New Yorker*, November 18, 2018; www.newyorker.com/news/news-desk/new-evidence-emerges-of-steve-bannon-and-cambridge-analyticas-role-in-brexit
5. "Leading European Right-Wing Populists Attend Koblenz Meeting," *Deutsche Welle*, January 21, 2017; www.dw.com/en/leading-european-right-wing-populists-attend-koblenz-meeting/a-37220481
6. Ben Westcott and Kathy Quiano, "'We Both Like to Swear': Duterte Makes Peace with US, Trump," CNN, November 10, 2016; www.cnn.com/2016/11/10/asia/duterte-trump-military-exercises/index.html
7. Conor Gaffey, "Steve Bannon's Long Struggle with the Catholic Church," *Newsweek*, September 11, 2017; www.newsweek.com/steve-bannon-60-minutes-pope-francis-catholic-church-663021
8. Gwynn Guilford and Nikhil Sonnad, "What Steve Bannon Really Wants," *Quartz*, February 3, 2017; qz.com/898134/what-steve-bannon-really-wants/
9. Ronald Radosh cited a conversation he had with Bannon in which the latter said, "I'm a Leninist. Lenin wanted to destroy the state, and that's my goal, too. I want to bring everything crashing down, and destroy all of today's establishment." Bannon says, however, that he doesn't remember saying such a "thing." Dan Evon, "Did Steve Bannon Describe Himself as a 'Leninist' Who Wants to Destroy the State?" Snopes, February 3, 2017; www.snopes.com/fact-check/bannon-leninist-destroy-state/
10. In this, Bannon owes much to Murray Rothbard, the Koch brothers, and other libertarian thinkers. See, e.g., Nancy MacLean, *Democracy in Chains* (New York: Viking, 2017).
11. Rudyard Griffiths, *Stephen K. Bannon and David Frum in Conversation* (Toronto: House of Anansi Press, 2018), eBook, p. 87.

12. Cas Mudde, *The Far Right Today* (New York: Polity, 2019), p. 7.
13. Cristina Ruiz, "Culture Ministry Failed to Vet Right-Wing Religious Group Close to Steve Bannon," *The Art Newspaper*, November 27, 2019; www.theartnewspaper.com/news/culture-ministry-failed-to-vet-right-wing-group
14. Madeleine Schwartz, "Steve Bannon: Election Was Italy's Version of Trump Vote," *Politico*, March 5, 2018; www.politico.eu/article/steve-bannon-italy-election-like-us-donald-trump-vote/
15. Kenneth P. Vogel, Jonathan Martin, and Jeremy W. Peters, "Led by the Mercers, Bannon's Allies Abandon Him," *The New York Times*, January 4, 2018; www.nytimes.com/2018/01/04/us/politics/bannon-mercer-trump.html; Jonathan Swain and Erica Pandey, "Exclusive: Steve Bannon's $1 Million Deal Linked to a Chinese Billionaire," *Axios*, October 29, 2019; www.axios.com/steve-bannon-contract-chinese-billionaire-guo-media-fa6bc244-6d7a-4a53-9f03-1296d4fae5aa.html
16. Paul Lewis, "The Mayfair Dinner that Brought Europe's Far Right Together," *The Guardian*, November 21, 2018; www.theguardian.com/world/2018/nov/21/secret-rightwing-gathering-europe-steve-bannon
17. Rachel Cooke, "Filmmaker Alison Klayman: 'Bannon Holds Court and People Come to Him,'" *The Guardian*, July 6, 2019; www.theguardian.com/film/2019/jul/06/alison-klayman-interview-steve-bannon-film-the-brink
18. Jon Lee Anderson, "Jair Bolsonaro's Southern Strategy," *The New Yorker*, March 25, 2019; www.newyorker.com/magazine/2019/04/01/jair-bolsonaros-southern-strategy
19. Cezary Podkul and Brian Spegele, "Steve Bannon, Chinese Critic Create Fund to Investigate Beijing," *Wall Street Journal*, November 20, 2018; www.wsj.com/articles/bannon-chinese-critic-create-fund-to-investigate-beijing-1542759820; Brian Schwartz, "Trump Ally Steve Bannon Is Making a Documentary 'Takedown' of Chinese Leader Xi as US Seeks 'Phase Two' Trade Deal," CNBC, January 29, 2020; www.cnbc.com/2020/01/29/trump-ally-steve-bannon-producing-film-takedown-of-chinas-xi-jinping.html
20. Nick Fouriezos, "Can This Conservative Bring Trumpism to Asia?" *Ozy*, March 20, 2018; www.ozy.com/politics-and-power/can-this-conservative-bring-trumpism-to-asia/85154/
21. Quoted in Larry Rosenthal, *Empire of Resentment: Populism's Toxic Embrace of Nationalism* (New York: New Press, 2020), eBook, p. 120.
22. Mohammad Ali, "Opposition People's Party Of Belgium Announces Dissolution," *UrduPoint*, June 19, 2019; www.urdupoint.com/en/world/opposition-peoples-party-of-belgium-announce-649194.html
23. In March 2021, Italy's Council of State ruled against Bannon, upholding the government decision to rescind the lease. Nicole Winfield, "Italy Court Blocks Bannon-Linked Plans for Populist Academy," Associated

Press, March 16, 2021; apnews.com/article/donald-trump-europe-italy-think-tanks-rome-b561c35eb9db0690fb242f31d256641d
24. See, e.g., Yasmeen Serhan, "Why Doesn't Steve Bannon Matter in Europe," *The Atlantic*, October 12, 2019; www.theatlantic.com/international/archive/2019/10/why-doesnt-steve-bannon-matter-in-europe/599917/
25. Alan Feuer, William K. Rashbaum, and Maggie Haberman, "Steve Bannon Is Charged With Fraud in We Build the Wall Campaign," *The New York Times*, August 20, 2020; www.nytimes.com/2020/08/20/nyregion/steve-bannon-arrested-indicted.html
26. McCay Coppins, "When the MAGA Bubble Burst," *The Atlantic*, November 7, 2020; www.theatlantic.com/politics/archive/2020/11/trump-bannon-election-party/617020/
27. Curt Devine, Donie O'Sullivan, and Kara Scannell, "Twitter Permanently Suspends Steve Bannon Account after Talk of Beheading," CNN, November 6, 2020; www.cnn.com/2020/11/05/tech/steve-bannon-twitter-permanent-suspension/index.html
28. Jennifer Jacobs, "Trump Reconciles With Ex-Strategist Steve Bannon in Talks on Election," *Bloomberg*, January 14, 2021; www.bloomberg.com/news/articles/2021-01-14/trump-reconciles-with-ex-strategist-bannon-in-talks-on-election
29. Lenin's "Bolsheviks" (meaning, the majority) was initially a minority party.

CHAPTER 1

1. "Tyminski in Peru: Spiritual Awareness, Then Cable TV," *The New York Times*, December 2, 1990; www.nytimes.com/1990/12/02/world/evolution-in-europe-tyminski-in-peru-spiritual-awareness-then-cable-tv.html
2. Stephen Engelberg, "A Rough Campaign Closes in Poland," *The New York Times*, November 24, 1990; www.nytimes.com/1990/11/24/world/a-rough-campaign-closes-in-poland.html
3. Juliusz Gardawski, "The Dynamics of Unemployment, 1990-2002," Eurofound, October 28, 2002; www.eurofound.europa.eu/publications/article/2002/the-dynamics-of-unemployment-from-1990-to-2002; "Poland: Gross National Income, 1970–2018," IvanStat; ivanstat.com/en/gni/pl.html
4. Mary Battiata, "Walesa Wins Presidential Vote in Poland," *The Washington Post*, December 10, 1990; www.washingtonpost.com/archive/politics/1990/12/10/walesa-wins-presidential-vote-in-poland/0bb28e48-2b33-4c92-b8de-0ff406c07583/
5. Joanna Berendt, "Lech Walesa Denounces Report Labeling Him a Communist Informer," *The New York Times*, January 31, 2017; www.nytimes.

com/2017/01/31/world/europe/poland-lech-walesa-communist-report.html?_r=0
6. John Feffer, "Welcome to the Birthplace of Trumpism," Foreign Policy In Focus, December 6, 2017; fpif.org/welcome-birthplace-trumpism/
7. I provide more detail on the rise and fall of liberalism in Eastern Europe in John Feffer, *Aftershock: A Journey into Eastern Europe's Broken Dreams* (London: Zed, 2017).
8. Julia Ebner, "Who Are Europe's Far-Right Identitarians?" Politico, April 4, 2019; www.politico.eu/article/who-are-europe-far-right-identitarians-austria-generation-identity-martin-sellner/
9. Benjamin Moffitt, *The Global Rise of Populism* (Stanford, CA: Stanford University Press, 2016), p 168. See also Michael Kazin, *The Populist Persuasion: An American History* (Ithaca, NY: Cornell University Press, 1998).
10. Philip Rucker and Robert Costa, "Bannon Vows a Daily Fight for 'Deconstruction of the Administrative State,'" *The Washington Post*, February 23, 2019; www.washingtonpost.com/politics/top-wh-strategist-vows-a-daily-fight-for-deconstruction-of-the-administrative-state/2017/02/23/03f6b8da-f9ea-11e6-bf01-d47f8cf9b643_story.html?no redirect=on
11. Stefano Bernabei and Giuseppe Fonte, "Italian Party Proposes Nationalising Central Bank for Minimal Cost," Reuters, February 2, 2019; www.reuters.com/article/italy-centralbank-bill/italian-party-proposes-nationalising-central-bank-for-minimal-cost-idUSL5N20G5P8
12. Freedom House, *Freedom in the World 2019*, p. 2; freedomhouse.org/sites/default/files/Feb2019_FH_FITW_2019_Report_ForWeb-compressed.pdf
13. WJP Rule of Law Project; worldjusticeproject.org/our-work/research-and-data/wjp-rule-law-index-2020
14. "Global Democracy Has Another Bad Year," *The Economist*, January 22, 2020; www.economist.com/graphic-detail/2020/01/22/global-democracy-has-another-bad-year
15. Marco Revelli, *The New Populism: Democracy Stares into the Abyss* (New York: Verso, 2019), eBook, loc 2190.
16. Viktor Orbán, speaking at commemoration of the outbreak of the 1848 Hungarian Revolution, March 15, 2018; www.kormany.hu/hu/a-miniszterelnok/beszedek-publikaciok-interjuk/orban-viktor-unnepi-beszede-az-1848-49-evi-forradalom-es-szabadsagharc-170-evfordulojan
17. Global Inequality Facts, Inequality.org; inequality.org/facts/global-inequality/
18. Tom Metcalf and Jack Witzig, "World's Richest Gain $1.2 Trillion in 2019 as Jeff Bezos Retains Crown," Bloomberg, December 27, 2019; www.bloomberg.com/news/articles/2019-12-27/world-s-richest-gain-1-2-trillion-as-kylie-baby-sharks-prosper

19. Half of this figure, however, is attributable to fluctuations in currency exchange. Dylan Matthews, "Are 26 Billionaires Worth More than Half the Planet? The Debate, Explained," Vox, January 22, 2019; www.vox.com/future-perfect/2019/1/22/18192774/oxfam-inequality-report-2019-davos-wealth
20. McKinsey Global Institute, *Poorer Than Their Parents: Flat or Falling Incomes in Advanced Economies*, July 2016; www.mckinsey.com/~/media/McKinsey/Featured%20Insights/Employment%20and%20Growth/Poorer%20than%20their%20parents%20A%20new%20perspective%20on%20income%20inequality/MGI-Poorer-than-their-parents-Flat-or-falling-incomes-in-advanced-economies-Full-report.ashx
21. Ibid., p. 4.
22. Isabel Ortiz, Sara Burke, Mohamed Berrada, and Hernán Cortés, *World Protests, 2006–2013* (New York: Friedrich Ebert Stiftung, 2013), p. 25; policydialogue.org/files/publications/World_Protests_2006-2013-Complete_and_Final_4282014.pdf
23. Katy Lee and Claire Sergent, "How Leftists Learned to Love Le Pen," *Foreign Policy*, February 7, 2017; foreignpolicy.com/2017/02/07/how-the-left-learned-to-love-le-pen-national-front-france-communists/; David Goodhart, *The Road to Somewhere* (London: Hurst and Co., 2017), p. 76.
24. Katrin Bennhold, "Workers of Germany, Unite: The New Siren Call of the Far Right," *The New York Times*, February 5, 2018; www.nytimes.com/2018/02/05/world/europe/afd-unions-social-democrats.html
25. David Ost, "The Attack on Democracy in Poland and the Response of the Left," *The Nation*, July 19, 2018; www.thenation.com/article/archive/attack-democracy-poland-response-left/
26. Dominique Soguel and Monika Rębała, "Why Poland's Illiberal Ruling Party Is Cruising toward Reelection," *Christian Science Monitor*, October 11, 2019; www.csmonitor.com/World/Europe/2019/1011/Why-Poland-s-illiberal-ruling-party-is-cruising-toward-reelection
27. Iain Duncan Smith, "The Nazis, Maggie, the Euro … Our Business Bosses Always Get It Wrong," *Daily Mail*, June 27, 2018; www.dailymail.co.uk/debate/article-5894297/IAIN-DUNCAN-SMITH-Nazis-Maggie-euro-business-bosses-wrong.html; George Monbiot, "Conservatives? No—Brexit Has Shown Us What They Really Are," *The Guardian*, July 25, 2018; www.theguardian.com/commentisfree/2018/jul/25/conservatives-brexit-big-business
28. Walden Bello, *Counter Revolution: The Global Rise of the Far Right* (Rugby: Practical Action Publishing, 2019) eBook, loc 2166.
29. Benjamin Bradlow, "Rightist Bolsonaro Takes Office in Brazil, Promising Populist Change to Angry Voters," *The Conversation*, December 21, 2018; theconversation.com/rightist-bolsonaro-takes-office-in-brazil-promising-populist-change-to-angry-voters-106303

30. Niall McCarthy, "The State of Global Trade Union Membership," *Forbes*, May 6, 2019; www.forbes.com/sites/niallmccarthy/2019/05/06/the-state-of-global-trade-union-membership-infographic/#3ce2b6f-22b6e
31. Jelle Visser, *Trade Unions in the Balance* (International Labour Organization, 2019), p. 14.
32. Radio Poland, "Trade Union Membership Falls to All-Time Low in Poland," May 16, 2013; archiwum.thenews.pl/1/9/Artykul/135797,Trade-union-membership-falls-to-alltime-low-in-Poland
33. Felix Richter, "50 Years of U.S. Wages, in One Chart," World Economic Forum, April 12, 2019; www.weforum.org/agenda/2019/04/50-years-of-us-wages-in-one-chart/; John Schmitt, Elise Gould, and Josh Bivens, "America's Slow-Motion Wage Crisis," Economic Policy Institute; September 13, 2018; www.epi.org/publication/americas-slow-motion-wage-crisis-four-decades-of-slow-and-unequal-growth-2/
34. Barbara Ehrenreich, *Fear of Falling* (New York: Pantheon, 1989).
35. Olga Khazan, "People Voted for Trump Because They Were Anxious, Not Poor," *The Atlantic*, April 23, 2018; www.theatlantic.com/science/archive/2018/04/existential-anxiety-not-poverty-motivates-trump-support/558674/
36. Lorenzo Marsili and Niccolo Milanese, *Citizens of Nowhere: How Europe Can Be Saved from Itself* (London: Zed, 2018), eBook, p. 484.
37. Robert Jansen, "Populist Mobilization: A New Theoretical Approach," in C. de la Torre, ed., *The Promise and Perils of Populism: Global Perspectives* (Lexington: University Press of Kentucky, 2015).
38. Ishaan Tharoor, "The Growing Urban-Rural Divide in Global Politics," *The Washington Post*, August 9, 2018; www.washingtonpost.com/world/2018/08/09/growing-urban-rural-divide-global-politics/
39. Walden Bello, *Counter Revolution: The Global Rise of the Far Right* (Rugby: Practical Action Publishing, 2019) eBook, loc 2818.
40. Arlie Russell Hochschild, *Strangers in Their Own Land* (New York: New Press, 2016).
41. Sam Pizzigati, "New Leadership for the IMF, Same Old Hypocrisy?" Inequality.org, January 11, 2020; inequality.org/great-divide/new-leadership-for-the-imf-same-old-hypocrisy/
42. John Feffer, "'Slowbalization': Is the Slowing Global Economy a Boon or Bane?" Foreign Policy In Focus, August 14, 2019; fpif.org/slowbalization-is-the-slowing-global-economy-a-boon-or-bane/
43. *The Economist*, "The Steam Has Gone out of Globalisation," January 24, 2019; www.economist.com/leaders/2019/01/24/the-steam-has-gone-out-of-globalisation
44. Ian Bremmer, *Us vs Them: The Failure of Globalism* (New York: Penguin, 2018), p. 45.
45. Mark Muro, Robert Maxim, and Jacob Whiton, "The Robots Are Ready as the COVID-19 Recession Spreads," Brookings, March 24, 2020; www.

brookings.edu/blog/the-avenue/2020/03/24/the-robots-are-ready-as-the-covid-19-recession-spreads/
46. Sabine Selchow and Mary Kaldor, "Subterranean Politics in Europe: an introduction," OpenDemocracy, October 12, 2012; www.opendemocracy.net/en/subterranean-politics-in-europe-introduction/; Interview with Mary Kaldor, July 18, 2019.
47. Sheri Berman, "Foreword," in *Why the Left Loses*, Rob Manwaring and Paul Kennedy, eds. (Bristol: Policy Press, 2018), p. 3.
48. David Neiwert, *Alt-America: The Rise of the Radical Right in the Age of Trump* (New York: Verso, 2017); "The Adkisson Manifesto," faith17983.wordpress.com/2015/05/31/the-adkisson-manifesto/
49. Will Bunch, *The Backlash* (New York: HarperCollins, 2010), pp. 10–11.
50. Bill Dedman, Mike Brunker and Monica Alba, "Hate Crime in America, by the Numbers," NBC News, June 18, 2015; www.nbcnews.com/storyline/charleston-church-shooting/hate-crime-america-numbers-n81521
51. Deborah Levine and Marc Brenman, *When Hate Groups March Down Main Street* (Lanham, MD: Rowman and Littlefield, 2019), p. 28.
52. Neiwert, op. cit., p. 261.
53. Dale Beran, *It Came from Something Awful: How a Toxic Troll Army Accidentally Memed Donald Trump into Office* (New York: All Points Books, 2019).
54. Marco Revelli, *The New Populism: Democracy Stares into the Abyss* (New York: Verso, 2019), eBook, p. 672.
55. "According to exit polls, Hillary Clinton won by 12 points among voters making less than $30,000 a year—53% to Trump's 41%—and by 9 points among people making between $30,000 and $49,999. Trump's support was the inverse. He won every group making $50,000 or more—albeit by smaller margins." Jeremy Slevin, "Stop Blaming Low-Income Voters for Donald Trump's Victory," Talk Poverty, November 16, 2016; talkpoverty.org/2016/11/16/stop-blaming-low-income-voters-donald-trumps-victory/
56. Erin Duffin, "Exit Polls of the 2020 Presidential Election in the United States on November 3, 2020, Share of Votes by Income," Statista, November 9, 2020; www.statista.com/statistics/1184428/presidential-election-exit-polls-share-votes-income-us/
57. Nicholas Lemann, "The After-Party," *The New Yorker*, November 2, 2020; www.newyorker.com/magazine/2020/11/02/the-republican-identity-crisis-after-trump
58. Cas Mudde, *The Far Right Today*, op. cit., p. 101.
59. Julia Blunck, "In Brazil, Bolsonaro's Fight Is Not Against Marxism, But Against Enlightenment Values," *New Statesman*, November 21, 2018; www.newstatesman.com/world/2018/11/brazil-bolsonaro-s-fight-not-against-marxism-against-enlightenment-values
60. Sixty percent of PDS supporters stated in 2000 that there were too many immigrants in Germany. Hans Georg Betz and Fabian Habersack,

"Regional Nativism in East Germany" in *The People and the Nation*, eds. Reinhard Heinisch, Emanuele Masetti, and Oscar Mazzoleni (New York: Routledge, 2019).
61. Venetia Rainey, "Dutch Elections: Rotterdam, a Diverse and Divided Cradle of Populism," *Middle East Eye*, www.middleeasteye.net/fr/news/rotterdam-divided-city-elections-geert-wilders-islam-496105981
62. Andrew Brown, "The Myth of Eurabia: How a Far-Right Conspiracy Theory Went Mainstream," *The Guardian*, August 16, 2019; www.theguardian.com/world/2019/aug/16/the-myth-of-eurabia-how-a-far-right-conspiracy-theory-went-mainstream?CMP=Share_iOSApp_Other
63. John Feffer, *Crusade 2.0* (San Francisco: City Lights, 2012).
64. Alex Ward, "Aung San Suu Kyi Meets with Hungary's Orbán to Lament their 'Growing Muslim Populations,'" Vox, June 7, 2019; www.vox.com/2019/6/7/18656603/aung-san-suu-kyi-viktor-orban-muslims
65. Jenni Evans, "Numbers Swell Outside UN offices in Cape Town as Foreign Nationals Demand Evacuation over Safety Fears," News24, October 17, 2019; www.news24.com/SouthAfrica/News/numbers-swell-outside-un-offices-in-cape-town-as-foreign-nationals-demand-evacuation-over-safety-fears-20191017
66. Cyril Bennouna, "Latin America Shuts Out Desperate Venezuelans but Colombia's Border Remains Open—for Now," *The Conversation*, October 7, 2019; theconversation.com/latin-america-shuts-out-desperate-venezuelans-but-colombias-border-remains-open-for-now-123307
67. "Ethnic Chinese Still Grapple with Discrimination Despite Generations in Indonesia," *The Straits Times*, March 19, 2017; www.straitstimes.com/asia/se-asia/ethnic-chinese-still-grapple-with-discrimination-despite-generations-in-indonesia
68. Mudde, *The Far Right Today*, p. 4.
69. Maïthé Chini, "Anti-'Cordon Sanitaire' Demonstration to be Held in Antwerp on Sunday," *The Brussels Times*, October 14, 2019; www.brusselstimes.com/belgium/73127/anti-cordon-sanitaire-demonstration-to-be-held-in-antwerp-on-sunday/; Khaled Diab, "Belgium's Record-Breaking Identity Crisis," *Al Jazeera*, September 9, 2020; www.aljazeera.com/opinions/2020/9/9/belgiums-record-breaking-identity-crisis
70. Eddy Wax, Arthur Neslen, and Laura Kayali, "Parliament Groups Vow to Stop Far-Right MEPs Chairing Committees," Politico, July 2, 2019; www.politico.eu/article/parliament-groups-vow-to-stop-far-right-meps-chairing-committees/
71. William Downs, "How Effective is the Cordon Sanitaire? Lessons from Efforts to Contain the Far Right in Belgium, France, Denmark, and Norway," *Journal of Conflict and Violence Research*, vol. 4, no. 1 (2002), p. 37.
72. Ian Black, "Europe Rallies against Haider Coalition," *The Guardian*, February 4, 2000; www.theguardian.com/world/2000/feb/04/austria.ianblack

73. Mudde, *The Far Right Today*, p. 138.
74. David Neiwert, *Alt-America: The Rise of the Radical Right in the Age of Trump* (New York: Verso, 2017), pp. 110–12.
75. Agnieszka Pikulicka-Wilczewska, "Polish Officials March with Nationalists on Independence Day," *Al Jazeera*, November 11, 2018; www.aljazeera.com/news/2018/11/polish-officials-march-nationalists-independence-day-181111093227508.html
76. David Holthouse, "Several High-Profile Racial Extremists Serve in the U.S. Military," *Intelligence Report*, Southern Poverty Law Center, August 11, 2006; www.splcenter.org/fighting-hate/intelligence-report/2006/several-high-profile-racist-extremists-serve-us-military; Leon Shane III, "White Nationalism Remains a Problem for the Military, Poll Suggests," *Military Times*, February 28, 2019; www.militarytimes.com/news/pentagon-congress/2019/02/28/white-nationalism-remains-a-problem-for-the-military-poll-shows/
77. Dave Philipps, "Coast Guard Officer Plotted to Kill Democrats and Journalists, Prosecutors Say," The New York Times, February 20, 2020; www.nytimes.com/2019/02/20/us/christopher-hasson-coast-guard.html; A.C. Thompson, Ali Winston, and Jake Hanrahan, "Ranks of Notorious Hate Group Include Active-Duty Military," ProPublica, May 3, 2018; www.propublica.org/article/atomwaffen-division-hate-group-active-duty-military; Lois Beckett, "How the US Military Has Failed to Address White Supremacy in Its Ranks," *The Guardian*, June 24, 2020; www.theguardian.com/us-news/2020/jun/24/us-military-white-supremacy-extremist-plot
78. "Germany: More Right-Wing Extremist Soldiers Uncovered than Previously Reported," Deutsche Welle, March 9, 2019; www.dw.com/en/germany-more-right-wing-extremist-soldiers-uncovered-than-previously-reported/a-47838341
79. Katrin Bennhold, "Germany Disbands Special Forces Group Tainted by Far-Right Extremists," *The New York Times*, July 1, 2020; www.nytimes.com/2020/07/01/world/europe/german-special-forces-far-right.html
80. Vicente Rubio-Pueyo, "Vox: A New Far Right in Spain," Rosa Luxemburg Foundation, June 2019; www.rosalux-nyc.org/vox-a-new-far-right-in-spain/
81. Anne Applebaum, "Want to Build a Far-Right Movement? Spain's Vox Party Shows How," *The Washington Post*, May 2, 2019; www.washingtonpost.com/graphics/2019/opinions/spains-far-right-vox-party-shot-from-social-media-into-parliament-overnight-how/
82. Eva Saiz, "Spain's Vox Gets Nearly €3m in Public Funds Despite Tough Talk on Subsidies," *El Pais*, March 13, 2019; english.elpais.com/elpais/2019/03/13/inenglish/1552465079_939994.html
83. Justus Bender, "Seid umschlungen, Millionen!" *Frankfurter Allgemeine*, July 1, 2018; www.faz.net/aktuell/politik/inland/warum-die-afd-die-erasmus-stiftung-gegruendet-hat-15668559.html?printPagedArticle=true#pageIndex_0

84. Gabriel Stargartder, "Bolsonaro Presidential Decree Grants Sweeping Powers over NGOs in Brazil," Reuters, January 2, 2019; www.reuters.com/article/us-brazil-politics-ngos/bolsonaro-presidential-decree-grants-sweeping-powers-over-ngos-in-brazil-idUSKCN1OW1P8
85. Anna Jean Kaiser, "Brazil Environment Chief Accused of 'War on NGOs' as Partnerships Paused," January 17, 2019; www.theguardian.com/world/2019/jan/16/brazil-environment-chief-accused-of-war-on-ngos-as-partnerships-paused; Monica de Boille, "The Amazon Is Burning. Bolsonaro Fanned the Flames," PIEE, September 3, 2019; www.piie.com/blogs/realtime-economic-issues-watch/amazon-burning-bolsonaro-fanned-flames
86. Josephine Huetlin, "Can German Activists Stop the Neo-Nazi Resurgence?" *The Daily Beast*, February 18, 2020; www.thedailybeast.com/can-german-activists-stop-the-neo-nazi-resurgence
87. Human Rights Watch, "Russia: Government vs. Rights," June 18, 2018; www.hrw.org/russia-government-against-rights-groups-battle-chronicle
88. Patrick Kingsley, "Orban and His Allies Cement Control of Hungary's News Media," *The New York Times*, November 29, 2018; www.nytimes.com/2018/11/29/world/europe/hungary-orban-media.html; Eva Balogh, "Hungary's National Tobacco Shops: Who Are the Happy Recipients of the Concessions?" Hungarian Spectrum, April 25, 2013; hungarianspectrum.org/2013/04/25/hungarys-national-tobacco-shops-who-are-the-happy-recipients-of-the-concessions/
89. Interview with András Bozóki, May 15, 2013; www.johnfeffer.com/hungarys-u-turn/
90. Kathryn Krawczyk, "Trump Just Joked about Being President for Life—for the 6th Time," *The Week*, July 11, 2019; theweek.com/speedreads/852099/trump-just-joked-about-being-president-life--6th-time
91. Rudyard Griffiths, *Stephen K. Bannon and David Frum in Conversation* (Toronto: House of Anansi Press, 2018), eBook, pp. 154, 177.
92. Hannah Allam, "Terrorist Or Hero? Politics Shape The Story Behind Antifa's Only Fatal Attack," NPR, July 22, 2020; www.npr.org/2020/07/22/894343496/terrorist-or-hero-politics-shape-the-story-behind-antifas-only-fatal-attack
93. Simon Murdoch, "Identitarianism in America," Hope Not Hate, February 12, 2018; www.hopenothate.org.uk/2018/02/12/identitarianism-in-america/
94. Kate Zernike, "In Power Push, Movement Sees Base in G.O.P.," *The New York Times*, January 14, 2010; www.nytimes.com/2010/01/15/us/politics/15party.html

CHAPTER 2

1. Mike Carter, "Purported Leader of Neo-Nazi Group Atomwaffen Wants Out of Detention in SeaTac; Feds Oppose Release," *Seattle*

NOTES

Times, May 22, 2020; www.seattletimes.com/seattle-news/crime/purported-leader-of-neo-nazi-group-atomwaffen-wants-out-of-detention-in-seatac-feds-oppose-release/

2. Intel Division, "Examining Atomwaffen Division's Transnational Linkages," *Cipher Brief*, May 20, 2020; www.thecipherbrief.com/column_article/examining-atomwaffen-divisions-transnational-linkages
3. Daniel De Simone, Andrei Soshnikov, and Ali Winston, "Neo-Nazi Rinaldo Nazzaro Running US Militant Group The Base from Russia," *BBC News*, January 24, 2020; www.bbc.com/news/world-51236915
4. Pete Williams and Erik Ortiz, "Days Before Virginia Gun Rally, FBI Arrests 3 Alleged White Supremacists," NBC News, January 16, 2020; www.nbcnews.com/news/us-news/days-virginia-gun-rally-fbi-arrests-3-alleged-white-supremacists-n1117271
5. Robert O'Harrow, Jr., "Rallies Ahead of Capitol Riot Were Planned by Established Washington Insiders," *The Washington Post*, January 17, 2021; www.washingtonpost.com/investigations/capitol-rally-organizers-before-riots/2021/01/16/c5b40250-552d-11eb-a931-5b162d0d033d_story.html
6. Olivia Rubin and Soo Rin Kim, "Nearly a dozen ex-military members among those arrested in connection with Capitol riot," ABC News, January 15, 2021; abcnews.go.com/US/dozen-military-members-arrested-connection-capitol-riot/story?id=75278680
7. Devlin Barrett and Matt Zapotosky, "FBI Report Warned of 'War' at Capitol, Contradicting Claims There Was No Indication of Looming Violence," *The Washington Post*, January 12, 2021; www.washingtonpost.com/national-security/capitol-riot-fbi-intelligence/2021/01/12/30d12748-546b-11eb-a817-e5e7f8a406d6_story.html
8. Spencer S. Hsu, Tom Jackman, and Devlin Barrett, "Self-Styled Militia Members Planned on Storming the U.S. Capitol Days in Advance of Jan. 6 attack, Court Documents Say," *The Washington Post*, January 19, 2020; www.washingtonpost.com/local/legal-issues/conspiracy-oath-keeper-arrest-capitol-riot/2021/01/19/fb84877a-5a4f-11eb-8bcf-3877871c819d_story.html
9. James Whitman, *Hitler's American Model* (Princeton: Princeton University Press, 2017).
10. David Mikics, "The Nazi Romance with Islam Has Some Lessons for the United States," *Tablet*, November 24, 2014; www.tabletmag.com/sections/arts-letters/articles/nazi-romance-with-islam
11. Both quotes from Shrenik Rao, "Hitler's Hindus: The Rise and Rise of India's Nazi-loving Nationalists," *Haaretz*, December 14, 2017; www.haaretz.com/opinion/hitlers-hindus-indias-nazi-loving-nationalists-on-the-rise-1.5628532
12. For background on Savitri Devi, see Alexandra Minna Stern, *Proud Boys and the White Ethnostate* (Boston: Beacon, 2019), pp. 36–37.

13. Anti-Defamation League, *Deafening Hate: The Revival of Resistance Records*, January 8, 2013; www.adl.org/news/article/deafening-hate-the-revival-of-resistance-records
14. Nick Chester, "Meet the Malaysian Neo-Nazis Fighting for a Pure Malay Race," Vice, May 18, 2013; www.vice.com/en_us/article/jmv73p/the-malaysian-nazis-fighting-for-a-pure-race
15. Adam Wright, "'Malay Power' Neo-Nazi Band Festival Cancelled in Malaysia's Ipoh City," *South China Morning Post*, March 20, 2019; www.scmp.com/lifestyle/arts-culture/article/3002515/malaysian-neo-nazi-bands-lined-kuala-lumpur-concert-similar
16. Par Saïd Mahrane, "Ce Camus Aui N'aime Pas L'étranger," *Le Point Politique*, October 14, 2013; www.lepoint.fr/politique/ce-camus-qui-n-aime-pas-l-etranger-14-10-2013-1743776_20.php
17. Thomas Chatterton Williams, "The French Origins of 'You Will Not Replace Us,'" *The New Yorker*, November 27, 2017; www.newyorker.com/magazine/2017/12/04/the-french-origins-of-you-will-not-replace-us
18. Bruno Chaouat, "The Gay French Poet Behind the Alt-Right's Favorite Catch Phrase," *Tablet*, August 27, 2019; www.tabletmag.com/jewish-news-and-politics/europe/290272/renaud-camus-great-replacement
19. Elaine Ganley, "Taboos Fall Away as Far-Right EU Candidates Breach Red Line," AP, May 16, 2019; apnews.com/f55b5bed3da04586b2136e6aa1c13351
20. David Harrison, "France's National Rally Links to Violent Far-Right Group Revealed," *Al Jazeera*, December 16, 2018; www.aljazeera.com/news/2018/12/france-national-rally-links-violent-group-revealed-181216092409471.html
21. Thomas Chatterton Williams, "The French Origins of 'You Will Not Replace Us,'" *The New Yorker*, November 27, 2017; www.newyorker.com/magazine/2017/12/04/the-french-origins-of-you-will-not-replace-us
22. Julia Clark, "Racial Attitudes Poll in Partnership with UVA Center for Politics, via Reuters/Ipsos," Ipsos, September 14, 2017; www.ipsos.com/sites/default/files/ct/news/documents/2017-09/2017%20Reuters%20UVA%20Ipsos%20Race%20Poll%209%2014%202017_0.pdf
23. PRRI, "Fractured Nation: Widening Partisan Polarization and Key Issues in 2020 Presidential Elections," October 20, 2019; www.prri.org/research/fractured-nation-widening-partisan-polarization-and-key-issues-in-2020-presidential-elections/
24. In early December 2020, Trump's approval rating stood at 39 percent, according to Gallup polling. Sam Cohen, "Gallup Poll: Trump's Job Approval Ratings Slide Lower, Same for Congress," *The Denver Channel*, December 23, 2020; www.thedenverchannel.com/news/national-politics/gallup-poll-trumps-job-approval-ratings-slide-lower-same-for-congress
25. Jeffrey Gettleman and Hari Kumar, "India Plans Big Detention Camps for Migrants. Muslims Are Afraid," *The New York Times*, August 17, 2019;

www.nytimes.com/2019/08/17/world/asia/india-muslims-narendra-modi.html
26. Akanksha Singh, "Why India's Citizenship Law Crosses the Line," CNN, December 31, 2019; www.cnn.com/2019/12/31/opinions/india-citizenship-law-crosses-line-singh/index.html
27. Eviane Leidig, "The Far-Right Is Going Global," *Foreign Policy*, January 21, 2020; foreignpolicy.com/2020/01/21/india-kashmir-modi-eu-hindu-nationalists-rss-the-far-right-is-going-global/
28. Maiara Folly and Robert Muggah, "How Brazil Can Do Better for Venezuela's Refugees," *Americas Quarterly*, December 18, 2018; www.americasquarterly.org/content/how-brazil-can-do-better-venezuelas-refugees?utm_campaign=clipping_institucional_dia_a_dia&utm_medium=email&utm_source=RD+Station
29. Daniel Okrent, "A Century Ago, America Built Another Kind of Wall," *The New York Times*, May 3, 2019; www.nytimes.com/2019/05/03/opinion/sunday/anti-immigrant-hatred-1920s.html
30. Michael Savage, "How Brexit Party Won Euro elections on Social Media—Simple, Negative Messages to Older Voters," *The Guardian*, June 29, 2019; www.theguardian.com/politics/2019/jun/29/how-brexit-party-won-euro-elections-on-social-media
31. Jennifer Rankin, "Nigel Farage Seventh on List of MEPs' Outside Earnings," *The Guardian*, July 9, 2018; www.theguardian.com/world/2018/jul/10/nigel-farage-seventh-on-list-of-meps-outside-earnings
32. Aurora Bosotti, "Nigel Farage Explains 'Brexit Would Not Have Happened' without One HUGE Change Made in '99," *Express*, January 28, 2020; www.express.co.uk/news/uk/1234404/Nigel-Farage-Brexit-news-European-Parliament-UK-leaves-EU-David-Cameron-latest-news
33. Rachel Farrell, "'Sit Down, Put Your Flags Away and Take Them with You'—Irish MEP McGuinness Cuts Off Farage during Final EU Speech," *Independent*, March 4, 2020; www.independent.ie/business/brexit/sit-down-put-your-flags-away-and-take-them-with-you-irish-mep-mcguinness-cuts-off-farage-during-final-eu-speech-38908197.html
34. Albert O. Hirschman, *Exit, Voice, and Loyalty* (Cambridge, MA: Harvard University Press, 1972).
35. Justin Salhani, "The Russian Billionaire Carrying Out Putin's Will across Europe," ThinkProgress, January 4, 2017; thinkprogress.org/putins-man-in-europe-a4fe6bb48d76/
36. Lionel Barber, Henry Foy, and Alex Barber, "Vladimir Putin Says Liberalism Has 'Become Obsolete,'" *The Financial Times*, June 27, 2019; www.ft.com/content/670039ec-98f3-11e9-9573-ee5cbb98ed36
37. Tess Own, "How a Small Budapest Publishing House Is Quietly Fueling Far-Right Extremism," Vice, May 30, 2019; www.vice.com/en_us/article/3k3558/how-a-small-budapest-publishing-house-is-quietly-fueling-far-right-extremism

38. Pablo Gorondi, "Hungary's Orban Critical of EU Leaders on Migration, Economy," AP, July 27, 2019; apnews.com/b89e682583014c7e8a1bf1cbb46e5dcf
39. Tim Hume, "Far-Right Extremists Have Been Using Ukraine's War as a Training Ground. They're Returning Home," Vice, July 31, 2019; www.vice.com/en_us/article/vb95ma/far-right-extremists-have-been-using-ukraines-civil-war-as-a-training-ground-theyre-returning-home
40. Tim Hume, "Italian Police Found an 11-foot Missile and Nazi Propaganda During a Far-Right Raid," Vice, July 16, 2019; www.vice.com/en_us/article/wjvm8y/italian-police-found-an-air-to-air-missile-and-nazi-propaganda-during-a-far-right-raidsomehow-it-gets-weirder
41. Jonathan Stevenson, "Hatred on the March," *The New York Review of Books*, November 21, 2019; www.nybooks.com/articles/2019/11/21/hatred-on-the-march/
42. Luke Baker, "Far-right Austrian leader visits Israel's Holocaust memorial," Reuters, April 12, 2016; www.reuters.com/article/us-israel-austria-strache/far-right-austrian-leader-visits-israels-holocaust-memorial-idUSKCN0X91NX
43. "Trump Again Cites Israel, Says 'Walls Work,'" *Haaretz*, February 9, 2017; www.haaretz.com/us-news/president-trump-walls-work-just-ask-israel-1.5431036
44. Dan Williams, "Israeli Minister Sees Gaza-Style Measures for U.S.-Mexico Border," Reuters, July 24, 2018; www.reuters.com/article/us-israel-usa-mexico-border/israeli-minister-sees-gaza-style-measures-for-u-s-mexico-border-idUSKBN1KE2E9
45. "Israeli Company Wins Bid to Help Secure US Border," *Jerusalem Post*, June 27, 2019; www.jpost.com/Israel-News/Israeli-company-wins-bid-to-help-secure-US-border-593847
46. "1,000 Israeli Soldiers to Arrive in Honduras to Train Troops, Police on Border Protection," Telesur, May 6, 2019; www.telesurenglish.net/news/1000-Israeli-Soldiers-To-Arrive-in-Honduras-to-Train-Troops-Police-on-Border-Protection-20190506-0014.html
47. Janene Peters, "Wilders Reiterates Trump Support While Calling for LGBT Rights, Gender Equality," NLTimes, January 23, 2017; nltimes.nl/2017/01/23/wilders-reiterates-trump-support-calling-lgbt-rights-gender-equality
48. Maresi Starzmann, "Green Fascism: A Far-Right Ecology Movement is on the Rise in Germany, And It's Spreading Here," *The Indypendent*, September 7, 2019; indypendent.org/2019/09/green-fascism-a-far-right-ecology-movement-is-on-the-rise-in-germany-and-its-spreading-here/
49. Alexander Clarkson, "Thought Populists Want to Kill the EU? It's Worse Than That," *Politico*, January 8, 2019; www.politico.eu/article/populist-attitude-to-eu-matteo-salvini-far-right/
50. Walter Laqueur and Christopher Wall, *The Future of Terrorism* (New York: St. Martin's, 2018), pp. 168–69; Sam Kestenbaum, "Among

White Nationalists, Catchy New Shorthand for the 'Jewish Question,'" *Forward*, December 21, 2016; forward.com/news/356773/among-white-nationalists-catchy-new-shorthand-for-the-jewish-question/
51. Audrea Lim, "The Alt-Right's Asian Fetish," *The New York Times*, January 6, 2018; www.nytimes.com/2018/01/06/opinion/sunday/alt-right-asian-fetish.html
52. Brendan O'Connor, "Here Is What Appears to Be Dylann Roof's Racist Manifesto," *Gawker*, June 20, 2015; gawker.com/here-is-what-appears-to-be-dylann-roofs-racist-manifest-1712767241
53. World Congress of Families, "WCF Letter to Viktor Orbán Congratulates Prime Minister on Historic Election Victory in Hungary," April 11, 2018; profam.org/world-congress-of-families-congratulates-viktor-orban-on-election-victory-in-hungary/
54. Claire Provost and Adam Ramsay, "Revealed: Trump-Linked US Christian 'Fundamentalists' Pour Millions of 'Dark Money' into Europe, Boosting the Far Right," OpenDemocracy, March 27, 2019; www.opendemocracy.net/en/5050/revealed-trump-linked-us-christian-fundamentalists-pour-millions-of-dark-money-into-europe-boosting-the-far-right/
55. Claire Provost, "Christian 'Legal Army' in Hundreds of Court Battles Worldwide," OpenDemocracy, December 13, 2017; www.opendemocracy.net/en/5050/christian-legal-army-court-battles-worldwide/
56. Rebecca Damante and Brennan Suen, "The Extremism of Anti-LGBTQ Powerhouse Alliance Defending Freedom," Media Matters, July 26, 2018; www.mediamatters.org/alliance-defending-freedom/extremism-anti-lgbtq-powerhouse-alliance-defending-freedom
57. Alberto Carosa, "'Human Rights Fanatic': A New Criminal Offense in Europe?" *The Catholic World Report*, July 16, 2015; www.catholicworldreport.com/2015/07/16/human-rights-fanatic-a-new-criminal-offense-in-europe/
58. European Citizens' Initiative, Wikipedia; en.wikipedia.org/wiki/European_Citizens%27_Initiative
59. Cole Parke, "The Right's 'Gender Ideology' Menace Rolls to Africa," Political Research Associates, May 4, 2018; www.politicalresearch.org/2018/05/04/the-rights-gender-ideology-menace-rolls-to-africa
60. Jo Becker, "The Global Machine Behind the Rise of Far-Right Nationalism," *The New York Times*, August 10, 2019; www.nytimes.com/2019/08/10/world/europe/sweden-immigration-nationalism.html
61. Interview with Susanne Götze, July 8, 2019. Stella Schaller and Alexander Carius, *Convenient Truths*, Adelphia, 2019; www.adelphi.de/en/system/files/mediathek/bilder/Convenient%20Truths%20-%20Mapping%20climate%20agendas%20of%20right-wing%20populist%20parties%20in%20Europe%20-%20adelphi.pdf
62. AJ Dellinger, "The 'Anti-Greta' German Teen Naomi Seibt Is Taking the Stage at CPAC 2020," *Mic*, February 26, 2020; www.mic.com/p/

the-anti-greta-german-teen-naomi-seibt-is-taking-the-stage-at-cpac-2020-22418341

63. Juliet Ellperin and Desmond Butler, "Anti-Climate Activist Praises Alt-Right Commentator at CPAC," *The Washington Post*, February 29, 2020; www.washingtonpost.com/climate-environment/2020/02/29/anti-climate-activist-praises-white-nationalist-cpac/
64. Jeremy Deaton, "Climate Deniers Are Embracing QAnon," Nexus Media News, September 24, 2020; nexusmedianews.com/climate-deniers-are-embracing-qanon-690a0eb69071/
65. Natashya Gutierrez, "State-Sponsored Hate: The Rise of the Pro-Duterte Bloggers," *Rappler*, August 18, 2017; www.rappler.com/newsbreak/in-depth/178709-duterte-die-hard-supporters-bloggers-propaganda-pcoo
66. Iain Marlow, "Meet the Man Leading Modi's Outreach to India's Huge Diaspora," Bloomberg, December 20, 2016; www.bloomberg.com/news/articles/2016-12-20/meet-the-man-leading-modi-s-outreach-to-india-s-huge-diaspora
67. Jeet Heer, "Donald Trump Is Holding a Rally With... Narendra Modi?" *The Nation*, September 20, 2019; www.thenation.com/article/archive/trump-india-modi/
68. Mairav Zonszein, "Israeli Extremists Are Making a Comeback—With the Help of US Tax Dollars," *The Nation*, February 26, 2019; www.thenation.com/article/archive/israeli-extremists-us-tax-dollars/
69. Zhaoyin Feng, "Why I Translate All of Trump's tweets into Chinese," BBC, August 9, 2019; www.bbc.com/news/world-us-canada-49092612
70. Kathleen Belew, *Bring the War Home: The White Power Movement and Paramilitary America* (Cambridge, MA: Harvard University Press, 2018), pp. 179–80.
71. Derek Thompson, "Why the Internet Is So Polarized, Extreme, and Screamy," *The Atlantic*, May 23, 2019; www.theatlantic.com/ideas/archive/2019/05/how-did-the-far-right-take-over-the-web/590047/
72. Hari Kunzru, "For the Lulz," *The New York Review of Books*, March 26, 2020; www.nybooks.com/articles/2020/03/26/trolls-4chan-gamergate-lulz/
73. Larry Rosenthal, *Empire of Resentment: Populism's Toxic Embrace of Nationalism* (New York: New Press, 2020), eBook, p. 70.
74. Matthew Rozsa, "QAnon Is the Conspiracy Theory that Won't Die," *Salon*, August 18, 2019; www.salon.com/2019/08/18/qanon-is-the-conspiracy-theory-that-wont-die-heres-what-they-believe-and-why-theyre-wrong/
75. Matthew Rosenberg and Jennifer Steinhauer, "The QAnon Candidates Are Here. Trump Has Paved Their Way," *The New York Times*, July 14, 2020; www.nytimes.com/2020/07/14/us/politics/qanon-politicians-candidates.html
76. Nellie Bowles, "Jordan Peterson, Custodian of the Patriarchy," *The New York Times*, May 18, 2018; www.nytimes.com/2018/05/18/style/jordan-peterson-12-rules-for-life.html; Benjamin Doxtdator, "Why Does

Jordan Peterson Resonate with White Supremacists?" A Long View on Education, April 14, 2018; longviewoneducation.org/why-does-jordan-peterson-resonate-with-white-supremacists/

77. Joe Mulhall, "Deplatforming Works: Let's Get On With It," Hope Not Hate, October 4, 2019; www.hopenothate.org.uk/2019/10/04/deplatforming-works-lets-get-on-with-it/
78. Drew Harwell and Jay Greene, "Video Giant Twitch Pushes Trump Rallies and Mass Violence into the Live-Stream Age," *The Washington Post*, October 17, 2019; www.washingtonpost.com/technology/2019/10/17/video-giant-twitch-pushes-trump-rallies-mass-violence-into-live-stream-age/
79. Tony Lin, "After New Zealand Massacre, Islamophobia Spreads on Chinese Social Media," *Columbia Journalism Review*, March 21, 2019; www.cjr.org/analysis/weibo-new-zealand-massacre.php
80. Juliette Legendre, "Far Right Groups Are Stumbling, But Their Rhetoric Is More Mainstream Than Ever," Foreign Policy In Focus, April 23, 2018; fpif.org/far-right-groups-are-stumbling-but-their-rhetoric-is-more-mainstream-than-ever/

CHAPTER 3

1. "Hungary illegally held asylum-seekers, ECJ rules," *Deutsche Welle*, May 14, 2020; www.dw.com/en/hungary-illegally-held-asylum-seekers-ecj-rules/a-53431848
2. Robert Mackey, "Hungarian Leader Rebuked for Saying Muslim Migrants Must Be Blocked 'to Keep Europe Christian,'" *The New York Times*, September 3, 2015; www.nytimes.com/2015/09/04/world/europe/hungarian-leader-rebuked-for-saying-muslim-migrants-must-be-blocked-to-keep-europe-christian.html?action=click&module=RelatedCoverage&pgtype=Article&region=Footer
3. Patrick Kingsley, "Hungary Criminalizes Aiding Illegal Immigrants," *The New York Times*, June 20, 2018; www.nytimes.com/2018/06/20/world/europe/hungary-stop-soros-law.html
4. Eva Balogh, "The Coronavirus Has Made Its Appearance in Hungary," Hungarian Spectrum, March 4, 2020; hungarianspectrum.org/2020/03/04/the-coronavirus-has-made-its-appearance-in-hungary/
5. Haris Zagar, "Far Right Uses Coronavirus to Scapegoat Refugees," *Mail & Guardian*, March 22, 2020; mg.co.za/article/2020-03-22-far-right-uses-coronavirus-to-scapegoat-refugees/
6. Laszlo Bruszt, "Viktor Orban: Hungary's Disease Dictator," *Balkan Insight*, April 23, 2020; balkaninsight.com/2020/04/23/viktor-orban-hungarys-disease-dictator/

7. Zach Beauchamp, "Hungary's 'Coronavirus Coup,' explained," Vox, April 15, 2020; www.vox.com/policy-and-politics/2020/4/15/21193960/coronavirus-covid-19-hungary-orban-trump-populism
8. Naomi O'Leary, "Calls for EU to Act as NGO Deems Hungary No Longer a Democracy," *The Irish Times*, May 7, 2020; www.irishtimes.com/news/world/europe/calls-for-eu-to-act-as-ngo-deems-hungary-no-longer-a-democracy-1.4247748
9. Marianna Biro and Zoltan Kovacs, "The Decade of Illiberalism—the 2010s in Hungary," *Index*, January 3, 2020; index.hu/english/2020/01/03/hungary_politics_2010s_top_ten_illiberalism/
10. Eva Balogh, "Orban's Dream: A Permanent State of Emergency," *Hungarian Spectrum*, May 27, 2020; hungarianspectrum.org/2020/05/27/orbans-dream-a-permanent-state-of-emergency/
11. Joseph Byrne, *The Black Death* (ABC-CLIO, 2004), p. 66; Joseph Stromberg, "A History of Slavery and Genocide Is Hidden in Modern DNA," *Smithsonian Magazine*, November 15, 2013; www.smithsonianmag.com/science-nature/a-history-of-slavery-and-genocide-is-hidden-in-modern-dna-180947707/
12. Steven Johnson, *The Ghost Map* (New York: Riverhead, 2007).
13. John Feffer, "What the Coronavirus Says About Us," Foreign Policy In Focus, March 18, 2020; fpif.org/what-the-coronavirus-says-about-us/
14. International Center for Not-for-Profit Law, COVID-19 Civic Freedom Tracker; www.icnl.org/covid19tracker/?locaton=&issue=5&date=&type=
15. Alan Greene, "State of Emergency: How Different Countries Are Invoking Extra Powers to Stop the Coronavirus," *The Conversation*, March 30, 2020; theconversation.com/state-of-emergency-how-different-countries-are-invoking-extra-powers-to-stop-the-coronavirus-134495
16. Christopher Miller, "This Leader Has Banned His Doctors From Saying The Word 'Coronavirus'—And Refuses To Admit There Are Any Cases," BuzzFeed, May 1, 2020; www.buzzfeednews.com/article/christopherm51/coronavirus-turkmenistan
17. Daniel Trilling, "Migrants Aren't Spreading Coronavirus—But Nationalists Are Blaming Them Anyway," *The Guardian*, February 28, 2020; www.theguardian.com/commentisfree/2020/feb/28/coronavirus-outbreak-migrants-blamed-italy-matteo-salvini-marine-le-pen; Joshua Kurlantzik, "Dictators Are Using the Coronavirus to Strengthen Their Grip on Power," *The Washington Post*, April 3, 2020; www.washingtonpost.com/outlook/dictators-are-using-the-coronavirus-to-strengthen-their-grip-on-power/2020/04/02/c36582f8-748c-11ea-87da-77a8136c1a6d_story.html; "These Are the 10 'Most Urgent' Threats to Press Freedom Amid the Coronavirus Pandemic," *Time*, April 1, 2020; time.com/5813095/press-freedom-threats-coronavirus-april-2020/
18. TraceTogether, www.tracetogether.gov.sg/

NOTES

19. Mark Zastrow, "South Korea Is Reporting Intimate Details of COVID-19 Cases: Has It Helped?" *Nature*, March 18, 2020; www.nature.com/articles/d41586-020-00740-y
20. Oren Liebermann, Michael Schwartz and Amir Tal, "Israel Is Deploying Spy Technology to Track the Virus, Prompting Fears of Privacy Invasion," CNN, March 18, 2020; www.cnn.com/2020/03/18/tech/israel-coronavirus-technology-intl/index.html
21. Ayelet Shachar, "Bio-Surveillance, Invisible Borders and the Dangerous After-Effects of COVID-19 Measures," OpenDemocracy, June 22, 2020; www.opendemocracy.net/en/pandemic-border/bio-surveillance-invisible-borders-and-dangerous-after-effects-covid-19-measures/
22. Selam Gebrekidan, "The World Has a Plan to Fight Coronavirus. Most Countries Are Not Using it," *The New York Times*, March 12, 2020; www.nytimes.com/2020/03/12/world/coronavirus-world-health-organization.html
23. White House, "Remarks by President Trump, Vice President Pence, and Members of the Coronavirus Task Force in Press Conference," February 27, 2020; www.whitehouse.gov/briefings-statements/remarks-president-trump-vice-president-pence-members-coronavirus-task-force-press-conference/
24. Harry Stevens and Shelly Tan, "From 'It's Going to Disappear' to 'WE WILL WIN THIS WAR,'" *The Washington Post*, March 31, 2020; www.washingtonpost.com/graphics/2020/politics/trump-coronavirus-statements/
25. Myah Ward, "Wilbur Ross Says Coronavirus Could Bring Jobs Back to the U.S. from China," Politico, January 30, 2020; www.politico.com/news/2020/01/30/wilbur-ross-coronavirus-jobs-109445
26. Rush Limbaugh, "Overhyped Coronavirus Weaponized Against Trump," The Rush Limbaugh Show, February 24, 2020; www.rushlimbaugh.com/daily/2020/02/24/overhyped-coronavirus-weaponized-against-trump/
27. Robert Costa, "As Much of America Takes Drastic Action, Some Republicans Remain Skeptical of the Severity of the Coronavirus Pandemic," *The Washington Post*, March 17, 2020; www.washingtonpost.com/politics/as-much-of-america-takes-drastic-action-some-republicans-remain-skeptical-of-the-severity-of-the-coronavirus-pandemic/2020/03/17/f8b199c8-6786-11ea-b313-df458622c2cc_story.html
28. Yasmeen Abutaleb, Josh Dawsey, Ellen Nakashima, and Greg Miller, "The U.S. Was Beset by Denial and Dysfunction as the Coronavirus Raged," *The Washington Post*, April 4, 2020; www.washingtonpost.com/national-security/2020/04/04/coronavirus-government-dysfunction/?arc404=true
29. Britta L. Jewell and Nicholas P. Jewell, "The Huge Cost of Waiting to Contain the Pandemic," *The New York Times*, April 14, 2020; www.nytimes.com/2020/04/14/opinion/covid-social-distancing.html

30. Nancy Cook, "In Crisis, Trump Team Sees a Chance to Achieve Long-Sought Goals," *Politico*, March 9, 2020; www.politico.com/news/2020/03/09/trump-team-policy-border-china-tax-124166
31. Nick Miroff and Josh Dawsey, "Trump Order to Paint border Wall Black Could Drive Up Cost $500 Million or More," *The Washington Post*, May 6, 2020; www.washingtonpost.com/immigration/trump-border-wall-black-paint/2020/05/06/dbda8ae4-8eff-11ea-8df0-ee33c3f5b0d6_story.html
32. Manuela Andreoni, "Brazilians turn against Bolsonaro for government's handling of coronavirus crisis," *Los Angeles Times*, March 22, 2020; www.latimes.com/world-nation/story/2020-03-22/brazilians-turn-against-bolsonaro-for-governments-handling-of-coronavirus-crisis
33. Tom Phillips, "Brazil's Jair Bolsonaro Says Coronavirus Crisis Is a Media Trick," *The Guardian*, March 23, 2020; www.theguardian.com/world/2020/mar/23/brazils-jair-bolsonaro-says-coronavirus-crisis-is-a-media-trick
34. Jihan Abdalla, "Brazil's Bolsonaro facing 'crisis moment' as coronavirus spreads," *Al Jazeera*, May 6, 2020; www.aljazeera.com/news/2020/05/brazils-bolsonaro-facing-crisis-moment-coronavirus-spreads-200504193650707.html
35. Tim Ross, "Johnson's War With Coronavirus Is No Joke Anymore," Bloomberg, March 28, 2020; www.bloomberg.com/news/articles/2020-03-28/johnson-s-war-with-coronavirus-is-no-joke-anymore
36. Richard Heydarian, "The Coronavirus and Rodrigo Duterte's Response," Council on Foreign Relations, April 14, 2020; www.cfr.org/blog/coronavirus-and-rodrigo-dutertes-response
37. Jason Gutierrez, "Leading Philippine Broadcaster, Target of Duterte's Ire, Forced Off the Air," *The New York Times*, May 5, 2020; www.nytimes.com/2020/05/05/world/asia/philippines-abs-cbn-duterte.html?action=click&module=RelatedLinks&pgtype=Article
38. Jovana Gec, Pablo Gorondi, and Vanessa Gera, "Dismantling Democracy? Virus Used as Excuse to Quell Dissent," *The New York Times*, March 30, 2020; www.nytimes.com/aponline/2020/03/30/world/europe/ap-eu-virus-outbreak-grabbing-power.html
39. Lorenzo Tondo, "Salvini Attacks Italy PM over Coronavirus and Links to Rescue Ship," *The Guardian*, February 24, 2020; www.theguardian.com/world/2020/feb/24/salvini-attacks-italy-pm-over-coronavirus-and-links-to-rescue-ship
40. Andrew Higgins, "The Theatrical Method in Putin's Vote Madness," *The New York Times*, July 1, 2020; www.nytimes.com/2020/07/01/world/europe/putin-referendum-vote-russia.html
41. Matt Ho, "How Hong Kong National Security Law Compares to Legislation in Other Countries," *South China Morning Post*, July 7, 2020; www.scmp.com/news/china/politics/article/3092041/one-law-two-systems-how-chinas-national-security-law-hong-kong
42. Tim Hume, "Coronavirus Is Giving Europe's Far Right the Perfect Excuse to Scapegoat Refugees," Vice, March 19, 2020; www.vice.com/

en_us/article/884bvv/coronavirus-is-giving-europes-far-right-the-perfect-excuse-to-scapegoat-refugees

43. Critina Grossner, "Anti-Lockdown Protests in Germany Infiltrated by Far-Right Extremists," *EuroActiv*, May 14, 2020; www.euractiv.com/section/coronavirus/news/anti-lockdown-protests-in-germany-infiltrated-by-far-right-extremists/
44. Nick Robins-Early, "Far-Right Politicians Are Using Coronavirus To Push Anti-Immigration Xenophobia," Huffington Post, February 28, 2020; www.huffpost.com/entry/far-right-coronavirus-europe_n_5e597431c5b601022110798b
45. Kiera Butler, "The Anti-Vax Movement's Radical Shift From Crunchy Granola Purists to Far-Right Crusaders," *Mother Jones*, June 18, 2020; www.motherjones.com/politics/2020/06/the-anti-vax-movements-radical-shift-from-crunchy-granola-purists-to-far-right-crusaders/
46. Anita Chabria, "Anti-Vaccine and Alt-Right Groups Team Up to Stoke Fears of COVID-19 Vaccine," *Los Angeles Times*, December 18, 2020; www.latimes.com/california/story/2020-12-18/anti-vaxxers-team-up-alt-right-against-covid-19-vaccine
47. Charlemagne, "Why Is Europe So Riddled with Vaccine Scepticism?" *The Economist*, December 12, 2020; www.economist.com/europe/2020/12/12/why-is-europe-so-riddled-with-vaccine-scepticism
48. Georgios Samaras, "Has the Coronavirus Proved a Crisis Too Far for Europe's Far-Fight Outsiders?" The Conversation, July 17, 2020; theconversation.com/has-the-coronavirus-proved-a-crisis-too-far-for-europes-far-right-outsiders-142415; John Lichfield, "The Other Loser in the French Elections," Politico, June 30, 2020; www.politico.com/news/2020/06/30/france-marine-le-pen-macron-346480
49. Cristina Ariza, "From the Fringes to the Forefront: How Far-Right Movements Across the Globe Have Reacted to Covid-19," Tony Blair Institute for Global Change, July 1, 2020; institute.global/policy/fringes-forefront-how-far-right-movements-across-globe-have-reacted-covid-19
50. Nolan McCaskill, "Trump, Governors Diverge on Mask Mandates," *Politico*, July 19, 2020; www.politico.com/news/2020/07/19/trump-governors-masks-371304
51. David Welna, "Pentagon Chief Rejects Trump's Threat To Use Military To Quell Unrest," NPR, June 3, 2020; www.npr.org/2020/06/03/868929288/pentagon-chief-rejects-trumps-threat-to-use-military-to-quell-unrest
52. Doug Brown, "A Constitutional Crisis in Portland," ACLU, July 18, 2020; www.aclu.org/news/criminal-law-reform/a-constitutional-crisis-in-portland/
53. Peter Baker, Zolan Kanno-Youngs, and Monica Davey, "Trump Threatens to Send Federal Law Enforcement Forces to More Cities," *The New York Times*, July 20, 2020; www.nytimes.com/2020/07/20/us/politics/trump-chicago-portland-federal-agents.html

54. "Protests Continue In Russia's Far East Over Arrest Of Local Governor," RFE/RL, July 19, 2020; www.rferl.org/a/more-protests-in-russia-khabarovsk-over-arrest-of-local-governor/30735947.html
55. Kareem Fahim, "Turkey's Crackdown on Political Opposition Finds a Favored Target: Elected Kurdish Mayors," *The Washington Post*, July 20, 2020; www.washingtonpost.com/world/middle_east/turkeys-erdogan-seeks-to-neuter-the-opposition-ousting-dozens-of-mayors-is-his-latest-move/2020/07/19/b624f574-bfb9-11ea-8908-68a2b9eae9e0_story.html
56. Archana Chaudhary, "Alcohol Fight Shows India's States Battling Modi for Virus Billions," Bloomberg, April 28, 2020; www.bloomberg.com/news/articles/2020-04-28/alcohol-spat-shows-india-states-battling-modi-for-virus-billions
57. "In One Month, STOP AAPI HATE Receives almost 1500 Incident Reports of Verbal Harassment, Shunning and Physical Assaults," Press Statement, Stop AAPI Hate, April 24, 2020; www.asianpacificpolicyandplanningcouncil.org/wp-content/uploads/Press_Release_4_23_20.pdf
58. Pete Wilson, "Missouri Man Planned to Bomb Hospital during Pandemic to Get Attention for White Supremacist Views," NBC News, March 30, 2020; www.nbcnews.com/news/us-news/missouri-man-planned-bomb-hospital-during-pandemic-get-attention-white-n1172346
59. Masood Farivar, "How Far-Right Extremists Are Exploiting the COVID Pandemic," VOA News, April 25, 2020; www.voanews.com/covid-19-pandemic/how-far-right-extremists-are-exploiting-covid-pandemic
60. Souad Mekhennet, "Far-right and Radical Islamist Groups Are Exploiting Coronavirus Turmoil," *The Washington Post*, April 10, 2020; www.washingtonpost.com/national-security/far-right-wing-and-radical-islamist-groups-are-exploiting-coronavirus-turmoil/2020/04/10/0ae0494e-79c7-11ea-9bee-c5bf9d2e3288_story.html
61. Hunter Walker and Jana Winter," Federal Law Enforcement Document Reveals White Supremacists Discussed Using Coronavirus as a Bioweapon," Yahoo News, March 21, 2020; news.yahoo.com/federal-law-enforcement-document-reveals-white-supremacists-discussed-using-coronavirus-as-a-bioweapon-212031308.html
62. Craig Timberg, Elizabeth Dwoskin, and Moriah Balingit, "Protests Spread, Fueled by Economic Woes and Internet Subcultures," *The Washington Post*, May 1, 2020; www.washingtonpost.com/technology/2020/05/01/anti-stay-home-protests/
63. Tess Owen, "The 'Boogaloo Bois' Are Bringing Their AR-15s and Civil War Ideology to the Lockdown Protests," Vice, May 8, 2020; www.vice.com/en_us/article/y3zmj5/the-boogaloo-bois-are-bringing-their-ar-15s-and-civil-war-ideology-to-the-lockdown-protests
64. Amanda Arnold and Claire Lampen, "What We Know About the Plot to Kidnap Gretchen Whitmer," *The Cut*, December 17, 2020; www.thecut.

com/2020/12/the-gretchen-whitmer-kidnapping-plot-what-we-know.html
65. Lori Hinnant, "$500K in Bitcoin Sent from France to US Far-Right Groups," Associated Press, January 15, 2021; abcnews.go.com/International/wireStory/500k-bitcoin-france-us-groups-75277316
66. Adam Taylor, "Trump's 'Stop the Steal' Message Finds an International Audience Among Conspiracy Theorists and Suspected Cults," *The Washington Post*, January 7, 2021; www.washingtonpost.com/world/2021/01/07/trump-qanon-stop-the-steal-japan/
67. Hannah Allam, "Vehicle Attacks Rise As Extremists Target Protesters," NPR, June 21, 2020; www.npr.org/2020/06/21/880963592/vehicle-attacks-rise-as-extremists-target-protesters
68. John Feffer, "Debunking Trump's China Nonsense," Foreign Policy In Focus, May 6, 2020; fpif.org/debunking-trumps-china-nonsense/
69. Emily Birnbaum, "California GOP Candidate Tweets Coronavirus Conspiracy Theories," *The Hill*, March 2, 2020; thehill.com/policy/technology/485427-california-gop-candidate-tweets-coronavirus-conspiracy-theories
70. Eric Cortellessa, "Conspiracy Theory that Jews Created Virus Spreads on Social Media, ADL says," *Times of Israel*, March 14, 2020; www.timesofisrael.com/conspiracy-theory-that-jews-created-virus-spreads-on-social-media-adl-says/; Daniel Estrin, "New Report Notes Rise In Coronavirus-Linked Anti-Semitic Hate Speech," NPR, April 21, 2020; www.npr.org/sections/coronavirus-live-updates/2020/04/21/839748857/new-report-notes-rise-in-coronavirus-linked-anti-semitic-hate-speech
71. Murali Krishnan, "Indian Muslims Face Renewed Stigma amid COVID-19 Crisis," *Deutsche Welle*, May 14, 2020; www.dw.com/en/indian-muslims-face-renewed-stigma-amid-covid-19-crisis/a-53436462
72. Billy Perrigo, "White Supremacist Groups Are Recruiting With Help From Coronavirus—and a Popular Messaging App," *Time*, April 8, 2020; time.com/5817665/coronavirus-conspiracy-theories-white-supremacist-groups/
73. "America's Far Right Is Energised by Covid-19 Lockdowns," *The Economist*, May 17, 2020; www.economist.com/united-states/2020/05/17/americas-far-right-is-energised-by-covid-19-lockdowns
74. Toby Vogel, "The Vulnerabilities of Schengen," *Politico*, May 18, 2011; www.politico.eu/article/the-vulnerabilities-of-schengen/; Kim Willsher, "European Far Right Calls for End to Open Borders after Berlin Suspect Shot," *The Guardian*, December 23, 2016; www.theguardian.com/world/2016/dec/23/european-far-right-end-to-open-borders-schengen-berlin-le-pen
75. Schengen Visa Info, "Only 11 Schengen Members Have Notified EU for Reintroduction of Internal Border Checks," March 21, 2020; www.schengenvisainfo.com/news/only-11-schengen-members-have-notified-eu-for-reintroduction-of-border-checks/

76. Lorenzo Tondo, "'Migrants Never Disappeared': the Lone Rescue Ship Braving a Pandemic," *The Guardian*, April 4, 2020; www.theguardian.com/global-development/2020/apr/04/migrants-never-disappeared-the-lone-rescue-ship-braving-a-pandemic-coronavirus
77. Mia Alberti and Vasco Cotovio, "Portugal Gives Migrants and Asylum-Seekers Full Citizenship Rights during Coronavirus Outbreak," CNN, March 30, 2020; www.cnn.com/2020/03/30/europe/portugal-migrants-citizenship-rights-coronavirus-intl/index.html
78. Nicolaj Nielsen, "Half of Refugees at German Camp Test Covid-19 Positive," EUObserver, April 16, 2020; euobserver.com/coronavirus/148072
79. Maurizio Massari, "Italian Ambassador to the EU: Italy Needs Europe's Help," *Politico*, March 10, 2020; www.politico.eu/article/coronavirus-italy-needs-europe-help/
80. Aimee Tsang, "E.U. Seeks Solidarity as Nations Restrict Medical Exports," *The New York Times*, March 7, 2020; www.nytimes.com/2020/03/07/business/eu-exports-medical-equipment.html
81. Chad Brown, "EU Limits on Medical Gear Exports Put Poor Countries and Europeans at Risk," Peterson Institute for International Economics, March 19, 2020; www.piie.com/blogs/trade-and-investment-policy-watch/eu-limits-medical-gear-exports-put-poor-countries-and
82. Luigi Scazzieri, "Trouble for the EU Is Brewing in Coronavirus-Hit Italy," Center for European Reform, April 2, 2020; www.cer.eu/insights/trouble-eu-brewing-coronavirus-hit-italy
83. Jennifer Rankin, "Coronavirus Could Be Final Straw for EU, European Experts Warn," *The Guardian*, April 1, 2020; www.theguardian.com/world/2020/apr/01/coronavirus-could-be-final-straw-for-eu-european-experts-warn?fbclid=IwAR3Rl2olVAeSOx_B_wrXcNBoRoMwROrde3qn7JsGscWMiVoq3zxuSN7xJWU
84. "Coronavirus: EU Leaders Reach Recovery Deal after Marathon Summit," BBC, July 21, 2020; www.bbc.com/news/world-europe-53481542
85. William Ophuls, "Leviathan or Oblivion" in Herman Daly, ed., *Toward a Steady-State Economy* (W. H. Freeman, 1973).
86. John Feffer, "How to Decide the Fate of the Planet," TomDispatch, July 30, 2019; www.tomdispatch.com/blog/176591/tomgram%3A_john_feffer%2C_how_to_decide_the_fate_of_the_planet/
87. "Trade Restrictions on Food Exports Due to the Coronavirus Pandemic," *The New York Times*, April 3, 2020; www.nytimes.com/reuters/2020/04/03/world/europe/03reuters-health-coronavirus-trade-food-factbox.html
88. Micah Zenko, "The Coronavirus Is the Worst Intelligence Failure in U.S. History," *Foreign Policy*, March 25, 2020; foreignpolicy.com/2020/03/25/coronavirus-worst-intelligence-failure-us-history-covid-19/
89. See, e.g., Samantha Power, "How the COVID-19 Era Will Change National Security Forever," *Time*, April 14, 2020; time.com/5820625/national-security-coronavirus-samantha-power/

90. Declan Walsh, "Autocrats' Quandary: You Can't Arrest a Virus," *The New York Times*, April 6, 2020; www.nytimes.com/2020/04/06/world/middleeast/coronavirus-autocrats.html; "Diseases like Covid-19 Are Deadlier in Non-Democracies," *The Economist*, February 18, 2020; www.economist.com/graphic-detail/2020/02/18/diseases-like-covid-19-are-deadlier-in-non-democracies

CHAPTER 4

1. Interview with Paul Spoonley, February 28, 2020.
2. OECD, *Society at a Glance 2011: OECD Social Indicators*, April 12, 2011, p. 99; www.oecd.org/berlin/47570353.pdf
3. Rawiri Taonui, "Is Christchurch the Capital of White Racism in New Zealand," *Waatea News*, June 20, 2019; www.waateanews.com/waateanews/x_news/MjE5ODk/Opinion/-Is-Christchurch-the-capital-of-white-racism-in-New-Zealand
4. Eleanor Ainge Roy and Michael McGowan, "New Zealand Asks: How Was the Threat from the Far Right Missed?" *The Guardian*, March 20, 2019; www.theguardian.com/world/2019/mar/21/new-zealand-asks-how-was-the-threat-from-the-far-right-missed
5. Interview with Ikhlaq Kashkari, May 11, 2020.
6. Interview with Rawiri Taonui, March 11, 2020.
7. Interview with Meng Foon, April 29, 2020.
8. See my analysis of the Breivik attacks in John Feffer, *Crusade 2.0* (San Francisco: City Lights, 2012).
9. Interview with Matt Nipert, April 2, 2020.
10. Anna Fifield, "New Zealand's Prime Minister Receives Worldwide Praise for Her Response to the Mosque Shootings," *The Washington Post*, March 18, 2019; www.washingtonpost.com/world/2019/03/18/new-zealands-prime-minister-wins-worldwide-praise-her-response-mosque-shootings/
11. Charlotte Graham-McLay, "New Zealand Man Gets 21 Months for Sharing Video of Christchurch Attacks," *The New York Times*, June 18, 2019; www.nytimes.com/2019/06/18/world/asia/new-zealand-video.html; Florence Kerr and Thomas Manch, "Arrested New Zealand soldier with far-right ties was questioned after March 15 attacks," *Stuff*, December 18, 2019; www.stuff.co.nz/national/118298650/arrested-new-zealand-soldier-with-farright-ties-was-questioned-after-march-15-attacks
12. Interview with Martin Cocker, March 12, 2020.
13. "Christchurch Call," www.christchurchcall.com/
14. "Joint Statement in Support of the Christchurch Call," May 2019; blogs.microsoft.com/wp-content/uploads/prod/sites/5/2019/05/Christchurch-Call-and-Nine-Steps.pdf

15. "Facebook Changes Prompted by Christchurch Call," *Otago Daily Times*, September 18, 2019; www.odt.co.nz/news/national/facebook-changes-prompted-christchurch-call
16. Sophie Davis, "Regulating Beyond the Christchurch Call," *The Regulatory Review*, December 31, 2019; www.theregreview.org/2019/12/31/davis-regulating-beyond-christchurch-call/
17. Eleanor Ainge Roy, "New Zealand Health Minister Demoted after Beach Visit Broke Lockdown Rules," *The Guardian*, April 6, 2020; www.theguardian.com/world/2020/apr/07/new-zealand-health-minister-demoted-after-beach-visit-broke-lockdown-rules
18. Charles Anderson, "Jacinda Ardern and Her Government Soar in Popularity during Coronavirus Crisis," *The Guardian*, April 30, 2020; www.theguardian.com/world/2020/may/01/jacinda-ardern-and-her-government-soar-in-popularity-during-coronavirus-crisis
19. Joseph Cox and Jason Koebler, "Why Won't Twitter Treat White Supremacy Like ISIS? Because It Would Mean Banning Some Republican Politicians Too," *Vice*, April 25, 2019; www.vice.com/en_us/article/a3xgq5/why-wont-twitter-treat-white-supremacy-like-isis-because-it-would-mean-banning-some-republican-politicians-too
20. Cas Mudde, *The Far Right Today*, op. cit., p. 143.
21. Michael Zeller, "Germany: Is Banning Far-Right Groups Enough?" OpenDemocracy, February 12, 2020; www.opendemocracy.net/en/global-extremes/germany-banning-far-right-groups-enough/
22. "German Far-Right Deputies Expelled over Clothing," BBC, June 13, 2012; www.bbc.com/news/world-europe-18429463
23. Cynthia Miller-Idriss, *The Extreme Gone Mainstream: Commercialization and Far Right Youth Culture in Germany* (Princeton: Princeton University Press, 2018).
24. Amy Labarrière, "The Story Behind Warsaw's New LGBT+ Declaration," URBACT, March 28, 2019; www.blog.urbact.eu/2019/03/warsaw-lgbt-declaration/
25. Russ Bynum, "Georgia Virus Law Tops 500; Mask Law Targeting Klan Waived," AP, April 14, 2020; apnews.com/2ef6615981f16ee75eabbe8c8f676da7
26. Institute for Constitutional Advocacy and Protection, *Prohibiting Private Armies at Public Rallies*, September 2020; www.law.georgetown.edu/icap/wp-content/uploads/sites/32/2018/04/Prohibiting-Private-Armies-at-Public-Rallies.pdf; Erika Bolstad, "Emboldened Far-Right Groups Challenge Cities, States," The Pew Charitable Trust, October 13, 2020; www.pewtrusts.org/en/research-and-analysis/blogs/stateline/2020/10/13/emboldened-far-right-groups-challenge-cities-states
27. *Not In Our Town*, www.niot.org/about-us
28. Lorenzo Tondo, "'Sardines' against Salvini: Italy's Fight against the Far Right," *The Guardian*, December 14, 2019; www.theguardian.com/world/2019/dec/14/sardines-pack-piazza-in-rome-for-protest-against-matteo-salvini

NOTES

29. Tom Philips, "Brazil's Left and Right Unite to Launch Pro-Democracy Manifesto," *The Guardian*, May 31, 2020; www.theguardian.com/world/2020/may/31/brazils-left-and-right-unite-to-back-pro-democracy-manifesto-bolsonaro#maincontent
30. Muri Assunção, "Despite Protests, Brazil President Jair Bolsonaro Visits Texas, Hangs out with Bush, Gets High Praise from Ted Cruz," *New York Daily News*, May 16, 2019; www.nydailynews.com/news/national/ny-bolsonaro-dallas-ted-cruz-protest-20190516-igbxayakpzhvvp3lzqwbjnv42e-story.html
31. Heather Stewart and David Smith, "Donald Trump Cancels London Visit amid Protest Fears," *The Guardian*, January 12, 2018; www.theguardian.com/us-news/2018/jan/12/donald-trump-visit-to-london-called-off-amid-fears-of-mass-protests
32. "That Baby Balloon Makes Me Feel Unwelcome in London, Complains Trump, Blaming Mayor," Associated Press, July 13, 2018; www.scmp.com/news/world/europe/article/2155074/baby-blimp-makes-me-feel-unwelcome-london-complains-trump-blaming
33. "Protesters briefly disrupt World Hindu Congress in Chicago," *Times of India*, September 8, 2018; timesofindia.indiatimes.com/world/us/protesters-briefly-disrupt-world-hindu-congress-in-chicago/articleshow/65730504.cms
34. Dan Plesch, *Human Rights after Hitler* (Washington, DC: Georgetown University Press, 2017), p. 158.
35. Alexandra Minna Stern, *Proud Boys and the White Ethnostate* (Boston: Beacon, 2019), p. 7
36. Jason Wilson, "Milo Yiannopoulos 'More than $2m in Debt,' Australian Promoters' Documents Show," *The Guardian*, December 3, 2018; www.theguardian.com/australia-news/2018/dec/03/milo-yiannopoulos-more-than-2m-in-debt-australian-promoters-documents-show
37. P.R. Lockhart, "Counterprotesters Vastly Outnumbered White Nationalists at Unite the Right 2," Vox, August 12, 2018; www.vox.com/2018/8/12/17681120/unite-the-right-rally-2018-washington-dc-counterprotest-charlottesville-anniversary-photos
38. Elena Cresci, "German Town Tricks Neo-Nazis into Raising Thousands of Euros for Anti-Extremist Charity," *The Guardian*, November 18, 2014; www.theguardian.com/world/2014/nov/18/neo-nazis-tricked-into-raising-10000-for-charity
39. Laurin-Whitney Gottbrath, "'Adopt a Nazi': How Groups Are Countering Neo-Nazis," *Al Jazeera*, August 25, 2017; www.aljazeera.com/indepth/features/2017/08/nazi-groups-countering-neo-nazis-170824072656258.html
40. "How YouTubers Are Deradicalizing Members of the Alt-Right," CBC Radio, September 6, 2019; www.cbc.ca/radio/tapestry/contra-1.5273072/how-youtubers-are-deradicalizing-members-of-the-alt-right-1.5273079

41. Petra Boumaiza, "Labor-Market Oriented Exit-Support Work to Combat Right-Wing Extremism: the XENOS Special Program, 'Exit to Enter' (Ausstieg zum Einstieg)" in Ralf Melzer and Sebastian Serafin, eds., *Right Wing Extremism in Europe* (Berlin: Friedrich-Ebert-Stiftung, 2013), p. 307.
42. Kristina Nauditt and Gerd Wermerskirch, "Lessons Learned: Can Germany's 'Labor-Market Oriented Exit Initiative' be Adapted for Other Countries?" in Ralf Melzer and Sebastian Serafin, eds., *Right Wing Extremism in Europe* (Berlin: Friedrich-Ebert-Stiftung, 2013), p. 410.
43. Jacob Davey and Julia Ebner, *The 'Great Replacement': The Violent Consequences of Mainstreamed Extremism* (London: Institute for Strategic Dialogue, 2019); www.isdglobal.org/wp-content/uploads/2019/07/The-Great-Replacement-The-Violent-Consequences-of-Mainstreamed-Extremism-by-ISD.pdf
44. Robert Klemko, "A Small Group of Sleuths Had Been Identifying Right-Wing Extremists Long Before the Attack on the Capitol," *The Washington Post*, January 10, 2021; www.washingtonpost.com/national-security/antifa-far-right-doxing-identities/2021/01/10/41721de0-4dd7-11eb-bda4-615aaefd0555_story.html
45. Zack Beauchamp, "Alex Jones, Pizzagate Booster and America's Most Famous Conspiracy Theorist, Explained," Vox, December 7, 2016; www.vox.com/policy-and-politics/2016/10/28/13424848/alex-jones-infowars-prisonplanet
46. Rachel Kraus, "2018 Was the Year We (Sort of) Cleaned up the Internet," Mashable, December 26, 2018; mashable.com/article/deplatforming-alex-jones-2018/
47. Jack Nicas, "Alex Jones Said Bans Would Strengthen Him. He Was Wrong," *The New York Times*, September 4, 2018; www.nytimes.com/2018/09/04/technology/alex-jones-infowars-bans-traffic.html
48. SimilarWeb; www.similarweb.com/website/infowars.com#social; accessed May 2, 2020.
49. Interview with Matt Nipert, April 2, 2020.
50. Joe Mulhall, "Deplatforming Works: Let's Get On With It," Hope Not Hate, October 4, 2019; www.hopenothate.org.uk/2019/10/04/deplatforming-works-lets-get-on-with-it/
51. Elizabeth Dwoskin and Craig Timberg, "Misinformation Dropped Dramatically the Week after Twitter Banned Trump and Some Allies," *The Washington Post*, January 16, 2021; www.washingtonpost.com/technology/2021/01/16/misinformation-trump-twitter/
52. Rachel Lerman, "Facebook Removes Hundreds of Boogaloo Accounts for 'Promoting Violence' in Coordinated Takedown," *The Washington Post*, June 30, 2020; www.washingtonpost.com/technology/2020/06/30/facebook-boogaloo-ban-accounts/
53. Blake Montgomery, "PayPal, GoFundMe, And Patreon Banned A Bunch of People Associated With The Alt-Right. Here's Why," Buzzfeed, August 2,

NOTES

2017; www.buzzfeednews.com/article/blakemontgomery/the-alt-right-has-a-payment-processor-problem; April Glaser, "The Swag Shop of the Far Right," Slate, February 7, 2019; slate.com/technology/2019/02/proud-boys-1776-shop-paypal-square-chase-removed.html; Julia Ebner, "The Currency of the Far-Right: Why Neo-Nazis Love Bitcoin," *The Guardian*, January 24, 2018; www.theguardian.com/commentisfree/2018/jan/24/bitcoin-currency-far-right-neo-nazis-cryptocurrencies

54. Interview with Martin Cocker, March 12, 2020.
55. Ian Bremmer, *Us vs Them: The Failure of Globalism* (New York: Penguin, 2018), p. 112.

CHAPTER 5

1. Robert Borosage, "The Battle in Seattle," *The Nation*, November 18, 1999; www.thenation.com/article/archive/battle-seattle/
2. systemicalternatives.org/2020/04/29/global-dialogue-for-systemic-change/
3. www.covidglobalsolidarity.org/
4. Stephanie Nebehay, "UN Labor Body Adopts #MeToo Pact Against Violence at Work," Reuters, June 21, 2019; www.reuters.com/article/us-un-labour-harassment/un-labor-body-adopts-metoo-pact-against-violence-at-work-idUSKCN1TM1CM
5. Dave Lee, "Acta Protests: Thousands Take to Streets across Europe," BBC, March 8, 2012; www.bbc.com/news/technology-16999497
6. John Feffer, "South Korea and the Politics of Patience," Foreign Policy In Focus, November 5, 2014; fpif.org/south-korea-politics-patience/
7. The Local, "Geneva's Local Currency Launches in Lausanne," June 10, 2016; www.thelocal.ch/20160610/genevas-local-currency-launches-in-lausanne
8. Manuel Perez-Rocha and Jen Moore, *Extraction Casino*, Institute for Policy Studies, April 2019; ips-dc.org/report-extraction-casino/
9. Natasha Lennard, "With Record Numbers of Displaced People, Deterrence Policies to Stop Their Movement Are Mass Murder," *The Intercept*, July 26, 2019; theintercept.com/2019/07/06/migration-open-borders-deterrence-mass-murder/

CHAPTER 6

1. Anna Lührmann and Staffan Lindberg, "A Third Wave of Autocratization Is Here: What Is New about It?" *Democratization*, Volume 26, Issue 7 (2019).
2. Shaun Walker, Tom Phillips, and Jon Henley, "End of Trump Era Deals Heavy Blow to Rightwing Populist Leaders Worldwide," *The Guardian*, November 11, 2020; www.theguardian.com/us-news/2020/nov/11/end-trump-era-blow-rightwing-populist-leaders-worldwide-biden-victory-brazil-hungary

3. Esty Dinur, "How El Salvador Won on Mining," *The Progressive*, April 1, 2018; progressive.org/magazine/how-el-salvador-won-on-mining/
4. Victor Mair, "How a Misunderstanding about Chinese Characters Has Led Many Astray," Pinyin.info, September 2009; www.pinyin.info/chinese/crisis.html
5. Andrew Freedman and Chris Mooney, "Earth's Carbon Dioxide Levels Hit Record High, Despite Coronavirus-Related Emissions Drop," *The Washington Post*, June 4, 2020; www.washingtonpost.com/weather/2020/06/04/carbon-dioxide-record-2020/
6. Ruby Russell, "Building Walls to Keep Climate Refugees Out," *Deutsche Welle*, April 11, 2019; www.dw.com/en/building-walls-to-keep-climate-refugees-out/a-48273469
7. Edward Barbier, "Rethinking the Economic Recovery: A Global Green New Deal," United Nations Environment Program, April 2009; wedocs.unep.org/bitstream/handle/20.500.11822/7727/-Rethinking%20the%20Economic%20Recovery_%20A%20Global%20Green%20New%20Deal-2009853.pdf
8. Matthew Taylor and Arthur Neslen, "Yanis Varoufakis: Green New Deal Can Unite Europe's Progressives," *The Guardian*, May 22, 2019; www.theguardian.com/world/2019/may/22/yanis-varoufakis-green-new-deal-can-unite-europes-progressives
9. Christopher Balding, "Asia Is the Right Place for a US 'Green New Deal,'" *Nikkei Asian Review*, August 7, 2019; asia.nikkei.com/Opinion/Asia-is-the-right-place-for-a-US-Green-New-Deal
10. Tom Athanasiou, "Only a Global Green New Deal Can Save the Planet," *The Nation*, September 17, 2019; www.thenation.com/article/archive/green-new-deal-sanders/
11. Justin Guay, "Coronavirus Bailouts Stoke Climate Change," *Foreign Affairs*, July 3, 2020; www.foreignaffairs.com/articles/united-states/2020-07-03/coronavirus-bailouts-stoke-climate-change
12. Ryan Brooks, "Thomas Friedman Coined 'The Green New Deal.' He's Happy With How It's Progressing." Buzzfeed, March 29, 2019; www.buzzfeednews.com/article/ryancbrooks/thomas-friedman-green-new-deal
13. Chantal Mouffe, *For a Left Populism* (New York: Verso, 2018).
14. David Goodhart, *The Road to Somewhere* (London: Hurst and Co., 2017).
15. Frances Brown, Saskia Brechenmacher, and Thomas Carruthers, "How Will the Coronavirus Reshape Democracy and Governance Globally?" Carnegie Endowment for International Peace, April 6, 2020; carnegieendowment.org/2020/04/06/how-will-coronavirus-reshape-democracy-and-governance-globally-pub-81470
16. Julian Borger, "Trump Scapegoating of WHO Obscures Its Key Role in Tackling Pandemic," *The Guardian*, April 8, 2020; www.theguardian.com/world/2020/apr/08/world-health-organization-coronavirus-donald-trump

Index

Abe, Shinzo, 3, 36
abortion, 58, 59, 75, 112
accelerationism, 79, 81
activism
    antifascist, 28, 42, 43, 98
    anti-globalization, 13, 23, 34, 85, 104–5
    anti-LGBT, 37, 58, 75, 94, 114
    anti-immigrant, 60
    anti-racism, 78, 81, 95, 116, 125, 127
    anti-vaccine, 74–5
    climate, 26, 104, 107, 109, 115–6, 117, 124, 129, 131–3, 134
    digital, 62–5
    economic justice, 22–3, 121–4
    migrant, 125–6
    regional, 110–3
    transatlantic, 1, 10, 97, 113
    trans-European, 118–9
    translocal, 113–5
    transnational left, 108–10
    transnational right, 55, 58–61
    youth, 124–5
    women's movement, 32, 111–2, 116, 125
Adelphi Institute, 60
Adhanom, Tedros, 81
Adkisson, David, 29
Afghanistan, 33, 51
Africa, 69, 73, 111, 128, 132
Ahn, Christine, 112
Airbnb, 114
Akuno, Kali 105–6
Algazi, Gadi, 12, 138–9
Alliance Defending Freedom International, 59, 75
Alperovitz, Gar, 24–5, 121

Alternative für Deutschland, 2, 39, 40, 48, 53, 74
alt-right, 1, 6, 8, 30, 48, 49, 58, 63, 74
Alvarez-Negretti, Giovanna, 103
Amazon, 90, 101, 122
ameliorationism, 79
American Civil Liberties Union, 77
anti-Americanism, 8, 77
anti-Asian sentiment, 79
anti-Communism, 18
anti-corruption, 13, 116
Anti-Counterfeiting Trade Agreement, 111
anti-globalism, 5, 43, 136
anti-immigrant discourse, 32–4, 49–50, 57, 87
anti-liberal politics, 17, 43, 54
anti-Semitism, 55, 58, 81
Ardern, Jacinda, 89–91, 135
Arktos, 54
Aryan, 46, 57
Asia, 34, 105, 112–3, 115, 132
Asia-Europe People's Forum, 113
Athanasiou, Tom, 131, 132–3
Atomwaffen Division, 44
Attac, 124
Auschwitz, 44
austerity economics, 18, 27, 84
Australia, 34, 38, 44, 55, 87, 88, 90
Austria, 2, 18, 31, 36, 40, 53, 55, 57, 93, 124
authoritarianism, 4, 11, 13, 19–20, 24, 75–9, 129
Azar, Alex, 71
Aziz, Nikhil, 115
Azov Battalion, 44, 55

Balogh, Eva, 67

Bannon, Steve, 1–10
  Breitbart News, 30, 64
  failures, 9–10
  global activism, 2–5, 50, 53, 130
  organizing the Movement, 6–8
  philosophy, 5, 19, 26, 78
  Trump ally, 1–2, 9, 41
Base, 44–5
Beam, Louis, 62
Beauchamp, Zack, 67
Beirich, Heidi, 37, 40, 46, 58, 62, 97
Belgium, 6, 7, 8, 35
Belhassine, Salma, 124–5
Bello, Walden, 24, 25, 30–1, 61, 119–20, 125
Benjamin, Medea, 113
Bennis, Phyllis, 105, 109–10
Beran, Dale, 30
Berdimukhammedov, Gurbanguly, 69
Berlusconi, Silvio, 7, 18, 21
Berman, Sheri, 28
Bharatiya Janata Party, 18, 61
Białystok, 37
Billings, 95
Bitcoin
  see cryptocurrencies
Black Lives Matter, 78, 81, 95, 125, 127
Boeve, May, 26, 107, 124
Bolsonaro, Jair, 3, 4, 18, 20, 31, 32, 39, 50, 57, 72, 78, 95–6, 131
Bond, Patrick, 128
Boogaloo Bois, 80, 101
Bozóki, András, 40–1
Brazil
  Afro-Brazilians, 111, 125
  anti-refugee sentiment, 50
  Chamber of Commerce award, 96
  civic resistance, 95
  climate crisis, 39, 131
  COVID-19, 72, 78
  criminalization of popular movements, 39
  family payments, 119
  right-wing populism, 3, 4, 8, 24, 128
  World Social Forum, 104, 105, 106–7
Breitbart News, 1, 2, 6, 62, 64
Breivik, Anders, 33, 88
Brennan, Brid, 11
Brexit, 2, 23, 51–2
Brimelow, Peter, 35
Brussels, 6, 8, 26
Bruszt, Laszlo, 67
Budapest, 42, 54, 58
Buddhism, 5, 34, 50
Budraitskis, Ilya, 53–4
Bundestag, 39
Bundeswehr, 38
Burke, Edmund, 5

Cambridge Analytica, 2
Camp of the Saints, 49
Camus, Renaud, 33, 48
Canada, 15, 16, 64
Cantanhêde, Eliane, 128
capitalism, 133–4
Capitol riot, 9–10, 45, 80
Carto, Willis, 47, 56
Catholic Church, 5, 20, 94
Chan-o-cha, Prayut, 19
Charlottesville
  see Unite the Right gathering
Cheong, Wooksik, 112
China
  authoritarianism, 73–4, 85, 137
  Belt and Road Initiative, 132
  COVID, 69–70, 71, 79, 81, 83, 136
  extremism, 64–5
  national security law, 73–4, 78
  regional issues, 113
Chow, Tobita, 120
Christchurch
  Call, 90
  shooting 33, 48, 87–91
Christianity, 20, 66, 68
  Christian Democrats, 27, 36, 93
  fundamentalists, 58–9

INDEX

CitizenGo, 59, 75
citizenship
  Europe, 17, 82
  global, 112
  India, 34, 50
  Israel, 50
  New Zealand, 87
  Portugal, 83
  Russia, 37
climate crisis, 20, 26, 38, 60, 85, 111, 114, 127, 128, 132–3, 137, 139
climate denialism, 38, 60–1, 124, 131
Clinton, Hillary, 1, 16, 30, 100, 147f
Cocker, Martin, 89–90, 102
Cohen, Ran, 36, 55, 116–7, 128
Cole, Kaleb, 44
Comet Ping Pong, 63
Communist Party, 15–6, 23, 27
conservatism, 6, 49
  funders, 80
  media, 30, 81, 100
  social conservatives, 58
Conservative Party, 23
conspiracy theories, 9, 15, 74, 99, 100
  China, 81
  COVID, 82
  globalists, 81
  see also QAnon
Cooperation Jackson, 105
Corbyn, Jeremy, 23, 27
cordon sanitaire, 35
coronavirus
  see COVID-19
corporations, 28, 105, 109, 114, 115–6, 122
COVID-19
  authoritarianism, 69–74, 85, 86
  bioweapon, 79
  borders, 60
  Brazil, 72
  China, 73–4
  climate, 131, 133
  economy, 27, 133, 136
  far right, 74–5, 82
  Global Solidarity Manifesto, 108

Israel, 73
Italy, 73, 83
national security, 86
New Zealand, 91
Philippines, 72–3
Russia, 73
United Kingdom, 72
United States, 4, 68, 71–2, 79
xenophobia, 34
cryptocurrencies, 102, 114–5
Czech Republic, 17, 93

Dandora landfill, 123
Davao, 61
Davos, 5, 105, 108, 123
deconstruction of administrative state, 19, 26, 58, 78
Demirovic, Alex, 56
democracy, 6, 30–1, 111, 117–120, 134–5, 139–140
  Brazil, 95
  challenges to, 11, 12, 18, 20, 41, 102, 116
  COVID-19, 69–70, 85–6
  democratization, 25, 122, 124
  economy, 114
  Hong Kong, 78
  Hungary, 54
  Trump, 41, 71–2, 77–8, 128
Democracy Index, 20
Democratic Party, 28, 29, 71, 77–8, 95, 108, 135
demography, 32, 33, 50, 57, 131, 138
  see also Great Replacement
deplatforming, 100–3
diaspora, 61, 111
DiEM25, 118, 132
digital organizing, 62–5, 82, 99–103
disinformation, 81, 101
  see also conspiracy theories
Dodik, Milorad, 54
Dove, Fiona, 23, 105, 113, 121, 122–3, 129
doxxing, 99
Duke, David, 47

Duque, Iván, 24
Duterte, Rodrigo, 3, 20, 24, 61, 72–3
Dwoskin, Elizabeth, 101

Earle, Ethan, 4, 107, 120, 128
Eastern Europe
  alliance with far right, 47, 52, 54–5
  economic reforms, 16–7, 22, 27, 82, 122
  right-wing populists, 2, 17
  trade unions, 24
Ebner, Julia, 60, 64, 99
economics
  COVID-19, 4, 74, 131, 136
  Eastern Europe, 16–7, 22, 27, 82, 122
  globalization, 12, 21–7, 28, 31, 104–5, 122
  inequality, 82, 86, 116, 123–4
  precariat, 122–3
  Trump, 71–2, 76
El Salvador, 128
England
  see United Kingdom
English Defence League, 33
environment
  activism, 26, 39, 60, 113, 115, 116, 124, 133, 134, 138
  far right, 57
  state power, 85–6
  trade, 112, 116
Erasmus Stiftung, 39
Erdoğan, Recep Tayyip, 3, 20, 41, 78
ethnopluralism, 49
Eurabia, 32
Europe
  Bannon, 6–8
  Brexit, 2, 23, 51–2
  civil society, 40, 59–61
  COVID-19, 66–8, 75
  economy, 56, 122, 132
  European Parliament, 28, 39, 51–2, 110, 118–9
  European Union, 82–4

far right, 2–3, 6–7, 29, 32–3, 34, 44, 48–9, 50–6, 59–61, 64, 74, 97
  Israel, 55–6
  migration, 32–3, 40, 48–50, 57, 62, 66, 73, 74, 82–3, 84, 125
  municipal organizing, 113–5
  Organization of Security and Cooperation in Europe, 110
  political parties, 35–6, 92–4, 118–9
  Russia, 53–4, 57
  see also Eastern Europe
Europe of Nations and Freedom, 52
Euroskepticism, 51, 111

Facebook, 9, 64, 97, 100, 101
  see also social media
Farage, Nigel, 7, 51–2, 55
fascism, 24, 25, 37, 44, 46, 50, 55, 57, 74, 93, 127
Fauci, Anthony, 9. 77, 81
Fearless Cities, 114
Federal Bureau of Investigation, 44–5, 55, 79, 80, 92
Feingold, Cathy, 109, 113, 121–2
Feldman, Matthew, 42, 50, 90
Fidesz, 28–9, 40, 54
Fight Inequality Alliance, 123
Finland, 2, 93
Five Star Movement, 7, 51
Floyd, George, 77, 81, 125
Foon, Meng, 88, 91
foreign agent law, 40
France, 2, 33, 48, 55, 75
Freedom House, 20, 54, 67
Freedom Party, 18, 36, 49, 53, 55, 93
Friberg, Daniel, 54
FridaysforFuture, 115, 124
Friedman, Thomas, 132, 134
Friedrich Ebert Foundation, 22
Furgal, Sergei, 78

Gab, 63, 101
Gamergate, 62

gender studies, 32
Germany
  climate change, 60-1
  constitution, 93
  constitutional court, 93
  COVID-19, 84
  East Germany, 76
  economy, 23, 82
  far right, 38, 47, 74, 93-4
  migration, 48-9
  political parties, 2, 33, 39, 40, 118
  World War II, 46
Ghiotto, Luciana, 111-2, 129
globalization, 12, 21-7, 28, 31, 104-5, 122
Global South, 18, 24, 72, 103, 106, 119, 125, 127, 137
Golwalkar, M.S., 46
Goodhart, David, 135
Götze, Susanne, 38, 60
Grajew, Oded, 106-7, 119
Gramsci, Antonio, 42
Grassroots Global Justice, 107-8
Great Replacement, 13, 33, 48-50, 56, 60, 87, 92, 99
  see also conspiracy theories
Greece, 82, 83
Green fascism, 57
Green New Deal, 13, 119, 130-4, 139-40
Green Party, 28, 118, 119, 135
Greene, Marjorie Taylor, 63, 93
Grillo, Beppe, 21, 31
Gruevski, Nikola, 54
gun control, 88, 89
Gupta, Sarita, 105, 107, 122
Guttal, Shalmali, 28, 121

Haidar, Jörg, 18, 36, 41
Harnwell, Benjamin, 7
hate speech, 89-90, 92, 94
Heartland Institute, 38, 61
Helsinki Citizens Assembly, 108
Heyerdahl, Barbarina, 4
Hinduism, 18, 20, 46, 50, 96

Hindu World Congress, 96
Hirschman, Albert, 52
Hitler, Adolf, 46, 48, 94, 97
Hochschild, Arlie, 26
Holocaust denial, 42, 47, 93
Honduras, 56
Hong Kong, 4, 73-4, 78
Horvat, Srećko, 106, 118, 121, 132-3
Houellebecq, Michel, 33
Hungary
  constitution, 67
  COVID-19, 66-8
  migration, 40, 66-7
  Islamophobia, 34
  Jobbik, 42-3
  Orbán, 4, 20, 28-9, 32, 40, 54, 66-8

identitarianism, 18, 38, 42, 48-9, 54, 56, 61, 62, 74, 130
Identity and Democracy Party, 52-3
illiberalism, 20-1, 43, 67, 102
immigration
  anti-immigrant discourse, 32-5, 37-8, 60, 74, 79, 135
  asylum, 41, 72, 81, 89
  asylum-seekers, 163, 170
  climate change, 60
  COVID-19, 66, 74-5
  policy, 125
  remigration, 48-9, 99
India, 3, 18, 46, 50, 61, 81, 96, 107
indignados, 22
Infowars, 62, 100
Institute for Strategic Dialogue, 82
internationalism, 5, 12, 45-7, 109-110, 137
International Labor Organization, 109
investor-state dispute settlement, 115-6
Iraq, 33, 105
Ireland, Phil, 55
Islam, 20, 59
Islamic State, 20, 92

Islamophobia, 33–4, 50, 55, 59, 88
Israel, 3, 8, 36, 50, 55–6, 61, 70
Italy, 2, 7, 8, 18, 21, 51, 53, 55, 73, 75, 82–4, 95

Japan, 11, 36, 46, 80, 112–3
Jaruzelski, Wojciech, 15
Jensen, Robert, 25
Jerusalem, 3
Jobbik, 42–3, 53
Johnson, Boris, 72
Jones, Alex, 100
Jovanovic, Zeljko, 59–60

Kaczyński, Jarosław, 17, 56–7
Kaldor, Mary, 28, 119
Kashkari, Ikhlaq, 87–8, 91
Kathuria, Mansi, 96
Kawasaki, Akira, 112–3
Kenya, 123
Khabarovsk, 78
Kiska, Roger, 59
Klayman, Alison, 7
Koblenz, 2
Koehler, Daniel, 37–8
Korean peninsula, 112–3
Ku Klux Klan, 94
Kurz, Sebastian, 36

labor, 120, 121–3, 136
Labour Party, 29, 30, 33, 34, 141, 152
laïcité, 33
Lander, Edgardo, 19, 123–4
Law and Justice Party, 23, 37, 56–7, 94
League of Rights, 87
Lega, 7, 20, 53
léman, 115
Lenin, 5, 10, 141f
Le Pen, Marine, 2, 23, 52
Leviathan, 85–6, 137, 139
Liberal Democratic Party, 11
liberalism, 6, 134
    anti-liberalism, 19–21, 28–9, 43, 54, 67, 117

liberal-conservative consensus, 13, 17
liberal internationalism, 54, 110, 137
neoliberalism, 21–8, 111, 132, 139
libertarianism, 100
Libertarian Party, 15
Libya, 33, 83
Limbaugh, Rush, 71
London, 7, 69, 96
Louati, Yasser, 10, 33
Lübcke, Walter, 93

Macedonia, 54
Maduro, Nicolas, 19
Mair, Victor, 130
Malaysia, 47
Malinowska, Magda, 122
Malofeev, Konstantin, 53
Manshaus, Philip, 33
Maori, 87, 91, 135
Marsili, Lorenzo, 25, 52, 106, 110, 113, 119, 130
Marxism, 129
Maso, Tchenna, 39
Massari, Maurizio, 83
mass shootings, 11, 33, 48, 64–5, 87–90, 92
Matveev, Ilya, 37, 53
Mazowiecki, Tadeusz, 15, 16
McCarthy, Joseph, 18
McGuinness, Mairead, 52
McKinsey, 22
Medical Freedom Patriots, 74
Mestrum, Francine, 120
MeToo, 116
Mexico, 9, 47, 56, 72, 107, 122
Michel, Charles, 84
middle class, 24, 25, 121, 123, 134
Middle East, 51, 109
migration
    see immigration
Milanese, Niccolo, 25
military
    bases, 115

INDEX

coups, 11, 19, 72
COVID-19, 86
far right, 38, 45
militarism, 8
military intervention, 33
Trump, 77-8, 95
Milosevic, Slobodan, 76
Modi, Narendra, 18, 20, 21, 31, 41, 50, 61, 78
Modrikamen, Mischaël, 6, 7, 8
Mouffe, Chantal, 134-5
Mudde, Cas, 6, 31, 35, 36, 92
Mueller, Jan-Werner, 35, 117
Mulhall, Joe, 101
multiculturalism, 49, 87
music, 47
Myanmar, 34, 50

Naidoo, Kumi, 102, 104-5, 109, 124, 126
name-and-shame tactics, 97-8
Nansen, Karin, 111, 117-8
Nardi, Jason, 114-5
nationalism, 8, 17, 56, 112
  Europe, 17
  India, 20
  masculinity, 32
  Russia, 37, 53-4
  white, 38, 48, 57-8, 61, 90, 98, 118
National Democratic Party (Germany), 93-4
National Rally, 18, 23, 49, 53, 75
national security, 86
national security law, 73-4, 78
Nauditt, Kristina, 99
Nazism, 6, 7, 44, 45-6, 57, 97
  Nazi symbols, 93-4
  neo-Nazis, 2, 6, 38, 44, 46-7, 48, 55, 58, 60, 64, 79, 80, 89, 98, 99
Nazzaro, Rinaldo, 44-5
Neiwert, David, 30
neoliberalism, 28, 111, 124, 129, 132
Netanyahu, Benjamin, 3, 8, 13, 36, 41, 50, 73
Netherlands, 2, 55, 122

New Delhi, 81
New Zealand, 11, 28, 33, 34, 38, 48, 64, 87-91, 113, 135-6
New Zealand First, 87, 135
NGOs, 40, 110, 121, 139
Nicaragua, 19, 20, 41
Nipert, Matt, 88-9, 90-1, 101
Norimatsu, Satoko, 36
North American Free Trade Agreement, 108, 112

Obama, Barack, 3, 29-30, 63, 137
Ocasio-Cortez, Alexandria, 119, 120
Occupy movement, 22, 23, 28, 106, 120
Okinawa, 115
Olomoofe, Larry, 42-3, 126
Online Progressive Engagement Network, 102-3
Ophuls, William 85
Orbán, Viktor
  climate change, 20
  COVID-19, 66-8
  economy, 40
  gender studies, 32
  globalism, 21, 28-9, 54
  immigration, 34, 66
  religion, 59
  southeast Europe, 54
Ortega, Daniel, 19, 20, 41
Ost, David, 23

Palestine, 55
pandemic
  see COVID-19
paramilitaries, 44-5, 55, 77-8, 94-5
Pardavi, Márta, 40, 54, 67-8
Park, Annabel, 118, 119
Park, Won-Soon, 114
patriarchy, 32, 112
Peace Boat, 112-3
Pegida, 33, 37
Pell, Herbert, 96-7
People's Democratic Party, 78
People's Party (Austria), 36, 54

People's Party (Denmark), 57
Perez-Rocha, Manuel, 47, 112, 116
Peters, Winston, 135
Petersen-Smith, Khury, 55, 125
Peterson, Jordan, 63
Philippines, 3, 20, 25, 30, 61, 72–3
Pierce, William Luther, 47, 56
Pieterse, Jan Nederveen, 19, 129–30
Pinochet, Augusto, 24
Pizzagate, 63
Plesch, Dan, 97
Poland
   civil society, 40
   constitutional court, 94
   election 1990, 15–7
   far right, 37, 56–7, 94
   Green New Deal, 119
   LGBT, 94, 114
   trade union, 24, 38, 122
police, 38, 45, 80, 81, 95, 125
Poor People's Campaign, 123–4
populism
   Italy, 21, 82, 95
   left-wing, 133–6
   right-wing, 5, 18–9, 22, 24, 35
   Russia, 53
   technology, 21
Portland, 77
Portugal, 83
Powell, Enoch, 18
precariat, 122–3
privatization, 17, 41
Proud Boys, 32, 45, 80
Putin, Vladimir, 4, 20, 37, 40, 53–4, 56–7, 73

QAnon, 45, 61, 63, 80, 101
quarantine, 69, 71, 72, 74, 136

racism, 11, 46, 49, 57, 79, 87, 88
Ramdas, Kavita, 32, 109
Ramos, Tarso, 58
Rappler, 73
refugees, 34, 50, 55, 66, 83, 114, 121, 125–6, 131

religious fundamentalism, 3, 5, 19–20, 32, 58–9
remigration, 48–9, 99
Republican Party, 27, 29, 30, 37, 42, 63, 81, 92, 128, 135
Revelli, Marco, 21
Ricks, Jenny, 123, 133
Rockwell, George Lincoln, 46–7
Rohingya, 34, 50
Roma, 17, 59–60
Roof, Dylann, 58
Rosenthal, Larry, 43, 51, 129
Ross, Wilbur, 71
Roth, Laura, 114, 120
Rousseff, Dilma, 107
Ruggiero, Renato, 104
Rule of Law Fund, 8
Rule of Law Index, 20
Russia
   authoritarianism, 40, 102
   civil society, 40
   constitution, 53, 73
   far right, 8, 44, 47, 53, 60
   Hungary, 29
   nationalism, 37, 53
   Poland, 56–7
   protests, 78
   revolution, 10
Ryan, Melissa, 31, 47–8
Rydliński, Bartosz, 57, 119

Saakashvili, Mikheil, 57
Salman, Mohammed bin, 19
Salvini, Matteo, 2, 7, 56, 73, 74
Sanders, Bernie, 5, 27, 108, 135
Sardines, 95
Sarrazin, Thilo, 49
Saudi Arabia, 19, 67, 116, 137
Sauer, Birgit, 32, 57
Savitri Devi, 46
Scazzeri, Luigi, 84
Schaffar, Wolfram, 24, 34, 85, 129
Schengen, 82–3
secret police, 16
Seibt, Naomi, 60–1

INDEX

Serbia, 17, 54, 66, 76
Shinagawa, Thaksin, 24
Shiva, Vandana, 104, 107, 115
shock therapy, 16, 17, 27
Singapore, 69
Slovakia, 17, 91
Slovenia, 17, 54
slowbalization, 26
Smith, Iain Duncan, 23
Smolensk, 57
Social Democrats, 23, 27, 28, 36
Socialist Party, 27
Socialist Reich Party, 93
Solano, Esther, 3
Solidarność, 15–16, 23, 24, 38
Soros, George, 60, 81
South Africa, 34, 38, 107, 124, 128
Southern Poverty Law Center, 97
South Korea, 69, 70, 112, 113, 119, 124, 132
sovereignty, 26, 52, 53, 54, 56, 85, 119, 134, 136, 137
Soviet Union, 33, 41, 53, 76
Spain, 38–9, 75, 76, 114, 134
Spencer, Metta, 117
Spencer, Richard, 8, 97
Spoonley, Paul, 87, 89
Standing Rock, 115
state capture, 40–1
state power, 13, 41, 69–70, 76–8, 85–6, 138
Stokfiszewski, Igor, 37, 40, 111, 114
Stormfront, 62
Strache, Heinz-Christian, 55
Strickner, Alexandra, 36
subterranean politics, 28
surveillance, 69–70
survivalism, 79, 100
sustainability, 113, 115, 116, 122
Suu Kyi, Aung San, 34
swastika, 92, 93
Sweden, 2, 7, 60
Sweden Democrats, 2, 7, 60
Switzerland, 115
Syria, 4, 18, 33, 51

Taiwan, 69, 78, 80, 115
Taliban, 33
Taonui, Rawiri, 88
Tarrant, Brenton, 88
technology, 21, 26–7, 56, 62–5, 69–70, 103, 114–5
Telegram, 82, 101
terrorism, 33, 42, 59, 82, 88, 89, 99
Texas, 44, 48, 96
Thackeray, Bal, 46
Thailand, 19, 24, 25, 34
Thompson, Derek, 62
Thor Steinar, 94
Thunberg, Greta, 60
Timberg, Craig, 101
Touré, Coumba, 111
trade unions, 15, 23, 24–5, 38, 105, 112, 120, 121–2
transnationalism
  see internationalism
transnational organizing, 2–10, 44–56, 58–65, 102–10, 115–7, 118–26, 128
trolls, 64, 99
Trump, Donald
  authoritarianism, 76–8, 128
  Bannon, 1–2, 6, 9–10, 41
  climate crisis, 131
  COVID-19, 70–2, 76–7
  deplatforming, 92, 101
  international influence, 3–4
  Muslim travel ban, 33–4
  popular support, 25, 49, 61
  QAnon, 63
  resistance to, 96, 114, 125
  far right, 30, 37, 75, 80–1, 137
Tunisia, 82, 122
Turkey, 3, 20, 41, 78, 83
Turkmenistan, 69
Turner Diaries, 47
Twitch, 63–4
Twitter, 9, 21, 30, 63, 90, 92–3, 99, 100, 101
Tymiński, Stan, 15–8

Ukraine, 31, 37, 44, 47, 55, 57, 76, 93

Unite the Right gathering, 65, 97, 102
United Kingdom, 2, 22, 23–4, 82, 93
United Nations, 5, 109–10
United States
    Constitution, 77, 94
    COVID-19, 71–2, 74, 76–8
    economy, 24–5, 123
    electoral politics, 27, 29, 37, 118
    far right, 44–5, 47, 49, 57–9, 61, 79–82, 94–5, 97–8, 100–1
    racial justice, 125
    Trump, 30, 35, 37, 71–2, 76–8
U.S. Congress
    2020 election, 81, 128
    impeachment of Trump, 10
    January 6 insurrection, 9–10, 45
    legislation, 132
U.S. Social Forum, 108

Vaquer, Jordi, 39, 52, 53, 54, 123
Varoufakis, Yanis, 132
Vila, Sol Trumbo, 27, 114
Vlaams Belang, 35
Vox Party, 38–9

Walsh, Declan, 86
Wannsee Conference, 7, 8
Warsaw, 94, 114
Wałęsa, Lech 15–6
Ward, Eric, 47, 49–50, 56, 118, 125–6
Wengui, Guo, 7, 8
Wermerskirch, Gerd, 99
Western civilization, 49, 55
white supremacy, 33, 38, 44, 46, 48, 55, 58, 62, 79, 82, 87–8, 92

Wiesner, Cindy, 108, 116
WikiLeaks, 30
Wilders, Geert, 2, 23, 52, 55, 57
women's movement, 32, 57, 62, 111–2, 125
Workers Party (Czech Republic), 93
Workers Party (Brazil), 107
working class, 24, 25, 30, 116, 122–3, 134
World Congress of Families, 58–9, 75
World Economic Forum
    see Davos
World Social Forum, 104–8, 121, 129, 132, 138
World Trade Organization, 105, 108
Wright, Joanne, 81
Wuhan, 81
Wunsiedel, 98

xenophobia, 34
Xi, Jinping, 19, 20, 73–4, 75

Yeats, William, 11, 14, 140
Yiannopoulos, Milo, 97–8, 101
Yockey, Francis Parker, 47, 56
YouTube, 9, 63, 98
Yugoslavia, 17, 76

Zelensky, Volodymyr, 31
Zeller, Michael, 93
Zhang, Chenchen, 64–5
Zhihu, 64
Zhirinovsky, Vladimir, 41
Zuckerman, Ethan, 29, 63–4

Thanks to our Patreon Subscribers:

Lia Lilith de Oliveira
Andrew Perry

Who have shown generosity and comradeship in support of our publishing.

Check out the other perks you get by subscribing to our Patreon – visit patreon.com/plutopress. Subscriptions start from £3 a month.

The Pluto Press Newsletter

Hello friend of Pluto!

Want to stay on top of the best radical books we publish?

Then sign up to be the first to hear about our new books, as well as special events, podcasts and videos.

You'll also get 50% off your first order with us when you sign up.

Come and join us!

Go to bit.ly/PlutoNewsletter